THE BALKAN REVOLUTIONARY TRADITION

THE BALKAN REVOLUTIONARY TRADITION

Dimitrije Djordjevic
and
Stephen Fischer-Galati

1981
Columbia University Press
New York

Library of Congress Cataloging in Publication Data

Dordević, Dimitrije, 1922–
The Balkan revolutionary tradition.

Includes bibliographical references and index.
1. Balkan Peninsula—History. 2. Revolutions
—Balkan Peninsula. I. Fischer-Galati, Stephen
A., joint author. II. Title.
DR37.D67   949.6   80-24039
ISBN 0-231-05098-4

Columbia University Press
New York   Guildford, Surrey
Copyright © 1981 Columbia University Press

To the subject and object of Balkan history—the peasant, for the hospitality offered to one of us in Serbia during the last war and, respectively, to the few who have recognized the true significance of revolutions in Balkan history

CONTENTS

PREFACE

Our book, *The Balkan Revolutionary Tradition*, has been long in the making. Dimitrije Djordjevic, as a member of the Belgrade Historical Institute, prepared the volume *Révolutions Nationales des Peuples Balkaniques, 1804–1914* as a contribution to the International Congress of the Historical Sciences held in Vienna in 1965. His work was totally independent of that of Stephen Fischer-Galati, who, also concerned with the significance of Balkan revolutionary activities, was working concurrently on revolutionary manifestations of the sixteenth, seventeenth, eighteenth, and twentieth centuries. In the seventies, as Dimitrije Djordjevic became a permanent member of the faculty of the University of California at Santa Barbara, we agreed to combine our efforts and to produce a comprehensive study of the Balkan revolutionary tradition in the historic perspective of the last five hundred years. That we have done in the present volume.

   Our book is based on a systematic review of the published documentation and literature on Balkan revolutions,

ix

and on extensive and intensive study of archival data contained in Western and Eastern European depositories. The chapters pertaining to the period 1804–1914 and the Conclusion were contributed by Dimitrije Djordjevic; the rest of the book is the work of Stephen Fischer-Galati. It was not our intention to write an exhaustive factual account of the history of the Balkan Peninsula and of its revolutions. Rather, it was, and is, our hope that the present volume will provide informative historical interpretations of the political and social revolutionary movements which sought to shape the course of the history of the Balkans and of the peoples of that part of the world.

The authors wish to express their gratitude to numerous colleagues and institutions for assistance rendered at various stages of their endeavors. Furthermore, Stephen Fischer-Galati wishes to single out the contributions of his wife Anne—who was first to recognize the significance of the topic—and of the John Simon Guggenheim Memorial Foundation and the American Council of Learned Societies for early support of the project; in turn, Dimitrije Djordjevic wishes to express his appreciation for his coauthor's efforts related to translating and editing significant parts of the original French text of his study.

Dimitrije Djordjevic
Stephen Fischer-Galati

INTRODUCTION

The notion that the Balkans have at all times been the "powder keg of Europe" has gained wide acceptance among historians and other students of world affairs. And, as that notion was expanded into a complete theory of revolution by communist historians and political leaders after World War II, it has become popular to view the history of the Balkan Peninsula as one of continuing revolutionary struggles directed against domestic and foreign oppressors by the peoples of that region.

The history of the Balkan Peninsula has indeed been turbulent by any standards but not more so than that of other parts of Europe or of the world for that matter. The turbulence was largely a function of the geographic location of the Peninsula and of the relentless struggle for control of Constantinople, of the Eastern Mediterranean, and of the Near and Middle East which has been waged by contenders for political and economic power. A Romanian chronicler of the seventeenth century, Grigore Ureche, offered as an explanation for the continuing misery of the Romanian provinces the fact that they were located "on the road of all evils." That explanation is accurate not only for the Romanian lands but for the lands of the Balkans as a whole. Frequent dislocations of unsettled political entities and of their populations caused by incessant wars, invasions, disease, and other evil things have plagued the Peninsula since the collapse of the *Pax Romana*. The ever growing crises of the Eastern Roman Empire made for constant instability, and the *Pax Ottomanica* of the sixteenth century was relatively short lived as the empire of the Ottomans itself became subject to the same pressures and crises which had led to the collapse of its predecessors.

The inability of the Ottoman rulers of the Balkans to cope with changing internal and external conditions and pressures, most of them generated by the opposing forces of Western capitalism and Eastern feudal theocracy, led to renewed unrest and revolutionary activity in the Peninsula. The character of the revolutionary manifestations which beset the Ottoman Empire since the closing years of the sixteenth century was unique to the Balkan Peninsula, as it reflected specific political and socioeconomic conditions of the region. The majority of the movements lacked any ideological foundations in keeping with the basic frustrations and desires of the overwhelmingly illiterate agrarian population. Before the nineteenth century they were mostly simple and spontaneous peasant movements, jacqueries directed against feudal landlords, Christian or Moslem. The underlying ideological foundation was the avenging of the humiliations inflicted upon the Christian population by the Infidel Turk but that foundation was, in fact, considerably weaker than generally assumed by historians of the Balkans. For there were many revolutionary manifestations directed by Moslem peasants against Moslem landlords and by Christian peasants against Christian landlords. By the nineteenth century, the ideological basis for revolutionary activity was proclaimed to be nationalism. The emerging leadership, whether petit bourgeois as in Serbia, commercial and intellectual as in Greece, or aristocratic as in the Romanian provinces, evoked the theme of independence from the Ottoman oppressors as the rationale for revolutionary, liberating, actions directed against the Porte. Thus, if any ideology could be found in Balkan revolutionary activities prior to the twentieth century, it was that of nationalism and of the war of national liberation. Social revolutionary manifestations occurred only to the extent to which the oppressed masses sought elimination of onerous feudal conditions. There were indeed no clearly definable or categorical social revolutionary manifestations or doctrines which emerged in the Balkan Peninsula before the present century. And even in our times, social revolutionary manifestations of purely Balkan origin have been invariably intertwined with a nationalist rationale. The current claims made by communist historians and political leaders that all revolutions in the Balkans were in fact forerunners of the great social revolutions which occurred in all countries of the Peninsula, other than Greece, in our times are invalidated by the historic evidence presented in the present volume. Instead, what emerges is the history of internal unrest, external subversion, internecine struggles, class conflicts—all embodied in vague and nebulous doctrines enunciated by occasionally idealistic and, more frequently, cynical exploiters of "objective conditions" of their own vision if not of their own making.

It may be interesting to speculate just where and how

the revolutionary manifestations which occurred in the Balkans would fit into the various analytical schemes and theses devised by students of revolution, such as Barrington Moore, Eric Wolf, Jean Chesneaux, Roland Mousnier, and other exponents of theoretical approaches. Yet, objectively, such speculation would serve no more useful purpose, perhaps, than trying to pattern the history of Balkan manifestations to fit the dogmatic theses propounded by contemporary Marxist historians and propagandists in Russia and Eastern Europe. The Balkan pattern, as indicated above and in the pages to follow, is simple and generic to essentially apolitical, paternalistic, isolated, religiously conservative agrarian societies. It would be difficult and unrealistic to provide profound theoretical explanations and to devise original terminology for what may be best qualified as elemental reactions and responses to political and social oppression or religious and nationalist propaganda.

Thus, in the last analysis, the history of the Balkans and of its revolutions was conditioned by the historical retardation of the region as much as by its unfortunate location. It is a history of occasional successes and ultimate failure. The goals of revolutionary leaders and participants have not been realized and are not likely to be realized in the foreseeable future, not even in non-Communist Greece. It is evident that the revolutionary goals of the Balkan peoples were not identical with those of participants in the great bourgeois revolutions of the eighteenth century. But it is also true that even their most modest goals—the attainment of well-being in a national state protective of the rights to property and liberty of its inhabitants—have not been achieved. And it is for these reasons that the rulers of the Balkan peoples who base their legitimacy on fulfillment of the revolutionary desiderata of their subjects are in constant fear of potential mass revolution.

The story of Balkan revolutions is thus not completed by this study since the "objective conditions" which have led to revolutionary activities in the past have not been eliminated. The *Pax Sovietica* has devised more effective means of control over the peoples of the Balkans than had either the Roman or the Turkish but it has been unable to eradicate the dissatisfaction and disaffection of the inhabitants of the Peninsula with conditions which cannot be described as fulfilling of their historic hopes and aspirations.

PAX OTTOMANICA AND HOLY WAR: THE REVOLT OF MICHAEL THE BRAVE

Historic evolution in the Balkan Peninsula, the "powder keg of Europe," has been a function of revolutionary activity. Historians and politicians, nationalist and Communist, have characterized that activity as "social" and "national" and have assigned specific connotations to each. "Social revolution" encompasses the entire range of violent actions, from rudimentary peasant uprisings to major movements designed to free the masses from social and economic oppression. "National revolution" is the "struggle for liberation" from foreign domination. In its ultimate form, the "war of national liberation," it is assumed to represent the total synthesis of the "social" and "national" revolutionary potential and aspirations of all inhabitants of the Peninsula.[1]

Revolutionary manifestations are deeply rooted in the history of the Balkan peoples. They are largely the reflection and result of a tradition of defiance of political authority inherent to societies devoid of well-defined institutions. The causative and corollary absence of legal means for the attainment and preservation of elementary socioeconomic and political justice, combined with tribal violence and long periods of foreign domination, antedate the Ottoman conquest and the reorganization of the Peninsula by the Turks in the fourteenth and fifteenth centuries. There is indeed a long tradition of revolution among the inhabitants of the Peninsula that may be traced to the Byzantine and pre-Byzantine eras. However, the problems relevant to violent socioeconomic and political transformations related to our times are directly and immediately connected with the history of the Ottoman Empire.[2]

The Turks did not necessarily create conditions propitious for revolutionary action but they did provide a rationale for it by virtue of their alien faith. The theme of ridding Balkan Christendom of the Infidel was the leitmotiv of opponents of the Ottoman order since the fourteenth century and the crusading efforts on behalf of, or with the aid of, the peoples under Turkish domination invariably trumpeted that theme. "Liberators" as diverse as the Varna crusaders, Leopold II, Peter the Great, Karageorge, the *Philike Hetairia,* Nicolae Bălcescu, Karavelov—to mention but a few—sought the support of the masses in the name of freedom from Moslem domination. But under the umbrella of anti-Ottoman action, the inciters to revolution were also seeking to encourage or exploit mass discontent caused by factors independent of the non-Christian nature of the Turkish regime.

It is noteworthy that the earliest revolutionary manifestations in the Turkish-occupied or dominated Peninsula, recorded at the beginning of the fifteenth century among Romanian peasants and Montenegrin, Albanian, and Bosnian tribesmen, were not directed against the Turks. The Moldavian and Wallachian peasants were reacting to stimuli generated by constant struggles for power among rival factions of the feudal oligarchy, while the mountaineers were merely pursuing the customary tribal warfare and brigandage so characteristic of Northern Albania, Montenegro, and the mountains of Bosnia. However, it should be noted that the nucleus of a new revolutionary group, specifically anti-Ottoman, had developed in the Peninsula shortly after the Turkish conquest. That group consisted at first of the aristocracy and clergy that fled before the onrushing Turkish forces, normally into Hungarian territory, men who either as crusaders or propagandists exhorted the Balkan peoples to rise against the Infidel. But such appeals went unheeded because not only the masses, but also the lay and spiritual leaders who remained in Turkish-ruled territories, had either made their peace with the Turks or were unwilling to risk Ottoman reprisals.

Any appraisal of the "objective conditions" for revolution against the Turk during the early years of Ottoman rule and, for that matter, until the middle of the sixteenth century must take into consideration the nature of the *Pax Ottomanica*.[3] If we were to accept the traditional view that Turkish rule was both oppressive and regressive and as such created from the very moment of conquest the "objective conditions" for "social" and "national" revolution, it would be necessary to concede that the only deterrent to militant action against the Moslem rulers was the certitude of defeat by the formidable conqueror. If, on the other hand, we were to accept the "revisionist" view that Turkish rule was in fact more benevolent and beneficial to the majority of the inhabi-

3

tants of the Peninsula than that which preceded the conquest, it would be necessary to concede that as long as Turkish rule was characterized by those attributes the "objective conditions" for revolution were unfavorable in the Ottoman Empire. Regrettably, there are no certain answers to these questions, since the evidence is either contradictory or nonexistent. In general, such evidence as there is tends to favor an interpretation that would stress "peaceful coexistence" among rulers and subjects. The *Pax Ottomanica* was a reality, perhaps an imperfect one, until such time in the sixteenth century when the possibilities of further territorial aggrandizement and the securing of unlimited wealth by military and commercial means were arrested. Thus it would appear that during the first century after the conquest of Constantinople, generally enlightened Ottoman policies and superior military strength precluded revolutionary action from within and prevented the subversion of actual or potential malcontents by foreign rulers inimical to the Ottoman Empire.

This is not to say that the revolutionary potential of the Balkan Christians, and even that of the Moslemized inhabitants of the Peninsula, had been eradicated by the Ottoman rulers during that century. As fiscal and economic exactions became more stringent after Suleiman the Magnificent's unsuccessful siege of Vienna and the subsequent expansion of the armed conflict between Habsburg and Turk, revolutionary activities directly attributable to, and directed against, Constantinople were recorded in areas where Ottoman control was insecure. Still, with the possible exception of the peasant revolt directed expressly against the Moldavian feudal aristocracy in the sixties, these activities could not be classified as actual "social" revolutions, anti-Turkish in origin or caused by a breakdown of the *Pax Ottomanica*. Nor could the occasional conspiracies involving local Albanian or Greek potentates or Romanian princes and representatives of Venice, the Habsburgs, or the Poles, which occurred before the battle of Lepanto, be regarded as more than plots by an unrepresentative leadership. It would indeed be difficult to look upon men like the Albanian usurper Ibrahim Beyoli of Busciati, or Greek *armatoles* like Bua Grivas, Drakos, and Malamos, or even the Moldavian voevod Peter Rareş as leaders of wars of liberation against the Infidel. But these occurrences, whether intrinsically "social" or "national" or not, were symptomatic of a decline in the power of the Turks, and in their authority and ability to maintain the viability of the Ottoman system.

After the death of Suleiman, and particularly after Lepanto, the external enemies of the Turks, primarily the Venetians and the Habsburgs, were prepared to exploit the weaknesses of the Porte by encouraging uprisings by disaffected or adventurous men who had also detected the decline in Turkish power. Internal and external conspirators alike were totally unconcerned with "social" revolution; if anything, they favored the eradication of the privileges which Turkish power had afforded to the peasant masses. The externally backed revolutionary movements were to be "wars of liberation" but only in the sense of their seeking the removal of Turkish rule by direct military action. The "objective conditions" for militant action of this kind were present in the "war of liberation" led by Michael the Brave of Wallachia in the

5

last decade of the sixteenth century. That revolt may thus be regarded as the initial link in the revolutionary tradition of the Balkans in modern times.[4]

In 1593 Emperor Rudolph II decided to pick up the gauntlet flung repeatedly by the Pasha of Bosnia during the continuous Ottoman violations of the Empire's territorial integrity and the first major war between the Austrians and the Turks broke out. In theory, the emperor and his allies in the Holy League were fighting a Holy War, the goal of which was the expulsion of the Infidel Turk from Europe. In practice, Rudolph appeared more interested in removing the immediate Turkish threat to the borders of the monarchy and in the possibility of seizing Transylvania from his ally Sigismund Báthory. Rudolph's true intentions were most clearly revealed in his relations with Wallachia and Moldavia.[5]

Since the death of Suleiman the Magnificent in 1566, and particularly after the Turkish debacle at Lepanto, the Habsburgs meddled in Romanian affairs to check the growth of Polish and Transylvanian influence in Moldavia and to prevent the transformation of Wallachia into a regular Turkish Pashalik. In was in that spirit that Ferdinand I and Maximilian II had supported such rulers as Despot Vodă or Ioan Vodă cel Cumplit in Moldavia in the sixties and the seventies. It was for similar reasons that the Austrians courted the Wallachian boyars who considered the incipient practice of direct appointment of voevods by the Porte as a prelude to formal Turkish takeover or, in any event, annulment of their right to elect the ruling prince. The wrath of the boyars was directed primarily against the *Phanariotes* in Constantinople, who

6

were held responsible for the promotion of their proteges to voevodeships in Wallachia and for the ensuing diminution of the power of the native aristocracy. The Habsburgs, motivated by expediency as they were, pursued seemingly contradictory policies in Moldavia and in Wallachia. In Moldavia they encouraged Ioan Vodă cel Cumplit to rally the masses in revolt against the boyars because the aristocracy pursued pro-Polish policies detrimental to Austrian interests. In Wallachia, on the other hand, the Austrians proclaimed themselves protectors of the boyars' traditional rights—broadened to include legal ownership of peasants—to counteract the rise of Turkish, Greek, and princely power. But this dissonant policy of encouraging consolidation of the power of the prince in Moldavia, and that of the boyar oligarchy in Wallachia, was unacceptable to the ultimate source of power in the Romanian provinces, the Ottoman Turks. The Porte regarded the Austrian maneuvers as inimical to its sovereign rights. To protect its interests it permitted the establishment, in remote Moldavia, of virtually hereditary voevodeships for the pro-Polish but anti-Austrian Movilă family pending restoration of full Turkish authority in that province. At the same time, Constantinople approved the recommendation of Andronicos Cantacuzenos that his protege Michael—the "Brave" of later times—be appointed voevod in Wallachia.[6]

Whatever hopes of restoration or maintenance of stability in the Romanian provinces might have been reflected in these Turkish decisions, they soon were to be frustrated by Rudolph and his ally Sigismund Báthory. As the anti-Turkish war began in 1593, Rudolph and Báthory mapped a strategy designed to secure Moldavian and Wallachian participation in the Holy League. The staff of emissaries of subversion

7

sent to Moldavia in the summer of 1594 under the direction of the Ragusan John de Marini Poli succeeded without much effort in winning over the ruler Aron Movilă and the boyars of Moldavia. The Polish monarchy consented to the agreement, which in its judgment did not prevent the exercising of Polish influence in that province.[7] Negotiations with Wallachia proved to be infinitely more complex. Sigismund Báthory, without Rudolph's or Michael's knowledge, sought to secure control over that province through unilateral concessions to the boyars. The boyar oligarchy, in return for Báthory's recognition of its traditional rights of election of voevods and his promise to allow legalization of serfdom, acknowledged the Transylvanian sovereign's overlordship in Wallachia and cast its lot on the Christian side. The understanding, legalized by the Treaty of Alba Iulia of May 1595—albeit without Michael's consent—constituted a de facto revolution against both Michael and Sultan Selim II.[8] The parties to the agreement of Alba Iulia also frustrated the concurrent negotiations between voevod and emperor by which Rudolph guaranteed hereditary rule to Michael and his heirs in return for acceptance of Rudolph's suzerainty and participation in the war of the Holy League. Impending retaliatory military action by the Turks, who regarded the Wallachians as rebels regardless of whose suzerainty they expressed preferences for, forced acceptance of the fait accompli by a threatened Michael and an unprepared Rudolph.

The development of potentially explosive situations in Wallachia may be traced back to at least twenty years prior to the outbreak of the Austro-Turkish war. The Porte, first independently and later under direct Greek influence, sought to maintain friction between boyars and voevods to preclude "national" conspiracies directed against the Turks. Internecine struggles for power between boyars and voevods were the rule during the last quarter of the sixteenth century. To resolve the struggles in their favor, the princes sought the support of the dissatisfied peasantry. The peasants, whose status had deteriorated because of internal conflict and external pressures, tended to side with the ruling princes whom they regarded as the protectors of their interests. From the very beginning of his rule, Michael posed as the champion of the peasant. His concern with the allegiance of the peasantry was initially prompted by his desire to consolidate the power of the ruler at the expense of the aristocracy and by his commitment to war against the Turk. In 1595, as prince and supreme commander of the armed forces of Wallachia, he did indeed summon the masses to the "war of liberation" against the Infidel.

During the early battles of the fall of 1595, the Romanian forces—consisting of mercenaries and peasants—scored decisive victories against the Turks and even withstood the major Ottoman attacks launched against them at Călugăreni and Giurgiu. But the peasantry's demand for redistribution of land in Wallachia was rejected by the boyars. Michael himself, as one of the country's leading landowners and as a military strategist dependent on the support of the mercenaries paid by Sigismund Báthory and controlled by his fellow boyars, sided with the aristocracy. The peasant forces were dissolved and serfdom was legalized. Desertions and fleeing into Turkish held territories were recorded by contemporary chroniclers who mentioned the jacqueries staged by the re-

9

bellious peasantry in Wallachia. The "war of liberation," albeit *sans* peasants, was pursued and even extended beyond Wallachia's frontiers.

In 1597 Michael's fame as a fighter of the Infidel had spread far beyond the frontiers of Wallachia.[9] The papacy hailed the voevod as the liberator of Balkan Christendom from the Turk. Greek writers in exile in Italy and Wallachia echoed the pope. More significantly, discontented Balkan leaders who had approached Rudolph and Báthory shortly after the outbreak of the war reiterated their desire to join the side of the allies. To them Michael was the "man of the hour," the galvanizer of anti-Ottoman action in the Balkans.

"Revolutionary" fervor was minimal in the Balkan Peninsula at the beginning of the Austro-Turkish war. Discontented or adventurous men were to be found in certain parts of the Ottoman Empire, but they were unrepresentative of the masses and the other social groups they claimed to represent. Nevertheless, they sought out either Rudolph or Báthory to secure support.[10] They were in turn encouraged by the allies' agents, most notably the Ragusian merchants Paolo Giorgio and John Marini Polli, who asked them to ready themselves for action at the proper moment. Given the limited means and aims of Rudolph and Báthory direct assistance, financial or military, was refused to all suppliants other than *hajduks* whose mobility and permanent war footing seemed worthy of minor sacrifices. Michael was assigned the task of supporting diversionary action in territories adjoining Wallachia when feasible but never at the cost of placing the Wallachian uprising in jeopardy. Throughout the duration of the war, extension of the conflict south of the Danube was assigned low priority by the allies. Still, appeals

10

for military assistance to potential allies could not be ignored by "crusaders against the Infidel."

Among the several requests for military aid which emanated from Bulgarian territory that issued by Dionisie Rally Paleologos, the Metropolitan of Trnovo, was the most significant.[11] Rally's activities were closely related to the successes of Michael the Brave and antedated the Wallachian voevod's invasion of Bulgaria, on Rudolph's orders, in 1595. The chronological sequence of Rally's movements appear to substantiate the contention that he had been in touch with Michael before establishing contacts with Rudolph and Sigismund Báthory and that his revolutionary schemes were in fact directed by the Romanian voevod. In 1595 the metropolitan went to Moscow to seek financial assistance from the Patriarchate and to sound out Feodor whether military support could be secured for Michael's revolt against the Porte. The countering of Catholic influences, exerted through Rudolph and Sigismund, was advanced as a cogent argument in favor of Russian action. Upon realization that Moscow would be unable to render any assistance during the unsettled conditions of the nineties, Rally informed Michael of the failure of his mission and appealed directly to Vienna for assistance; whereupon Rudolph authorized military intervention by the Romanian voevod on his behalf. Rally's schemes appear to have had no support from the Bulgarian population of Trnovo and to have been initially unrelated to the negotiations conducted between Austrian agents and some thirty Trnovo merchants who seemed disposed to seek Austrian patronage.[12] His mission to Moscow was undertaken at the behest of a Phanariote faction in Constantinople—the same faction that had sponsored Michael's nomination to the Wallachian throne—which was bent on securing Russian support against Austrian, Polish, and Transylvanian inroads into Orthodox territories as well as support for Michael's struggle against the boyars. It was thus, initially, not expressly directed against the Turks. The conclusion of the Treaty of Alba Iulia and Michael's subsequent commitment to action against the Turks found Rally caught in a web of international intrigues from which he could not easily extricate himself.

It is indeed noteworthy that the voevod's crossing of the Danube into Bulgarian territory in 1596, following early victories against the Turks, was not accompanied by insurrections in the occupied territory or anywhere else on Bulgarian land; on the contrary, Bulgarians joined the Turkish forces which rallied against the Wallachian's retinues. Michael's raid—for such it was—did however encourage the "merchant group" headed by Theodore Balina, Pavel Djordjić, and Peter Sorkochević. The merchants' demand for funds, based on the claim that the Bulgarian masses were ripe for revolution, was rejected by the Habsburgs in 1596. However, Emperor Rudolph held out the hope of a "liberating" expedition, to be led by Michael the Brave, sometime in the future. Balina and his associates were ready for action in 1598 as Michael's forces again crossed the Danube. But the mercenaries and *hajduks* who comprised the "liberating force" were more concerned with plunder than with liberation. The apathetic Bulgarian peasantry turned "counterrevolutionary" as soon as peasant land and belongings were ravaged by Michael's hordes. In the face of opposition by the Bulgarian peasantry, and in view of the unexpected opportunities for political gain arising from the sudden abandonment of the Transylvanian throne by

Báthory, Michael ordered his forces to invade Transylvania and abandon the war of liberation against the Turk south of the Danube. A desperate attempt by the Bulgarian conspirators to prolong the war in the Balkans, which took the form of a minor uprising in Trnovo, collapsed before the onslaught of the Ottoman forces, marching on orders from the Porte to rid Wallachia of Michael. The objective conditions for staging an effective uprising, or even as little as an anti-Turkish military diversion, were clearly absent in Trnovo or anywhere else on Bulgarian territory in the nineties of the sixteenth century.

Similarly adventurous insurrectionary plans or actions, stimulated primarily by vain promises from agents of the Holy League and by the military successes of Michael, were also brought to the attention of Rudolph or Báthory. But as a rule, the allies shied away from commitments of military support. Among the various schemes, the most noteworthy for its lack of realism was the Albanian conspiracy initially concocted by the ambitious Ibrahim Bejoli, the Moslemized tribal leader of Busciati.[13] In 1571, Ibrahim did in fact seize control of the Scutari pashalik, only to be forcibly evicted by the Turks a few years later. In 1597 survivors of Ibrahim's regime sought Rudolph's support for renewal of hostilities against the legitimate Pasha of Scutari. The emperor was as noncommittal to the demands of the Albanian conspirators as to those of Bishop Vissarion of Trebinje, in Herzegovina, or of Bishop Athanasie of Macedonia, who had submitted plans for diversionary revolutionary action in the Balkans during the previous years. Lack of resources and well-founded skepticism regarding the ability of would-be organizers to carry out their promises accounted for Rudolph's negativism. As far as Rudolph was concerned, only Michael and the Wallachian boyars and a few tribesmen and *hajduks* were fighters worthy of support in the "war of liberation" against the Turks in the Peninsula.

The *hajduks*, the age-long mountaineers, plunderers, and opponents of any organized form of government, realized from an early date the opportunities opened to them by the war of the Holy League. It would be difficult to credit the *hajduks* and their guerrilla tactics with any patriotic notions. Nor could these fighters be regarded as the vanguard of the revolutionary Balkan peasantry. Still, in return for weapons and supplies provided by Rudolph, Báthory, and Michael, and the certitude of benefits derived from organized brigandage, leaders and followers from the mountains of Bosnia and Herzegovina—men like Deli Marko, Georgi Rat, Baba Novak, Sava Temišvarat—readily sided with, and were assigned specific tasks by, the allies. Baba Novak, Deli Marko and their retinues raided Sofia in 1595 en route to joining Michael's forces. This action carried out by some 2,000 men, like Deli Marko's raiding of Plevna in the spring of 1596 with some 1,500 men, was not coordinated with the activities of Rally, Balina or Djordjić. Instead of rallying the peasantry to revolution against the Turk, the *hajduks'* actions were instrumental in driving the peasants into the arms of the enemy. Yet, no matter what their status and motivations, the *hajduks* represented a direct threat to the security of the masses and of the Turkish government and, as such, were a disrupting force which could be used by foreign enemies of the Porte bent on creating diversions in times of war. Such diversions as were staged during 1593 and 1606 were not insignificant in military terms. The *hajduks'* activities delayed the transmission of supplies and immobilized Ottoman forces that could have

14

been used to greater advantage, particularly during the early years of the war, against the Wallachians.

The revolutionary activities of tribal leaders were more limited. Several Montenegrin clans tentatively offered assistance to Rudolph from as early as 1595, in return for subsidies which the emperor was both unprepared and unable to pay. Only Grdan, the voevod of mountainous and remote Nikšić in the Herzegovina, militantly reaffirmed his chronic defiance of Turkish authority in 1596 and sought assistance from the Austrians in the following year. Rudolph, however, was convinced that Grdan's actions could be pursued independently of any such support and declined to finance the rebellion, at the risk of precluding similarly diversionary actions by other tribes traditionally opposed to political stability.

Anti-Turkish revolutionary plans and manifestations in the Balkans were by-and-large terminated by the end of 1598. The most perseverant opponents of the Ottoman order after that date remained the *hajduks*, whose disrupting activities continued in full force until the end of the Austro-Turkish war in 1606. The least active or dangerous were Grdan and later imitators of his techniques. Unable to secure Austrian aid, the voevod of Nikšić ceased the insurrection pending the appearance of more propitious conditions or more generous supporters. Michael the Brave himself sought reconciliation with the Turks after 1598. Anxious to exploit the rivalry between Rudolph and Báthory over control of Transylvania, the voevod offered his services to Constantinople, provided that the Porte would recognize him as the legitimate ruler of Wallachia, Moldavia, and Transylvania, albeit as a loyal vassal of the sultan. Michael's assassination, presumably on Rudolph's orders, in the fall of 1601, frustrated his plans.[14] It did not end the Wallachian uprising against the Turks. Michael's successor, Radu Şerban, defied Turkish authority by continuously meddling in Transylvanian affairs as an agent of the Habsburg emperor for a number of years after the death of his predecessor.

Almost as unstable were Moldavian conditions after Báthory's abdication in 1598 and the consequent deepening of Poland's involvement in the struggle for power in Transylvania. The fear of extension of Habsburg power into Moldavia resulted in the Polish leader Zamoiski's seeking substitution of Polish for Turkish suzerainty in Moldavia.[15] Invitations of rebellion against the Turks were extended concurrently also by Rudolph and by Michael the Brave. The showdown occurred in 1598 when the Wallachian voevod, ostensibly acting as Rudolph's vassal but in fact seeking direct control of Moldavia himself, invaded that province. The removal of the reliably pro-Polish Movilă dynasty, which was accompanied by persecution of boyars faithful to Poland, resulted first in military counteraction against Michael by Zamoiski and later in an Ottoman offensive directed against all conspirators, foreign and domestic. Yet the military weakness of the Turks precluded their crossing the Danube. They were thus unable to check the revolt against their authority and left the Moldavian arena open to the forces of Zamoiski, Rudolph, and Michael, and their respective retinues of boyars. The struggle ended in Poland's favor owing to Rudolph's primary commitment to Transylvania and Michael's inability to oppose Zamoiski's forces without imperial support. The Porte, however, rejected Polish claims to suzerainty and regarded Moldavia as an area of primary revolutionary activity against Ottoman authority. By supporting factions of the

Moldavian aristocracy opposed to Polish hegemony, the Porte was able to retain a modicum of control over the province at the cost of continuous turmoil and sedition. For nearly a quarter of a century after the termination of the war of the Holy League in 1606, Moldavia was in a state of semipermanent revolution against Constantinople.

Thus, at the beginning of the seventeenth century, the Ottoman rulers had to face the reality of their inability to control subversive, even revolutionary, activities fomented or encouraged by foreign enemies in the Romanian provinces and among *hajduks* and other mountaineers. However, that realization did not cause great alarm in Constantinople. The fluidity of the international situation and the essential reliability of the masses throughout the Balkan Peninsula allowed the Turks to take advantage of the objective conditions for stability which were implicitly recognized by the signatories of the Treaty of Sitvatorok, on the basis of the status quo, in 1606.

·2·

REVOLUTIONARY MOVEMENTS
IN THE SEVENTEENTH
CENTURY:
NATIVE ROOTS AND FOREIGN
INCITEMENT

Historians concerned with the seventeenth century believe that the Turks were unable to differentiate between "national" manifestations directed against the Ottoman Empire during "Holy Wars" and social unrest, which could have been exploited to the advantage of the sovereign power. Had the Turks, it is argued, been able to make such distinctions and had they avoided simplistic solutions which merely aggravated internal tensions and increased the potential for revolutionary action, social or national, the bases of Ottoman strength and of political stability in the Balkan Peninsula could have been secured. Although the validity of these contentions is questionable, since the Porte' was in fact aware of the problems it had to face in the Balkans even if it was more often than not impotent to solve them to its satisfaction, it is true that the measures taken by Constantinople to retain or restore control in the Peninsula in general and in the Romanian provinces in particular were ineffectual and usually also self-defeating.[1]

After 1615 the Porte appeared determined to invest as rulers in Wallachia and Moldavia only voevods whose reliability was confirmed by the Phanariote colony in Constantinople. The Romanian hospodars were allowed to maintain small standing armies to fend off plots by all enemies of the Porte, foreign or domestic. The military forces consisted of Serbian mercenaries and native infantry and cavalry contingents, the size of which depended on the voevod's means and Turkish estimates of his needs. The first such force was established during the rule of the Wallachian Matei Basarab, in the thirties of the seventeenth century, when the Porte became apprehensive over the activities of Polish, Cossack, Transylvanian, and Habsburg plotters against the security of the Romanian provinces and, by extension, of the Ottoman Empire itself. The self-defeating nature of this measure was soon evident as both Matei Basarab and his Moldavian contemporary Vasile Lupu abused the confidence placed in them by the Porte.[2] Throughout his rule of some twenty years, Matei Basarab was in subversive contact with Ferdinand of Austria, George Rákoczi of Transylvania, the Polish monarchy, and even with Venice, alternately pledging his allegiance to one, another, or all.[3] Vasile Lupu, also for twenty-odd years, befriended such proven enemies of the Turks as the Romanovs and the Venetians while constantly warring with Matei and even concluding a matrimonial alliance with the celebrated Cossack hetman Bogdan Khmelnitsky.[4] From the standpoint of the suzerain state, the Ottoman Empire, such collusion with parties inimical to the Porte was treasonable if not outright revolutionary. But the Turks were too weak to transform the Romanian provinces into pashaliks in the seventeenth century and hence tolerated the constant shift in allegiance by voevods, and by aristocratic factions loyal to the hospodars, as long as Ottoman suzerainty was not actually usurped by one or another of the Empire's enemies.

The anarchic conditions inherent in the political instability of the Romanian provinces, aggravated by the frequent devastation of substantial parts of Wallachia and Moldavia by Turkish, Tatar, Cossack, and Polish raiders, or by the native and mercenary armies maintained by the voevods themselves, also contributed to the deterioration of economic conditions and to the corresponding increase in the revolutionary spirit and activities of the Romanian peasantry. In the seventeenth century, peasant jacqueries were, as a rule, controllable by the forces available to voevods and boyars and were normally not directed against the Turks. The peasant movements may properly be qualified as basic social revolutionary actions directed against the feudal aristocracy. The majority of these have no history. One, however, the so-called Şeimeni Revolt of 1655 has been ascribed major significance by students of revolution because of its ostensible contribution to the history of "social" and "national" revolutionary activities in the Balkan Peninsula.[5]

The revolt was triggered off by the mercenaries, the so-called Şeimeni, and by other military formations used by Matei Basarab, which were threatened with dissolution after the death of the voevod in 1654. It was originally directed against the new Wallachian hospodar Constantin Şerban, who ordered the dissolution at the behest of the Porte, and against the boyars who, like the Turks, favored the disbanding of armed forces which were outside their control. The Şeimeni and their armed colleagues were joined by a substantial segment of the Wallachian peasantry, whose looting and murdering of boyars was apparently prompted by the ruthless enforcement of the adverse fiscal measures enacted during the last years of Matei Basarab's rule. The interests of the peasantry did not coincide with those of the military rebels nor is there any evidence to support the thesis of a collaborative military-peasant effort directed against foreign and domestic oppressors. The peasants' revolt was strictly antifeudal in character and was originally directed only against the boyars. The peasants' loyalty to Constantin Şerban proved to be unfounded, as the voevod—at the urging of the boyars and with the consent of the Porte—called on George Rákoczi of Transylvania for military assistance. Rákoczi's forces defeated the rebels at Şoplea in June 1655 and the mopping-up operation, conducted with the military assistance of the Pasha of Silistra and of the new Moldavian hospodar Gheorghe Ştefan, ever fearful of the spreading of the Wallachian uprising into Moldavia, ended in the fall of that year.

The effects of the events of 1655 were far-reaching. The Ottoman reliance on foreign armies for the quelling of a peasant uprising invited external intervention in the Empire's internal affairs. Indeed, after 1655 the voevods of Wallachia either by choice, or by necessity, sided with the princes of Transylvania in military actions involving the Turks.[6] Constantin Şerban and his immediate successor, Mihnea III, were both deposed as rebels by the Porte for their collaboration with Rákoczi. Subsequent rulers of Wallachia—men like Grigore Ghica, Radu Leon, Antonie din Popeşti, and other handpicked representatives of the Porte—also betrayed their suzerains, either by siding with enemies of the Turks on their own volition or by being forced into complicity by foreign enemies of the Porte.[7]

More difficult to ascertain is the effect which Turkish reliance on Rákoczi and active participation in the quelling of the Şeimeni rebellion had on the Wallachian peasantry. It has been argued that the peasantry nurtured no ill-feelings toward the Porte prior to 1655, in that it blamed the Romanian boyars and not the Ottoman Turks for the gradually deteriorating conditions of feudal servitude. The Turkish intervention, direct through the Pasha of Silistra and indirect through Rákoczi's forces, allegedly shattered the illusions of the peasantry with respect to the Porte's goodwill and introduced a "national" element in the social revolutionary manifestations of the Wallachian masses.[8] It is difficult to assess the validity of such contentions for lack of actual data. But it seems most doubtful that any "national" element may be found in the political and social manifestations of the period, whether directed against the Porte and its supporters, or against the feudal aristocracy alone, by either rulers or ruled. Grigore Ghica's defection to the Austrian side in 1664, following loyal pursuit of the war on the side of the Turks until that time, should be ascribed to opportunistic realism rather than to any sense of national consciousness or responsibility. Similarly the pro-Polish, pro-Austrian, pro-Transylvanian, and even pro-Russian activities of Ghica's successors prior to the long Christian war against the Turks, which commenced at the gates of Vienna in 1683 and ended at Karlowitz some sixteen years later, appear to be devoid of "national" contents. At most, they reflected a growing lack of

23

confidence in the military abilities and political future of the Ottoman Turks in Europe. And this was also true for Moldavia, where the defection of princes like Gheorghe Ştefan, Eustaţiu Dabija, or Ştefan Petriceicu to enemies of the Porte, at various times before 1683, cannot rightly be interpreted as "national" manifestations directed against the suzerain Ottoman power.

Subversive activities of a revolutionary nature were not localized in the Romanian provinces. Outside these provinces, however, conspiracies and uprisings occurred infrequently, the revolutionary forces were ill-defined, and until late in the seventeenth century, the manifestations were ineffectual. More often than not, revolts and conspiracies were engineered by outside forces and occurred in times of international conflicts involving the Ottoman Empire. They took place most frequently in areas remote from Turkish control but, significantly, they were invariably directed against the Turks.

The largest number of anti-Turkish actions took place in Greek lands but their significance is not commensurate with their frequency. Sporadic uprisings by *armatoles* and by inhabitants of the Peloponnesos in the early part of the seventeenth century failed to secure the support of the masses or to upset the Porte. Even the most elaborate anti-Turkish action, devised in 1611 by Greeks in the pay of Spain, failed to achieve its limited objectives. The so-called conspiracy of the Duke of Nevers, Charles II of Gonzaga, and his Greek followers, directed by Bishop Dyonisios of Trikala, was notable for its adventurism and not for its revolutionary qualities.[9] According to the chronicler Lenormant, Charles II sought the support of Dyonisios and of the Maniat corsairs in his attempt to liberate the Balkan Peninsula and to restore the Byzantine Empire with himself as emperor. If we are to believe Lenormant, a meeting of clergymen, summoned by the bishop, which included delegates from all parts of the Peninsula, except the Romanian provinces, assembled in Kuci territory in Albania, in 1614, to devise a master plan for a general uprising against the Infidel. A mission was sent to Pope Paul V to apprise the pontiff of the likelihood of an uprising by some 160,000 Balkan Christians in support of Charles's plans for restoration of the Byzantine Empire. The ensuing planning by Charles and his supporters is shrouded in mystery, most likely because of its insignificance. The chronicler's allegation that a formidable fleet was readied by the duke, with papal support, in 1620 is unsubstantiated by any other evidence. It is known, however, that contacts were maintained between the Duke of Nevers and the Maniats, the Bishop of Arta, and the Bishop of Jannina between 1614 and 1620. It is also known that a few ships, presumably donated by Spain, were available to Charles in 1620 but their number and seaworthiness were both limited. At best, the vessels could offer protective cover for the incessant acts of piracy committed by the Maniats and their fellow pirates from Dalmatia, the Uskoks. In any event, we are told that the Duke of Nevers abandoned his plans in 1620. No reason for his decision is offered by Lenormant but it seems fair to assume that the pirates on whom he relied lacked the vision expected of "national" and "social" liberators and that the bishops of Arta and of Jannina themselves could not move the peasants and shepherds comprising their flocks into revolutionary action against the Turks.

Subsequent attempts at rebellion against the Turks, inspired by the Venetians and utilizing the corsairs of Mane as instruments for the execution of the Signoria's plans, met with a similar fate.[10] Thus the Maniats' raid on Kalamata, financed by Admiral Morosini during the Candian War in 1669, failed to arouse the inhabitants of the Morea to revolutionary action against the Porte.

Revolutionary manifestations in other parts of the Balkan Peninsula were also inconsequential. With the exception of the perennial defiance of Ottoman authority by Montenegrin and by certain Albanian and Bosnian tribes and of minor jacqueries elsewhere, no insurrectionary activity as such was recorded prior to the war of the Holy League which began in 1683. However, the number and variety of utopian plans for ridding the Balkans of the Infidel, with the assistance of the inhabitants of the Peninsula, increased markedly during the seventeenth century. And it was for the Catholic clergy and laymen who placed their confidence in the Spanish and Austrian Habsburgs, in the Jagellonians, in the Papacy, and even in the Signoria to become the moving force behind the various blueprints for "liberation" of Balkan Christendom.[11]

The role of the Catholics became potentially significant after 1615. The consular and commercial privileges secured by Austria through the Treaty of Vienna of that year facilitated proselytizing activities by Franciscans in certain areas of Albania, Bosnia, and Bulgaria inhabited by Catholic groups. One of the largest Catholic communities in the Balkans was located in Bulgarian territory at Čiprovec. There, an original nucleus of some 4,000 Saxon immigrants of the preconquest period, which constituted the core of the trading community, had grown in size over the years through conversion of the wealthier members of the Bulgarian Orthodox

26

population to Catholicism. By the middle of the seventeenth century, the size of the Catholic population, as well as the development of Austrian political interest in Ottoman affairs, resulted in the establishment of the archbishopric of Marcianopolis and of the eparchies of Skopje and Ochrida. Less elaborate were the activities of the Catholioo in Boonia, wheie the Franciscans' work was directed by the Papacy rather than by the Habsburgs. Nevertheless, Pope Clement VIII had been instrumental in developing close ties between Bosnian catholicism and Rome, Venice, and Spain.

The economic, cultural, and—by extension—political activities of the Catholic nations and of the Papacy itself precipitated the formulation of appeals for "liberation" by coreligionaries in the Balkan Peninsula. In 1625 the Bosnian Catholics sent a certain Fra Francesco Bertucci to Philip IV to inform the Spanish monarch of the readiness of the Albanian and Bosnian people to support a crusade against the Infidel.[12] It is doubtful that Bertucci's action was inspired by the existence of potential revolutionary activity in Albanian or Bosnian territories. Rather, his was a fishing expedition designed to ascertain the correlation between anti-Turkish propaganda, freely distributed by agents of Spain, Venice, and the Papacy, and possible Catholic action against the Porte. Philip IV impressed upon Bertucci, as he did upon Bertucci's nephew Fra Christof Tarnowski in later years, Spain's lack of interest in military action against the Turk.[13] Little is known about Bertucci's subsequent activities. Tarnowski, however, would not take no for an answer from Philip and from other Catholic luminaries, such as the Staathalter of Naples, the Duke of Alba and others, and decided to ally himself with such notorious adventurers and fictitious claimants to the Ottoman throne as the so-called Sultan Jacchia, as well as Kaspar Scioppio, in common efforts to persuade Ferdinand II of Austria and Wladislaw of Poland to subsidize a war of liberation against the Porte. All these efforts were to no avail. However, after the outbreak of the Candian War the Venetians were not adverse to enlisting the support of Jacchia in their own efforts to seek the assistance of Montenegrin Orthodox and of Albanian Catholic tribes or of Maniat corsairs to cut off Turkish access to Bocca Cattaro and reduce the effectiveness of the Turkish fleet and land forces in areas of strategic importance.

The Signoria's Provedittore of Cattaro negotiated an agreement with the Vladika of Montenegro in 1649, whereby Venice recognized and guaranteed Montenegro's independence while the Montenegrins agreed to join the Venetian forces in common military action against the Infidel. Similar agreements were also concluded with the tribes of Brda and Northern Albania.[14] The value to Venice of these treaties was limited, since its allies' interests differed markedly from its own. The Montenegrins were singularly concerned with extracting reassurances from the Porte that it would not interfere with the de facto independence which Montenegro had enjoyed since the fifteenth century, but which appeared threatened by the Porte's insistence of the Vladika's fulfilment of his obligations of vassalage. The Porte's prompt acceptance of the continuation of the status quo in Montenegro resulted in an equally prompt Montenegrin betrayal of Venice. Similarly, the ever-rebellious Bosnian and Northern Albanian tribes interpreted their agreement with the Signoria as a mandate for plundering Turks and Christians alike. The Venetians' interest in the Balkans declined considerably as a result of these experiences and reached its nadir after the death of the Wallachian hospodar Matei Basarab, the Signoria's last hope for military assistance by Balkan plotters and malcontents.

The Romanian ruler did hold out the possibility of concerted military action against the Porte by his own forces, and by other fighting men in the Peninsula, on the basis of an elaborate Bulgarian scheme for a Venetian-led crusade against the Infidel.[15] The Bulgarian plan was devised by several Catholic merchants and churchmen from Čiprovec headed by the Archbishop of Marcianopolis, Peter Parchevich. The architects of the plan advocated a war of liberation to be directed by Matei Basarab who, in the likely event of victory, would become the ruler of liberated Bulgaria as "Prince of the Orient." Matei facilitated contacts between Parchevich and Christian rulers befriended by the hospodar, including Wladislaw IV of Poland, from as early as 1648, but the Bulgarians' mission to the courts of Poland, Austria, and Spain met with failure. Only Venice offered encouragement in keeping with the Western principle of dissuading diversionary actions in the Balkans except in times of war or in areas adjacent to the belligerents' frontiers. It is doubtful, however, that the Venetians were at any time too sanguine about the feasibility of meaningful diversionary action by such unknown quantities as the Čiprovec conspirators or by such known scoundrels as Romanian hospodars. In any event, Parchevich's scheme if not stillborn came to naught with Matei's death.

Subversive and insurrectionary plans concocted within or outside the Peninsula, even when not utopian, could not, short of general war, lead to effective action against the

29

Porte. The establishment of relations among common enemies of the Ottoman Empire did, however, pave the way to
actual cooperation during the protracted war of the Holy
League of 1683–1699 and in all wars thereafter. Of greater
significance is the fact that the planners of revolution in the
Balkans failed to devise any practical mode whereby the
peasantry's growing disaffection with Ottoman rule could be
harnessed in a war of liberation against the Turk. This failure
raises fundamental questions regarding the revolutionary climate in the Peninsula in the seventeenth century.[16]

The hypothesis that religious differences between the
Catholic powers seeking the support of the Balkan masses
and the Orthodox masses themselves militated against collaboration against the Turk is unsubstantiated by the evidence. Restraining anti-Catholic sentiments did prevail in
certain parts of the Peninsula but, in general, the relations
between Orthodox and Catholics were harmonious. Other
factors are more pertinent in accounting for the peasants' ab-
stention from revolutionary activities directed against the
Turks. The Balkan village was habitually peaceful in the seventeenth century and the occasional jacqueries which occurred during that century were directed against specific
local abuses and not against Constantinople. The increase in
the power of local Ottoman officials and landholders subsequent to, and symptomatic of, the decentralization and decline of the Porte's authority was not identified by the masses
with a centrally directed anti-Christian policy that had to be
combated through concerted action. Increases in taxation
and the increase in the numbers of privately owned estates,
čiftliks, at the expense of the Ottoman fiefs, timars, were
still localized phenomena in the seventeenth century. It is

true that the growing frequency and duration of wars between the Porte and foreign powers, at least during the second half of the century, did affect the peasantry's security and economic status. But it is extremely doubtful that the masses' political consciousness was sufficiently high to appreciate the shift in the balance of power in Eastern Europe, or to warrant their joining potential liberators from what to the peasantry was still a tolerable social, economic, and political order. It is also doubtful whether the Orthodox parish priests who ministered to the political and spiritual needs of Balkan Christendom, ostensibly as the maintainers of the Christian spirit of revenge against the Infidel, were successful in winning many converts for that cause. Nor is there much reason to subscribe to the oft-repeated view that the folk ballads which comprised the oral, anti-Turkish, tradition of the Balkan peoples did in fact awaken the masses from their traditional political slumber.

More relevant to the study of the Balkan revolutionary tradition is the rise in the number and activities of *hajduks,* klephts, and *armatoles* in the seventeenth century.[17] This phenomenon should not be interpreted, however, as a reflection of the revolutionary attitude of the masses. Significantly, that increase was most marked in the Romanian provinces and in Greek territories. In the former, onerous fiscal practices combined with devastation resultant from war, drove villagers into the mountains and, as such, into the ranks of the outlaws. In Greek lands the phenomenon is to be explained primarily by the gradual transformation of the "protectors of peace"—the *armatoles*—into brigands, or klephts, chiefly because of the Turks' inability to pay for the *armatoles'* services and the corollary increase in the opportunities for brigandage afforded by war. Thus, in the seventeenth century, anti-Turkish actions within the Peninsula, while reflecting the shift in the economic and political balance of power in the East, were primarily a function of war. The leaders of Poland, of the Habsburg Empire, of Venice, or of the Cossacks and their accomplices, the princes of Wallachia and of Moldavia, or the bishops of Montenegro were far more influential in determining the course of revolutionary action in the Balkans than were a Parchevich, a Jacchia, or a Tarnowski. For the Porte, the danger of coordinated revolutionary action remained distant also because of the lack of communication and coordination of the efforts of actual or potential "liberators." As long as *hajduks* and klephts were recognized less as friends and allies and more as enemies by the Balkan peasantry, as long as the masses did not associate local abuses with an anti-Christian policy directed by Constantinople, as long as external enemies of the Porte would not consciously and persistently seek the support of the peoples of the Peninsula in their anti-Turkish ventures, the sporadic efforts of churchmen, whether Catholic or Orthodox, or of *hajduks,* klephts, and *armatoles* to upset the Ottoman order by revolutionary action were doomed to failure. In fact, closer coordination of internal and external interests and efforts were recorded only during the war which began in 1683.

During the period 1683–1699, revolts, uprisings, conspiracies, betrayals and other forms of anti-Turkish action manifested themselves, for the first time, throughout the Peninsula. Serbia, Bosnia, Albania, Bulgaria, the Romanian provinces, and Greece were all engulfed, at one time or another, in the wave of upheavals unleashed by the war. The generating force of most movements were the Habsburgs, who, gradually, as the war progressed, sought the support—often at gunpoint—of various members of the Balkan community. Other fomentors of revolutionary action included Poland, Venice, and Russia.

As usual, the focus of revolutionary activity was in the Romanian provinces, where conflicting Austrian and Polish interests converged.[18] Austrians and Poles were both seeking control over Moldavia and Wallachia and encouraged wars of liberation in both provinces. Preliminary negotiations with the voevod of Wallachia, Şerban Cantacuzino, and that of Moldavia, Gheorghe Duca, began in 1682. However, the Austrian and Polish offers were too niggardly for Cantacuzino and Duca, who consequently joined the Turks in the siege of Vienna. Duca made the wrong choice, because the majority of the Moldavian boyars sided with Sobieski after the unsuccessful siege of 1683. A coup engineered by the pro-Polish boyars dethroned Duca, who was replaced by Poland's man Ştefan Petriceicu. In 1684 the Tatars, acting on behalf of the Porte, restored Turkish suzerainty and removed Petriceicu. With the tide of the war turning again the following year, the Moldavian aristocracy replaced the new ruler, Dimitrie Cantacuzino, with the more pliant Constantin Cantemir. Cantemir and the boyars recognized pro forma the suzerainty of the Porte over Moldavia. The boyars leaned strongly toward Poland, while the voevod favored close relations with Poland, the Habsburgs, and Russia. Cantemir was able to maintain himself in power until 1693, when the boyars, by then fearful of Poland's growing territorial ambitions in Moldavia, sought

33

an accommodation with Constantinople. The Porte, anxious to secure Moldavia, confirmed the elective character of the Moldavian throne and reconfirmed the oligarchic powers of the aristocracy. Constantin Duca was thereupon restored to the throne, only to be removed once more in 1696, when the boyars decided that the Austrians were stronger than the Turks. A pro-Austrian ruler, Antioh Cantemir, was thereupon elected as voevod. He was deposed in 1700, when the boyars decided to reconsider their position vis-à-vis the Porte in the light of the Treaty of Karlowitz.

The impotent Porte had to tolerate these continuous challenges to its authority in Moldavia, but it could reconcile itself to the situation because of its enemies' inability to reach agreement on the division of the spoils. The situation in Moldavia, where Leopold I opposed the annexation of the province by Poland, had its counterpart in Wallachia, where the Poles were just as adamant against Austria's gaining possession of that province. The pattern of intervention and subversion in Wallachia closely resembled the Moldavian. Şerbyan Cantacuzino, the voevod, and the majority of the boyars remained loyal to the Porte even after the Ottoman withdrawal from Vienna. Several missions by Grof Ladislas Csáky to Bucharest failed to persuade Cantacuzino to cast his lot with the Habsburgs. Veterani's victories in Hungary and Leopold's celebrated appeals to Balkan Christendom for revolution against the Porte also had no effect on the Wallachian ruler. Cantacuzino's position was determined less by fears of Turkish reprisals than by Vienna's insistence on Wallachia's becoming a vassal state of the Empire. Immediately after his death, however, his successor, Constantin Brâncoveanu had to accept Austria's terms under the threat of occupation of

34

the province. The treaty of vassalage and military support of 1688 was repudiated by Brâncoveanu in 1689 upon receipt of military aid from the Turks. The subsequent occupation of Wallachia by the forces commanded by Ludwig von Baden and General Heissler was short-lived. In 1690 the Austrians withdrew in the face of a joint Ottoman-Tartar counterattack. Brâncoveanu immediately restated his formal allegiance to Constantinople, but by this time he was ready and willing to engage in concurrent negotiations with Austria, Poland, and Russia—all viewed as possible claimants to suzerainty over Wallachia at the end of the war. His new attitude was also dictated by the political actions of the boyars, which reflected a maturing of political ideology in the Romanian provinces.

Since the beginning of the seventeenth century, the boyars of the Danubian provinces were united in their common opposition to Greek infiltration and to the imposition of limitations by the Porte on their right to elect the ruling princes.[19] Removal of all obstacles to the retention of their oligarchic position was the essence of the political theory of the Romanian aristocracy. The attainment of these goals was more feasible in Moldavia than in Wallachia. The Moldavian aristocracy held trump cards which the Wallachian lacked. One was the support of the Cossacks, which reached its zenith during the days of Bogdan Khmelnitsky and Vasile Lupu. When that support began to wane a few years later, as a consequence of the ascendancy of Moscow, the Moldavian nobility turned toward Russia. However, early contacts with Moscow yielded no results. A treaty of vassalage concluded in 1654 between Gheorghe Ştefan of Moldavia and Czar Alexis was never implemented for lack of genuine Russian concern for the problems of Moldavia.[20] A similar agreement of some twenty years later also remained a dead letter. In 1688 Constantin Cantemir assured Moscow of Moldavia's support in the event of Russian military intervention in the Romanian provinces, but, again, no commitment could be secured from Moldavia's neighbor to the east.

The adverse geographic location did not allow the boyars of Wallachia to exercise the same options. The Wallachians' choice was strictly between Austria and the Porte. The agreement of 1689 tended to favor collaboration with Austria but caution dictated a pro-Turkish attitude. Except for a small pro-Austrian group, the Wallachian aristocracy—fearful of outright incorporation of the Danubian provinces into the Habsburg Empire—favored neutrality during the War of the Holy League. And these fears were not allayed by the Austrians' victories over the Turks. The Wallachians' caution was justified at Karlowitz but even so the Turks remained suspicious of the ostensible loyalty displayed by the Romanian aristocracy during the conflict. The constant intrigues by covert anti-Turkish groups, the omnipresent threat of subversion and revolution, were all too well-known to the Porte and were considered all the more dangerous because of the overt revolutionary manifestations which occurred in other parts of the Peninsula during the long war of the Holy League.

The Holy League had failed to commit the Romanian provinces to revolutionary action against the Porte but succeeded in fomenting such action elsewhere. As the Austrian armies crossed the Danube, the until-then cautious and reticent Montenegrins, Serbs, Bosnians, and Albanians agreed to cast their lot with the Habsburg forces.[21] The Austrians succeeded where the Venetians had failed during the early

36

stages of the war. The Signoria's appeals to Albanians and Bosnians went unanswered. Venice was in no position to match the extravagant promises contained in Leopold's proclamation to Bosnians and Albanians of September 1687—promises which prompted the Piperi, Klementi, Kuci, and other Albanian and Bosnian tribes to stage meaningful diversionary raids against Turkish forces in Bosnia and Herzegovina. The emperor's assurances of military support and recognition of the tribes' traditional rights, privileges, and liberties were by themselves of less significance in swaying the Bosnians and Albanians than the prospects of reaping financial benefits from direct cash subsidies and the opportunities for looting inherent in Austrian military action. That the tribesmen's motivations were not heroic or distinctly anti-Turkish is acknowledged by both Piccolomini and his successor, the Duke of Holstein, who as commanders of the Austrian forces found themselves subject to harassment which their so-called allies had been traditionally meting out to the Turks.[22] The Austrian leaders' attempts to coordinate the common war effort was bitterly opposed by the Bosnians and Albanians: within a few months the war of liberation against the Infidel degenerated into one against the Habsburgs. Similarly, the Montenegrins, who had extended token support to their theoretical old-time ally Venice from as early as 1684, and who had fought in earnest upon receipt of funds and renewed assurances from the Signoria in 1687, were not adverse to entertaining the overtures and receiving the gifts emanating from Austrian agents. But as the Montenegrins were opposed to discipline and centralized planning, their diversionary actions directed against the Turks ceased by 1690.

The risks inherent in commitment to one or another of the participants in an anti-Turkish war were rather minimal for the Montenegrin, Albanian, and Bosnian tribes. But this was not true for the Serbs. Several factors militated against Serbian commitment to the allies. Serbian leaders such as the patriarchs of Peć, or knezes, or voevods had a long record of jealousy guarding their essentially privileged status in the Ottoman Empire. They remained manifestly suspicious of Austria's motivations in the eighties, since they all shared the fear that an Austrian victory over the Turks would not necessarily be beneficial to Serbian interests. Patriarch Arsenje, the spiritual and political leader of the Serbs, was particularly insistent on securing firm guarantees of Austrian respect of "traditional Serbian rights" as the price of revolt against the Porte.[23] From as early as 1684, the patriarch, conscious of the threat to Serbian neutrality, engaged in preliminary pourparlers with the weakest and least dangerous member of the Christian coalition, Venice. The lack of encouragement received from the Signoria—desinterested in involvement in areas remote from the sea—made him all-the-more fearful of the necessity of having to deal with Austria. He therefore turned to Russia. His messenger to Moscow asked for Russia's intervention on behalf of the Serbs for liberation from the Turk and prevention of "forcible union" with Catholic Austria. The Russians' polite refusal was intercepted by the Austrians, who threatened Arsenje with deposition lest he agreed to casting the Serbs' lot with the imperial forces. In the absence of alternatives, the patriarch consented. But the Serbs' military ineffectiveness—a reflection of their anti-Austrian feelings and lack of interest in pursuing the war against the Turks—forced Leopold's hand. Indeed, the possibility of

38

disintegration of the allied forces because of the inaction of the forcibly impressed Serbs and opportunistic Albanians and Bosnians prompted the issuance of the celebrated Proclamation of April 1690, whereby the emperor promised support to all members of Balkan Christendom against the Turks and guaranteed to all freedom of worship, exemption from taxation, and political autonomy under Austrian sovereignty.[24] These privileges were subsequently extended, on Arsenje's request, to all those who might be forced to seek asylum in Austrian lands. The emperor's deed did not bolster the Serbs' fighting spirit, particularly after the withdrawal of the Austrian forces from the Peninsula in the same year. It did, however, make possible the mass migration of Patriarch Arsenje and some 90,000 of his followers into Habsburg territories, also in 1690, an event which marked the de facto cessation of revolutionary activity in Serbia, Albania, Bosnia, and Montenegro.

Arsenje's circumspection and precautionary measures were justified. His mistrust of the Austrians had been augmented by Habsburg actions in Bulgaria in 1688 and betrayal of their own "man in Serbia," George Branković.[25]

The Bulgarian and Serbian movements were theoretically coordinated through the utilization by Leopold I of a certain George Branković. This presumed descendant of the Serbian despot of the fifteenth century acted as the emperor's emissary of revolution in the Peninsula, urging action against the Turk to avenge his ancestor's honor and obtain the restoration of Vouk's empire from "Ossek to Belgrade," of course, under George's rule. The effectiveness of his appeal to the Bulgarians is open to question, as the evidence would favor a more pragmatic explanation for the outbreak of the uprising in Bulgarian territory in 1688. At that time, a group of Bulgarian Catholics headed by a certain George Pejačević decided to join the allied forces headed by Veterani, Heissler, and Czáky as these crossed the Danube. An imperial proclamation guaranteeing autonomy to liberated territories or asylum to unsuccessful rebels was read to the inhabitants of the focal point of the uprising, the town of Čiprovec, by Pejačević and his immediate followers.[26] Only a minimal number of Bulgarian peasants, however, put their faith in the Čiprovec rebels and their external allies. The caution was justified, since the military commanders, whose commitment to Bulgarian liberation did not match Leopold's and Branković's professions, soon left the rebels at the mercy of the Turks. The Bulgarians' fate was shared by Branković but at the hands of the Austrians. In 1689 he was convicted for conspiring with Russia and with Arsenje and for the consequent failure of the Bulgarian venture.

The only part of the Peninsula where revolutionary activities were carried out independently of direct or indirect Austrian pressure was the area inhabited by Greeks.[27] Venetian entreaties to the Greeks, reinforced by the Signoria's conquest of Navarino, Nauplia, and the Morea, resulted in the Athenian primate's submission to Venice in 1687. The act of submission was not regarded as revolutionary by the Porte, which wisely sought the support of "its subjects" in the war of liberation from Venetian oppression. A large number of Athenians who had joined the Venetians in 1687 heeded the Turkish appeal in that they returned to Athens following the Venetian withdrawal from the Morea. The other supporters of the Signoria's plans for liberation of the Peninsula from the Infidel, the traditionally restless and rebellious Maniats and

40

the unruly klephts and *armatoles,* were both ineffectual and unreliable allies, since their primary goal was the plundering of Venetians, Turks, and Greeks alike. By 1699 when the Treaty of Karlowitz brought the War of the Holy League to an end, all revolutionary activity had ended in Greek territories and, for that matter, throughout the Balkan Peninsula.

The internationalization of Balkan problems and the corollary increase in revolutionary manifestations by the Balkan peoples, which had occurred during that prolonged conflict and—to a lesser degree even earlier in the seventeenth century, did nevertheless represent a new and significant dimension in the Balkan revolutionary tradition. Whereas it is true that alteration of the status quo through revolutionary action was not desired by the majority of the inhabitants of the Peninsula or by their leaders, the passive attitude of the Balkan peoples did not necessarily reflect satisfaction with the Ottoman order. It is fair to say that the peoples of the Peninsula found the alternate solutions provided by the Christian "liberators" equally unsatisfactory. The external fomentors of revolutionary activities, conspiracies, or sedition and their agents or supporters in the Peninsula were unable to rally the masses to action against the Infidel. The Austrians and Poles, when confining their activities to the Romanian provinces, utilized boyar factions for the attainment of their goals. In collaborating with the feudal aristocracy, they alienated the oppressed peasant population. The Venetians sought the support of unruly tribesmen, pirates, and brigands, whose activities—directed against the native population as much as against the Turks—failed to generate mass support. But even when external powers sought the collaboration of trusted native elements, spiritual leaders in particular, the masses

41

could not be aroused to revolt against the Porte. It would be erroneous to assume that the people's reticence was a reflection of religious considerations. Rather, the lack of response to propaganda, whether emanating from Catholic or Orthodox sources, was a reflection of general apathy toward change. In short, the masses' attitude was supremely pragmatic based on personal and local considerations. Jacqueries, and the joining of *hajduk* or similar bands remained the fundamental manifestations of mass discontent with abuses, no matter by whom perpetrated.

The motivations of the *hajduks,* klephts, *armatoles,* tribesmen, and other "free" elements that disturbed the peace of the Balkans in the seventeenth century also belie the myth of their anti-Turkish crusading spirit and heroism. Their manifestations were primarily anti-Turkish, because these popular heroes operated within the Ottoman Empire. But their "revolutionary" activities could just as well be qualified as anti-Christian, since, in fact, they were also directed against fellow Christians in the Peninsula and against external crusaders, be they Venetian, Austrian, or anyone else. Significantly too, the clergy—traditionally credited with at least maintaining the spirit of opposition to the Turk if not directly fomenting overt anti-Ottoman manifestations—does not mirror its assigned image. With rare exceptions, the Orthodox churchmen were passive members of the Christian community who favored maintenance of the status quo. And even the more militant Catholic priests and missionaries did not emulate Peter Parčević or encourage subversion by their coreligionaries. Indeed, the only Catholics who manifested revolutionary tendencies were merchants and churchmen in Bulgarian territory, but their number was small and their

42

revolt occurred only in time of war. And for that matter, even the most active political figures of the Balkans—the Romanian voevods and boyars—were neither crusaders nor necessarily anti-Turkish. For them, subversion, conspiracy, and revolt were dictated by selfish considerations ultimately related to the safeguarding of prerogatives.

External intervention in Balkan affairs did not directly generate or enhance the revolutionary spirit of the Balkan peoples. In fact, because of their extreme cynicism and frequent reliance on suspect elements, the policies of the Christian powers could not secure the support of the inhabitants of the Peninsula. The significance of external intervention in the Balkan revolutionary tradition lies elsewhere. The continuing warfare which characterized the seventeenth century in the Ottoman Empire adversely affected all levels of Balkan society. The gradual extension of the areas of combat from the Romanian provinces, early in the century, to almost every part of the Peninsula by the century's end committed an increasingly larger number of inhabitants of the Balkans to military action against the Turk. War also brought devastation to large areas, displacement of populations, changes in boundaries, and fundamental shifts in the balance of power in Eastern Europe. The *Pax Ottomanica* had been gravely disrupted in the seventeenth century and ended de facto at Karlowitz. To prevent its own destruction, the Porte was to destroy the *Pax Ottomanica* de jure in the eighteenth. At that time, the alternatives proffered by foreign enemies of the Porte, which had been rejected in the seventeenth century, became attractive to the peoples of the Peninsula. At that time too, the native, spontaneous manifestations of discontent both multiplied and assumed a clearly defined anti-Ottoman character. The search for alternatives at all levels of society gained momentum after Karlowitz. And it was that search which altered the character of revolution in the Peninsula in the years antedating the French Revolution and Napoleonic France.

·3·

REVOLUTIONARY MOVEMENTS
IN THE EIGHTEENTH CENTURY

The peace treaty of Karlowitz did not engender enthusiasm or optimism among the inhabitants of the Balkan Peninsula or among their leaders. Restoration of the status quo ante had brought with it the realization that the traditional modus vivendi with the Porte had to be continued. That much was understood also by Constantinople. No immediate tightening of controls or exceptional fiscal exactions were imposed, as no exacerbation of latent dissatisfaction was deemed desirable. If anything, the Turks, disoriented by military defeats and apprehensive over the continuing conflict with Peter the Great, chose to magnify the advantages enjoyed by the Christian population under Ottoman rule by sowing mistrust in Austrian, Venetian, and Russian policies. The attempts to placate the rayas were, however, undermined by the Porte's growing financial and political dependence on the Phanariote Greeks, particularly in the Romanian provinces and in Serbian territories. No wonder then that disaffected Serbs approached Peter the Great with a view to securing financial

45

and military support against the Turks and against the Porte's principal agent, the Greek successor to Arsenje, Patriarch Kolonikos. In all likelihood, the advice of patience given by the czar to one of the Serbian spokesmen, Sava Vladislavić—the alleged author of the Petrine proclamation to Balkan Christendom of 1711—reflected his own views and ambitions more than the hopes and aspirations of the Serbian masses, but it apparently did salve the anti-Greek and anti-Ottoman sentiments of the Serbs. This is not to say that Sava Vladislavić himself spoke for all Serbs any more than the Moldavian hospodar Dimitrie Cantemir spoke for his Romanian subjects. Indeed, Cantemir's negotiations with the Russian monarch, which eventually led to the dual Moldo-Wallachian rebellion against the Porte, were only partially representative of Romanian dissaffection with foreign rule. And this was also true of the tribal leaders of Montenegro and of Herzegovina who concocted plots directed against the Turks. It is within this frame of reference, therefore, that the reaction of the Balkan peoples and of their leaders to the first major Russian intervention in Balkan affairs must be considered.[1]

The much-heralded appeal to Balkan Christendom issued by Peter in March 1711 was calculated to achieve the same ends as Leopold's declaration of nearly a quarter-of-a-century earlier. Peter's experts on Balkan affairs, a Serbian émigré group headed by Sava Vladislavić, provided the very same formula for liberation which had proven its worthlessness in the days of Leopold. The czar's repetition of the emperor's stereotypes merely illustrated his lack of understanding of the realities of conditions in the Balkans. Peter, on the basis of assurances received from his principal agent in the Peninsula, the Montenegrin prince-bishop Danilo Pe-

46

trović, and of tentative political agreements with Dimitrie Cantemir, the Moldavian hospodar, succumbed to the temptation of exploiting what he was made to believe was massive expectation by revolutionary-minded Christians of a clarion call to an anti-Ottoman crusade.[2] Russian comprehension of the mood of the Balkan peoples and of the motivations of their leaders was minimal. Had not Dimitrie Cantemir promised from as early as 1710 the unconditional armed support of all Moldavians and even committed Constantin Brâncoveanu, his Wallachian confrere, to the war of liberation? Had not Danilo, as well as the Herzegovinian chieftain Miloradović and even Vladislavić himself, assured the czar and his agents of unlimited cooperation and certain victory? Apparently Peter relied on the promises of the Moldavian ruler, which, of all, proved to be the most ephemeral. Indeed Cantemir had no assurances of support from Brâncoveanu or even from Brâncoveanu's enemies among the Wallachian boyars. He and Peter deluded themselves into believing that a sudden and swift attack through Moldavia would induce the opportunistic Wallachian hospodar and his entourage to side with the Russo-Moldavian coalition. The czar should have been more circumspect about Cantemir's motives. Mihai Racoviță, Cantemir's predecessor, had requested aid from Russia after Poltava, ostensibly to fight the Turks but actually to use against the Phanar and those Moldavian boyars who sought his removal from power. Cantemir—in no small measure responsible for Racoviță's banishment by the Porte—used more sophisticated arguments to attain the same goal. The negotiations between the czar and the prince, initiated in 1710 and completed by the Treaty of Lusk in April 1711, revealed Cantemir's price. The czar had to confirm and

47

guarantee the traditional, but for a long time eroded, absolute powers of the Moldavian sovereign. In return, Cantemir promised to deliver the support of the Moldavian peasants, who regarded the voevod as the protector of their interests, as the continuator of the antiboyar and, as such, reformist tendencies of Mihai Racoviţă. Cantemir was gambling on what he believed to be superior Russian military power, while Peter gave credence to the overdrawn picture of the military weakness of the Turks. It was that belief which apparently tipped the scale in Peter's ultimate decision more than the advice of his brain trust or the messages received from his Montenegrin supporters.[3]

The outcome of Peter's venture is well-known. Less well-known is the fact that Cantemir's prognostications were exceedingly optimistic. The peasantry was either prevented from acting by an alert boyardom, or acted in a most desultory manner when it became evident that neither Cantemir nor the czar were actually committed to emancipation or reform. The notion of the emancipator-czar was readily debunked by the aristocracy, including those boyars who had temporarily—before the inevitability of defeat became evident—cast their lot with Cantemir and the Russians. The Montenegrins and Herzegovinians who rose after Peter's summons fared no better. Lack of support from the czar, the Peć patriarch, and the Balkan peasantry restricted the uprisings to Montenegro and southern Herzegovina. Short-lived and ineffectual as all these anti-Turkish activities were, they nevertheless made the Porte more apprehensive and the Phanar more greedy.[4]

The Russo-Turkish war of 1711 and Cantemir's uprising were turning points in the history of the Romanian provinces. The formal termination of rule by native princes and the instauration of outright Phanariot despotism were the immediate and direct consequences. The Turks' primary motivation was the securing of a controllable counterrevolutionary leadership in Moldavia and Wallachia. But the Porte was also ready to strengthen Phanariot administrative power in general. Through appointments to key clerical and lay positions throughout the Ottoman Empire, it sought not only to immobilize would-be conspirators but also to stabilize the tottering Ottoman economy. The Turkish policies did indeed provide a modicum of internal stability until the favored Greeks abused their privileges and powers.

It would be erroneous to ascribe the relative internal tranquility to Phanariot cunning and Ottoman restraint alone. Other factors, most notably the blunders committed by rival European powers, contributed to the short-lived restauration of a fragile *Pax Ottomanica*. The Phanariots did actually challenge the primacy of vested interests throughout the Peninsula, particularly in the Romanian provinces. The outright appointment of Greek hospodars to the provincial thrones after 1714 alienated the Romanian aristocracy in Wallachia and Moldavia. Elsewhere in the Balkans, the Greeks usurped the rights of the native clergy and of the rising commercial class. Nevertheless, this disaffection with Greek rule and power did not engender violent action against the Phanariots or their Turkish protectors, partly because of comparable disenchantment with would-be, or actual, foreign "liberators," and partly—as was the case in the Romanian provinces—because of the Phanariots' advocacy of agrarian and fiscal reforms. For instance, Nicolae Mavrocordat was able to frustrate the anti-Ottoman conspiracy organized by former followers of Constantin Brâncoveanu during the Austro-Turkish war of 1716–1718 by, inter alia, diverting the anger of the masses through promises of social and economic betterment. And the strategy of the Austrians, both during and after the war which ended by the Treaty of Passarowitz, helped the cause of the Phanariots. The Habsburgs had been unresponsive to the wartime demands of the boyars for restoration of their traditional privileges, so abused by the Phanariot rulers, and their stock declined even further after Passarowitz because of their abusive treatment of the aristocracy of Little Wallachia, the Romanian territory incorporated into the Habsburg Empire in 1718.[5]

In fact, in Little Wallachia, the Austrians' attitude toward the Romanian boyars so alienated the Romanian aristocracy in that province, and in Wallachia and Moldavia as well, that even the pro-Austrian boyars sought the support of Russia in their struggle for maintenance of privileges. Most striking in this respect were the demarches of Russia's principal agent in Moldavia, the boyar Lupu Anastasă, who asked the Russians in the name of fellow aristocrats to restore the historic rights of all Romanian boyars in the event of war between Russia and the Ottoman Empire. But such contacts were limited, both because of Russian inaction and Turko-Greek vigilance.[6]

Similar and equally inconsequential conspiracies and intrigues occurred also in other parts of the Peninsula, but the majority of the potential leaders were either war-weary, or discouraged, or at peace with the Porte. The Greek primates had been granted virtual autonomy by Constantinople after the Venetians' withdrawal from the Morea. The Phanar was privileged and prosperous. The Serbians' revolutionary spirit was blunted by their experiences with the Habsburgs both before and after 1718. Still, the rallying of Balkan Christendom to action against the Turk remained an essential concept of Austrian and Russian planners and was once more put into practice on the eve of a new war against the Turks, which began in 1736.

The principal conspirators and activists in this round of warfare were the Moldavians and the Albanians. The Moldavian activities focused on supplying intelligence to the Russians and establishing a basis for native military assistance to Russian troops. The pro-Russian boyars, a cautious minority headed by Lupu and the Duca brothers, sought the collaboration of the even fewer known Wallachian supporters of a pro-Russian course. Joint delegations sent to Russia requested both military intervention and political guarantees for the boyal oligarchy. The Russians did raise the question of independence for the Romanian provinces—albeit under Russian protection—at the Nemirov Congress in 1737 and held out vague promises of liberation at "the right moment." It was evident to Turks and Romanians that the liberation of the provinces was of secondary interest to the Russians at that time. The Romanian boyar groups thereupon assumed the role of mediators between the Porte and St. Petersburg, hoping to strengthen their own positions at the end of the war, no matter what its ultimate outcome. Only in 1739, when the possibilities of a separate peace seemed remote and the Russians invaded Moldavia, did the Moldavian "intermediaries" join the Russian forces and sign an agreement with General Munnich, by which Moldavia's independence "under Russian protection" was won. The short-lived Russo-Moldavian convention of September 1739 also reconfirmed the

51

"old feudal rights" of the boyars and clergy, which resulted in the abandonment of the common anti-Turkish war effort by the peasantry. The peasants had been suspicious of the Russians from the very beginning of the campaign, despite the standard proclamation of liberation of Balkan Christendom issued by the advancing armies. A few joined General Mannstein's forces but most remained loyal to Grigore Ghica's commanders until the Phanariot hospodar gave up the uneven fight and fled the province. Evidently the Greek policy of divide and conquer, of supporting the peasant against the native boyar, had been more effective than generally assumed. It would, however, be inaccurate to ascribe the Russians' withdrawal from Moldavia to lack of cooperation by the Romanian masses. Rather, the Austrians' signing of the separate peace treaty of Belgrade led to Russia's coming to terms with the Porte. But the Russian withdrawal broke the back of the pro-Russian boyar party, whose members either accompanied the Russian forces across the Dniester, or made last-minute shifts of allegiance back to the Porte, or were summarily executed by the restored Phanariots. By contrast, the Wallachian conspirators abandoned all activities after Nemirov, a few adopting instead a policy of collaboration with Austria. However Mavrocordat, the hospodar, commanded the confidence of the Porte and of the masses and, for that matter, was tolerated by the majority of the Wallachian aristocracy as well. To the boyars, the Phanariot regime was ultimately preferable to an Austrian one, since the Greeks were more corruptible and the Porte weaker than reformist Vienna. Besides the Austrians did not encourage sedition in Wallachia, concentrating instead on exploiting the revolutionary potential of the Southern Slavs and of the Albanians.[7]

It is by no means clear whether the contacts between Vienna and the Albanian and Herzegovinian tribal leaders— or for that matter, with the Patriarch of Peć—were initiated by Austrian agents or by would-be beneficiaries from Austrian military intervention in the Peninsula. That Vienna maintained agents in areas of potential collaboration is known but the effectiveness of those agents is not. Sedition and similar pro-Austrian revolutionary manifestations were generally opposed in times of peace even by perennial disturbers of tranquility in the Ottoman Empire. However, it was more than mere coincidence that immediately after the outbreak of hostilities between Austria and the Porte, solicitants from various Southern Slav and Albanian areas appeared in Vienna to pledge the support which Austrian agents had previously sought in vain. The first suppliants were Albanian tribal leaders from Novi Bazar, followed in turn by yet another Patriarch of Peć (Arsenje IV), by a few Serbian knezes—headed by Stephan Brvenicsky and Athanasie Rašković—and by several minor tribal leaders from Bosnia, Herzegovina, and Macedonia. By the spring of 1737, all were committed to supporting the Austrian armies. The tribal leaders' demands, when limited to arms and money, were readily met by Vienna. But the patriarch and the knezes were no longer satisfied merely with shallow proclamations of liberation of Balkan Christendom or promises of asylum in the event of military withdrawal. They now sought formal guarantees in the event of victory or defeat and, in the case of the knezes, also recognition of their independence following liberation; and, in the case of the patriarch, appointment to Karlowitz in the event of failure of the anti-Turkish crusade.

Both sides negotiated in bad faith. The Austrians were

promised military support by 30,000 rebels were they to accept these terms, to which they readily acquiesced, in the knowledge that neither side was prepared to fulfill its obligations. In actual combat the number of rebels gathered between 1737 and 1739 (exclusive of professional fighters like the Klementi and Piperi) numbered less than 2,000 and their military effectiveness was nil. The concept of liberation was not deeply rooted in the areas committed to support the Austrian effort, although it is certain that the Austrian forces also deterred potential warriors from joining the "liberators." The general fiasco, culminating in the abject concessions made by the Austrians at Belgrade in 1739, justified the reticence of the skeptics. But the direct and indirect consequences of the abortive political and military moves made in the various parts of the Peninsula during the war were to affect the revolutionary climate and potential for a long time to come.[8]

The alarming prospect of further Austro-Russian ventures that would make more effective use of the Christian population prompted retaliatory action by the Porte against actual and potential supporters of "liberators." The Turks were particularly alarmed by the constant restiveness of the Albanian and Herzegovinian tribes, and of the Greek klephts and *armatoles*—all operating in an uncontrollable area of the Peninsula. Constantinople therefore decided to seek forcible mass conversion to Islam of the Christian mountaineers of Albania, Herzegovina, and adjoining Greek territories. The task was entrusted to the loyal Albanian Pasha Mehmet Bushatlya and some lesser associates, who pursued the extermination-conversion campaign with great vigor but relatively little success. If most of the Brda tribes were defeated and numerous members Moslemized, victory proved ephemeral, as the Ottoman forces were unable to exercise effective control over the treacherous mountaineers. The constant skirmishes with the Greek *armatoles* and clephts, which soon involved regular mountain tribes like the Mirdites and Souliotes, merely increased the levels of unrest and lawlessness along the ill defined Albanian-Greek frontier. In fact, Mehmet's activities caused the number of anti-Ottoman guerrilas to increase even in neighboring Montenegro and generally exacerbated relations between Moslem and Christian elements in the mountainous areas of the southwest. In this area, at least, retaliation invited counter-retaliation and opened the door to Austrian and Russian agents much more widely than before the ill-fated events of the late thirties. Indeed, in the fifties and early sixties, as discussions between a plethora of Russian and Austrian agents and the mountaineers were renewed, the response of the latter was far more positive than in the past.[9]

In other parts of the Peninsula—even where partial collaboration with the enemy had been manifest—Ottoman reprisals were less severe, though by no means inconsequential. In Serbia, for instance, following Patriarch Arsenje's departure to assume the Karlowitz diocese, the patriarchal see was staffed with reliable Greek elements as a guarantee against a repetition of the events of 1737. Peć's inability to become a rallying force for discontented Orthodox Serbs, however, was apparent to the Porte, which resisted Greek pressures for outright abolition of the Patriarchate. Constantinople also stopped short of ordering more than routine punitive measures against the Serbian population. Nevertheless, the power of the Greek element in the Peninsula was considerably strengthened after 1740. The spreading of Phanariot influence was not confined only to the Romanian provinces and Serbia: it reached even Bulgarian territories. Promises of greater revenues through Phanariot economic activity in the Peninsula, combined with the Phanar's ability to convince the Porte that the strengthening of the Orthodox *millet* would arrest subversion, facilitated Greek infiltration into coveted ecclesiatic posts and into urban economic centers of the Peninsula after 1740. The abolition of the patriarchates of Peć and Trnovo in the later sixties was indicative of the success of Phanariot policies, designed to build a state within a state in a declining Ottoman Empire.[10] Nowhere were the Phanariots more successful, however, than in the Romanian provinces. The Greek hospodars of Moldavia and Wallachia vigorously pursued their campaign of destroying the pro-Russian and pro-Austrian boyar groups, in order to consolidate their own control over the economic and political life of the provinces. The rapid promotion of fellow Phanariots to boyardoms, following execution of the native aristocracy accused of plotting with the enemies of the Porte, exacerbated the basic hostility of the Romanian boyars to Greek rule. By the sixties, the Moldavian and Wallachian aristocracies were far more responsive to Russian overtures than they had been thirty years earlier. The anger of the boyars was, of course, also enhanced by the continuation of the practice of issuing, and occasionally implementing, decrees favoring the peasant at the expense of the master. Constantin Mavrocordat's actions on behalf of the Romanian peasantry, culminating in the theoretical abolition of serfdom by the middle of the century, could not be implemented because of boyar opposition. However, they incensed the Romanian aristocracy and raised the expectations of the peasantry sufficiently to trigger off

56

several bloody local jacqueries.[11] The aims of the Greeks were attained also in Greek territories as such. The primates' position in the Peloponnesos, and that of the merchants in the islands, were considerably strengthened in the eighteenth century as a result of concessions made by Constantinople after Passarowitz and of their close collaboration with a benevolent Porte. Still, the peace which the Turks had been able to maintain through repression and concessions in the forties and fifties was severely and by-and-large successfully jolted by the Russians in the sixties.

The striking feature in the renewal of the Russian offensive against the Ottoman Empire through incitement to revolution of discontented elements in the Peninsula was the change in the nature and location of would-be supporters. The Russians fared badly among the Albanian tribes, Serbians, and even Montenegrins. Their success in the Romanian provinces was even more limited than in the thirties. By contrast the response to Russian entreaties was unexpectedly enthusiastic in several parts of the Greek peninsula. There were good reasons for this.

Turkish reprisals carried out against the Albanians accounted for these peoples' reticence to side with Russia. The abolition of Peć was clearly a factor in Serbian hesitation. But the evasiveness of the traditionally pro-Russian and revolt-oriented Montenegrins reflected a change in outlook among the constantly restless tribesmen. It is apparent that by the time the celebrated Russian mission of Dolgorouki reached Montenegro in 1769 to seek support against the Porte, the Montenegrin leaders had decided to raise their price for collaboration. This novel attitude had been noticeable as early as the thirties. It became more pronounced during the early fif-

57

ties, following the temporary termination of the perennial military conflict with the Turks over the payment of *haradj*. By 1754 a majority of the tribal leaders had decided that the payment of the head tax, as a token of vassalage, was more than compensated for by the de facto granting of autonomy to Montenegro by an Osman III tired of constant guerrilla warfare in the Black Mountain. The Montenegrin decision was also prompted by the inefficiency of Russian financial support of their cause. The repeated missions to Moscow undertaken by Montenegrin delegates in search of financial aid for allegedly religious purposes met with only nominal success. The sums provided by the Patriarchate were inconsequential, even in comparison with those paid by the Venetians, and the likelihood of increments in times of crisis appeared doubtful. The Austrians themselves, although leaning toward disengagement in the Peninsula after 1740, were ready to provide more adequate remuneration than the Russians. As a consequence, Dolgorouki, the fearless agent dispatched by Orlov to Cetinje in 1769, encountered enormous difficulties before wresting promises of participation from pro-Russian chieftains. Those opposed to cooperation with Russia, led by the self-styled Peter III of Russia, the notorious impostor, and Venetian agent Stephen Mali, proved to be more accurate in their estimate of Russian reliability than the gullible traditionalists headed by Bishop Sava Petrović. In fact, Dolgorouki's departure without the fleet which was to assist the Montenegrins in the common war of liberation proved the foolishness of Petrović's followers, who by then had committed the Montenegrins to anti-Ottoman action.[12]

Greater enthusiasm was generated in Greek territories by what proved to be empty promises voiced by Russia's chief agents Papazolis and Papadopoulos. The primates and commercial leaders in the Morea were particularly naïve and susceptible to the fraudulent entreaties of the Russians. Tempted by the promised redistribution of Ottoman lands and capital to the Greeks at the end of the war against the Porte; and believing that Orlov's fleet, which was to anoint the warriors, was indeed a major instrument of war, the Greek leaders in the Morea were unaware of the cynicism of Gregory Orlov and of his masters in St. Petersburg. For the Russian aim was simply to stage a diversionary move in the Morea to allow decisive military action against Turkish forces in the Romanian provinces, and to make use of Moreote harbors as Orlov's fleet advanced toward Constantinople. The Spahiotes of Crete were also deceived by Russian propaganda, as were the Maniats, klephts, and *armatoles*—all ready to avenge the abuses of which the Turks and the Albanians were deemed guilty.

It is indeed noteworthy that the peasantry was most reluctant to lend support to collaborationist primates and mountaineers. The primates were unpopular because of the growth of their powers after Passarowitz; the mountaineers, because of their indiscriminate plundering of peasant property. The clergy too displayed strong opposition to adventurous moves. The prospect of usurpation of the traditional rights of the Greek church by the Moscow Patriarchate in the event of Russian victory was as feared as the desecration of church property by mountaineers in times of war, or the certitude of Turkish reprisals in case of military defeat.

The skeptics were right. The revolt, poorly organized and devoid of mass support, did not provide the diversion required by the Russians. The Orlov brothers' often desperate at-

59

tempts to rally the native forces were successful only in the southern Peloponnesus, at least until the Albanians reached the scene of the conflict. The decimation by loyal Albanian forces of the land armies assembled by the Greeks caused the immediate withdrawal of the fleet from Mane and, within three months, the total collapse of the ineffectual uprising.[13]

In the Romanian provinces alone was the show of Russian power impressive. But Russia's successes were determined more by the strength of her armed forces than by effective collaboration with native revolutionary-minded, anti-Turkish elements. Prior to the occupation of Moldavia and Wallachia in 1769, the Phanariot princes Grigore Callimachi and Grigore Ghica resisted all propositions made by such masterful Russian agents as Zancoroff or Cernakaps. Collaboration with Russia was envisaged only after the appearance of the Russian armies in the provinces and thus could not assume the form of a preliminary uprising as had been envisaged by St. Petersburg. The hospodars were, moreover, circumspect about Russia's sincerity, aware as they were of Catherine's agents' contacts with the anti-Phanariot Romanian aristocracy. Thus, the realistic Phanariots decided to withhold all assistance until the outcome of the Russo-Turkish conflict became clear. The aristocracy, whether Greek or native, endorsed this policy for similar reasons. The occupation of Moldavia and Wallachia resulted in the immediate endorsement by hospodars and boyars of the Russian proclamation of liberation of Balkan Christendom from the Infidel. The Moldavian aristocracy requested, and obtained, Russia's guarantee of its "historic feudal privileges" to be enjoyed under Russian suzerainty in an autonomous Moldavia ruled by a boyar oligarchy. This formula was inspired by Callimachi's apprehension and execution by a suspicious Porte shortly before the Russians crossed the Dniester. In Wallachia, the boyars demanded outright incorporation of their province into Russia, on the assumption that the provisions of the Charter to the Nobility were to be extended also to them. The Wallachians sought to protect themselves against Ghica, whose own terms for participation were hereditary rule in an autonomous Wallachia under Russian suzerainty. The Russians cynically agreed to all demands, since they regarded Romanian allegiance and possible military support essential for both propaganda and strategic purposes. Unfortunately, from the standpoint of all conspirators, the would-be gun fodder—the Moldavian and Wallachian peasants—seemed less than eager to cooperate. Interpreting Russia's proclamation as a promise of freedom from servitude—an impression not dispelled by either Ghica or the Russian propagandists and field commanders—they flocked to the Russian banner. When, however, they realized that the Russians' and boyars' aims were actually opposed to their own interests, the peasants turned their wrath on the boyars. Plundering, murder, burnings became fairly frequent in 1770, forcing retaliatory action by the aristocracy. The Romanian peasantry did not know of Pugachev but the Russian occupying commanders must have watched nervously over the Romanian jacqueries, which continued throughout the years of occupation.[14]

These problems notwithstanding, the possibility of utilizing sympathetic boyar factions and hospodars as auxiliary or direct agents of Russian subversion in the Balkan Peninsula was actually increased after 1774. The Treaty of Kuchuk Kainardji theoretically condoned Russian intervention in Romanian affairs to the degree of legitimizing cooperation between St. Petersburg and Romanian enemies of the Porte. The Romanian provinces were indeed earmarked as foci of intrigue and subversion against Constantinople through a variety of clauses included in the celebrated peace treaty. The right of the Imperial Court to "remonstrate" in the Romanians' favor in the event of Turkish failure to "provide humane and generous government" in Moldavia and Wallachia was as dangerous to the Porte as the provision allowing the "Ministers of the Imperial Court to make representations" on behalf of all Balkan Christians against abuses by Constantinople. Combined with the further right of appointment of Russian consuls anywhere in the Peninsula—allegedly for the proper conduct and supervision of commercial affairs— these provisions established the bases for synchronization of potential revolutionary activities, for organizing and financing uprisings and other forms of subversion under Russian auspices. The general "forgiveness" clauses contained in article XVI, guaranteeing freedom from reprisal to all who rebelled against the Porte or collaborated in any way with Russia during 1768–1774, tended to encourage cooperation with Russia by all parties interested in altering the existing order. But, at the same time, it also alerted the Porte and its supporters, domestic and foreign, to the enormous threat to the internal stability of the Empire posed by the provisions of the Treaty of Kuchuk Kainardji. The Turks' decision to disregard the terms offensive to their interests could only delay but not prevent the reorganization and reorientation of the forces engaged in the struggle for maintenance of the status quo or its alteration in a manner favorable to their individual group or class interests. Indeed, the impact of the settlement of 1774 on Ottoman affairs, domestic and foreign, was such as to represent the dawn of a new era in Balkan revolutionary activity.[15]

The Treaty of Kuchuk Kainardji, symbolic of continuing and intensified Russian presence in the Balkans—and as such, of further undermining and usurpation of the fading power of the Porte within the Empire itself—was, in these respects, less significant than the reactions which it engendered in Constantinople, in the Balkans, and among the European powers concerned with Balkan affairs. It ushered in a period of reappraisal by certain members of the sultan's entourage of the need for reform and for reassessment of the traditional relationships between Moslems and Christians. Whereas the reform movement did not assume much significance before the accession of Sultan Selim III in 1789, it did nevertheless seek political rather than military solutions to the problems of the Porte's subjects, whether Christian or Moslem.[16] In a sense, the Turkish reform movement was more modern and more cognizant of the realities of change in the Balkans than were the Russian solutions envisaged in the latter part of the eighteenth century. The reformers in Constantinople realized, albeit superficially, that the level of political consciousness and resultant aspirations of the Christian inhabitants of the Balkans had been elevated during the eighteenth century both before the after Kuchuk Kainardji. The rather simplistic solutions which the Russians imposed in 1774 took little account of the socioeconomic and corollary political changes which had occurred among substantial segments of Balkan Christendom. The millet which Russia sought to protect for St. Petersburg's benefit was disintegrating under the impact of forces which the Russians failed to understand. The political idiom of Romanian aristocrats; of Greek and Bulgarian tradesmen; of Serbian knezes, voevods, and merchants; and above all of the Phanariots and other wealthy Greek primates and entrepreneurs, was definitely more secular, more modern than that of the Russian nobility and even of the bureaucracy. These Balkan groups, exposed as they were at one time or another to Austrian influences to contacts with Western tradesmen, and on occasion intellectuals of the Age of Enlightenment, sought and frequently secured a power base of their own in dealings with the Porte and its representatives in the Peninsula. They were no longer the rayas of the sixteenth and of the seventeenth centuries, no longer the meek suppliants of aid from Russia for the liberation of Balkan Christendom from the Infidel. Balkan Christendom to them was differentiated by classes and wealth, a view more sophisticated than that entertained by the Russian "liberators." [17]

It is true that the actual uprisings and revolutionary conspiracies recorded in the eighteenth century bore a marked resemblance to those of the previous century. But that situation can best be accounted for by the participation in revolutionary activities of those elements of Balkan society which had been least exposed to external contacts of the "new kind," or who stood to gain—such as the Romanian boyars—nonmodern, in fact feudal, privileges from collaboration with the Russians. The Turkish reformers were aware of these transformations in their Empire's body politic but were unable to provide solutions that would secure a basis for accommodation with the politically, economically, and socially more advanced rayas. This because of the devastation of the Ottoman Empire during the prolonged conflict of 1768–74; and the resultant deterioration of Ottoman authority over substantial segments of Moslem-dominated territory, over the Janissaries and other military and semimilitary formations, over provincial administrators, and for that matter over substantial segments of the Moslem population as such. The Porte, even after the accession of the reformist Selim III, was obligated to heed—if not to cater to—Moslem prejudice, to respond to outcries by the masses and by political and military figures identified with an an anti-Christian tradition, who thought in terms of avenging the humiliation of Moslem power by the Infidel through continuation of the uneven struggle between the powerful Russian armies and the outmoded and ineffectual Turkish forces.

If the Porte failed to win over the Christians by its reformist moves even after Selim's assumption of power, it was not because of ignorance of the changes which had taken place within the Christian community during the eighteenth century. Similarly, if the Habsburg reformers of the latter part of the eighteenth century—including as enlightened a despot as Joseph II—failed to exploit the changing realities of Balkan political and socioeconomic life, it was because those changes were in a state of uneven growth and in flux, particularly during the last decades of that century. But the essential factor which the Russians generally ignored, which the Porte failed to grasp fully, and which the Austrians also realized only in part, was the secularization of Balkan political consciousness and theory or, at least, the redefinition of political goals by elements not identified with medieval feudal practices. Political change in the Peninsula was not necessarily to be attained by revolutionary means; accommodation with the Porte had its proponents too. But to the vast majority of those who sought liberation from the Turkish yoke, the formulas used prior to Kuchuk Kainardji seemed obsolete. This was true of the elemental revolutionaries, such as tribesmen, klephts, *armatoles,* and peasants, who had lost faith in external liberators and unfulfilled assurances. It is indeed noteworthy that collaboration by the politically underdeveloped forces in the Balkans with Austria and Russia during the anti-Turkish war of 1787–1792 was minimal. This was also true of the politically advanced elements in the Peninsula, who were contemplating a change in the Ottoman order by revolutionary means. The Austrian and even the Russian formulas for liberation per se were inadequate, because they subordinated the interests of Balkan Christendom to those of the Habsburg and Russian empires. New formulas had therefore to be found. They were not found immediately in the French experience of the eighteenth century, but the political secularism of the West—even in the watered-down versions which prevailed in various parts of the Habsburg Empire—was to provide a major element in the synthesis of political ideology which emerged in the Peninsula during the years of the French Revolution. More Balkan than Western in form and contents, yet materially different from those which the Habsburgs had prescribed early in the eighteenth century and the Russians in the later seventeen-hundreds, the formulas concocted in the Balkan Peninsula had to be swallowed, with explosive results, by Turks, Austrians, Russians, and other interested parties in the nineteenth century.

·4·

THE REVOLUTIONS OF THE
EARLY NINETEENTH CENTURY

The political consciousness of the individuals who sought political and social change in the Balkan Peninsula rose significantly in the age of "democratic revolutions." Whether—as has often been suggested—there was an organic link between eighteenth-century Western European and American revolutionary ideologies and practices and the development of revolutionary thought and plans in the Balkans is more difficult to ascertain. It is true that members of trading and intellectual communities living outside the Peninsula, or exposed to external ideological contacts, were cognizant of the progressive ideas enunciated by the men of the Enlightenment and of the changes which occurred in revolutionary France after 1789. But it seems fair to say that with few exceptions—most notably those of Greek intellectuals such as Rhigas Pheraios and Adamantios Kóraes, members of the Phanariot circles in Constantinople and in the Romanian provinces, and Southern Slav and Romanian intellectuals living outside the confines of the Ottoman Empire—awareness

67

of the actual achievements and extended implications of French revolutionary theory and practice made little headway in the Peninsula. This is not to say that even uneducated, pragmatic, Balkan leaders such as Serbian military figures exposed to Austrian influences, or Albanian pashas ready to collaborate with the French, or anyone in position to exploit favorable circumstances created by French military action directed against the Habsburg and Ottoman empires, were unwilling to pay lip service to the democratic and nationalistic dogmas which emanated from pre-Napoleonic and Napoleonic France.

It would be erroneous to regard the first major revolutionary manifestation which occurred in the Balkans at the beginning of the nineteenth century—the Serbian revolution of 1804—as an offshoot of the French Revolution. Rather, the Serbian uprising should be considered as an expression of indigenous exasperation over the ever-increasing abuses perpetrated by military and political units of the declining Ottoman Empire against the Serbian people—exasperation which assumed revolutionary proportions at a time propitious for challenging the authority of the Porte. In a sense, the Serbian revolution may be regarded as a forerunner of the national and social "liberation movements" which occurred throughout the Peninsula during the nineteenth century. It should be remembered, however, that each of the Balkan revolutions of that century reflected specific circumstances and conditions prevailing in various parts of the Peninsula; and also that, more often than not, the Balkan movements were only marginally related to Western revolutionary ideologies and practices and, for that matter, even to the revolutionary experience and aspirations of other inhabitants of the Peninsula.

The Serbian Revolution

The Serbian insurrection, led by that epic personality of the Serbian renaissance Karadjordje, started on the fourteenth of February 1804 in Sumadija as a direct reaction to the terrorism of the Belgrade Janissaries.[1] The revolt rapidly spread to the entire pashalik of Belgrade. The first detachments of insurrectionists consisted of companies of *hajduks* and refugees armed with Austrian contraband weapons or with arms seized from the Turks.

In its initial stages, the insurrection assumed the form of a limited struggle against the *Dahis,* who defied the authority of the Porte. As the scope of the uprising expanded in a manner detrimental to the interests of the Porte, two Ottoman armies were despatched from Bosnia and Bulgaria to crush the rebels. The rebels, however, defeated the Turkish forces at Ivankovac in 1805, and at Mišar and Deligrad in 1806, and even took Belgrade by assault in January 1807. The outbreak of the Russo-Turkish war in December 1806 facilitated the cause of the insurrection as the rebels, flushed with success and in anticipation of Russian support, enunciated a political program which demanded independence for Serbia.[2] This demand was reiterated in their rejection of the Porte's own request that they participate in the war against Russia. The reasons for the continued struggle were conveyed to the Russian commander at Jassy in 1808: the insurgents were determined to reestablish the historic Serbian state and unify

69

all Serbs under Ottoman and Austrian domination. That goal motivated Karadjordje's rejection of Turkish peace initiatives in 1807 and his launching of a major offensive toward the Sandjak in 1809, aimed at joining with Montenegro and spreading the revolution to Bosnia.

Since the events in Europe and the Napoleonic campaigns were of greater concern to the Great Powers than the Serbian insurrection, the Serbian movement soon became totally dependent on specific relationships among Russians, Austrians, and Turks. With Russian help, the insurgents scored victories at Stubik and Malajnica in 1807, and at Varvarin and Loznica in 1810, but their successes were related to the operations of the Russian armies on the Danube. Napoleon's Russian campaign brought the tenuous Russo-Serbian collaboration to a standstill, much to the detriment of the Serbs. The Russo-Turkish peace of Bucharest of 1812 anticipated the eventual autonomy of Serbia but negated the existence of a Serbian state.[3] The Serbs refused to accept the terms of the treaty and continued the struggle for independence; however, with little success. Three Ottoman armies came from Bosnia, Niš, and Vidin to break the Serbian resistance, entering Belgrade in October 1813. Thus, after nearly ten years of fighting, Serbia was reconquered.

The Russo-Turkish war and the Serbian revolution, however, had destroyed the Ottoman feudal system in the Pashalik of Belgrade, which precluded restoration of prerevolutionary conditions. This was demonstrated by the continuing revolutionary activities of the *hajduks,* by the attempted rebellion of Hadji Prodan Gligorijević in September 1814, by the activities of Serbian emigres to Austria, and finally by the erruption of the second Serbian insurrection, under the lead-

70

ership of Miloš Obrenović, in April 1815.[4] The Turks were defeated at Rudnik, Palež, and Čačak and were forced back into urban locations as the countryside was recaptured by the rebels. Nevertheless, the rebels—faced with the certitude of Ottoman military reaction, lacking the support of any Great Power, burdened with problems related to devastation, famine, and disease, as well as shortages of equipment and supplies—opted for a different course of action than that pursued in 1804. The first insurrection sought to achieve independence; the second was to settle for autonomy. The first insurrection counted on the support of Russia and of other Great Powers; the second was dependent on its own resources. No matter what the tactics, the struggle for the recognition of Serbia's autonomy from 1815 to 1830 was one of wearisome negotiations with the Porte, which resulted in the Convention of Akkerman of 1826, the Treaty of Adrianople of 1829, and the *Hatti şerif* of 1830, which secured Ottoman recognition of the goals of Miloš Obrenović and his followers.[5]

The Serbian insurrection of 1804 had the corollary effect of developing aspirations for national emancipation in territories inhabited by Southern Slavs. The insurrection had secured support from *hajduks* and from volunteers from other Southern Slav lands, who also supplied war matériel to Serbia. It is important to note that in spite of war losses the population of liberated Serbia doubled between 1804 and 1813, mostly because of immigration from neighboring provinces settled by Serbs.

The activities of the Serbian insurgents had both Southern Slavs and Balkan aspects. Immediately after the first Serbian victories in 1805–6, the Austrian authorities complained that Serbs from the Voivodina were leaving southern

71

Hungary for Serbia to help the insurgents.[6] These "fugitives" provided Serbia with its first functionaries, diplomats, teachers, and professors. Serbian merchants in Austria furnished money and war matériel to the rebels also. Two peasant rebellions directed against oppression by feudal landlords and bureaucratic abuses by Austrian authorities were closely linked to the Serbian insurrection. The first, the so-called Rebellion of Tican—named after its leader—broke out in Srem in 1807 and had ties to the activities of Luka Lazarević, Stanoje Glavaš, and Mladen Milovanović, all active participants in the Serbian uprising.[7] The second, which occurred in the Banat village of Krušica and is known as the Rebellion of Djak, was triggered off by events in Serbia.[8] Both rebellions were, however, readily crushed by Austrian forces.

Agrarian unrest and peasant movements were also recorded in Slavonia and Posavina.[9] As Karadjordje's victories became known in Croatia, too, officers and soldiers attached to the Commandant-General of Slavone-Srem and of Croatia deserted to Serbia and became volunteers in Karadjordje's forces. Serbian merchants in Trieste and Senj supplied funds and food to the Serbian insurgents. The Serbian revolutionary leaders sought union with Montenegro and the Sandjak of Novi Bazar and were anxious to spread the revolution into Bosnia and Herzegovina. The Serbian military plan for 1807 included the staging of an insurrection in Bosnia, and in 1809 Karadjordje's offensive recorded victories over Turkish forces in the Sandjak near Nova Varoš and Sjenica. The Serbian efforts in Bosnia did not go unanswered. *Hajduk* companies were established in Bosnian territory as far as Sarajevo and the Krajina of Bosnia, while volunteers from Bosnia and Herzegovina joined Serbian detachments. Tribes from Herzegovina and the mountains of northern Albania, such as the Drobnjak, Kuči, Piperi, Bjelopavlići, and Klimenti, also joined in the struggle between 1805 and 1807.[10] In 1807 an insurrection broke out in the Bosnian Podrinje and another one, known as the Rebellion of Jančić, occurred in Krajina in 1809.[11]

The insurgents also had contact with Montenegro.[12] In the spring of 1804, and again in 1806, the Serbs solicited military collaboration from the Montenegrin Bishop Peter I. A Montenegrin incursion into Herzegovina directed toward Trebinje and Nikšić was, however, repulsed by the Ottomans in 1807. Serbian and Montenegrin detachments collaborated in 1809 in the Sandjak. Moreover, also in 1809, Bishop Peter I renewed the offensive against Nikšić as Karadjordje was forced to withdraw Serbian contingents to face the Ottoman offensive against Serbia.

Aside from these activities supportive of the uprising in Serbia, the Serbian revolution also generated actions among other peoples in the Balkan Peninsula. The Austrian historian Kallay, for instance, stated that all Christian inhabitants of European Turkey regarded the Serbian insurrection as their very own.[13] This solidarity reflected the community of interests shared by the oppressed Balkan peasantry and was symptomatic of the general ferment which prevailed in the Balkans at the beginning of the nineteenth century.

In Bulgarian territory, for instance, the activities of the *kirdjale* rebels and corollary feudal anarchy had alienated the Bulgarian masses.[14] The Serbian insurgents decided to exploit that situation by spreading the insurrection into neighboring Ottoman pashaliks. The defeat which the Serbian forces inflicted on those of Pazvant-oglu, in February 1806,

73

near Soko Banja did, however, result in a bloody masacre of the population of Vidin by Pasvant-oglu's followers. Again, after the victory of Deligrad in 1806, the Serbian insurgents entered the Bulgarian region of Belogradčik which triggered off peasant movements in the region of Vidin. Further possibilities for collaboration appeared at the time of the Russo-Turkish war in 1806. Sofronie Vračanski created a Bulgarian committee for liberation in Romania. Bulgarians, Serbians, and Romanians fought in the Russian army. In 1810 a Bulgarian detachment was formed, which took part in military operations in the Danube region. Bulgarian detachments fought as volunteers in eastern Serbia. Serbo-Bulgarian detachments neared Sofia in 1807 and stimulated jacqueries in western Bulgaria and *hajduk* activity in the Balkan, Vitoša, and Rodope mountains. According to a Russian correspondent, after the conclusion of the Russo-Turkish armistice at Slobozia in August 1807, 4,000 Bulgarians went to Serbia; of these, 800 actually joined the insurrectionist forces. According to a report of Karadjordje's emissary to Napoleon, Rade Vučinić, a Bulgarian delegation had suggested to the Serbs the staging of common military action against the Turks in 1810. The collapse of the Serbian insurrection in 1813, however, ended, albeit temporarily, all forms of collaboration between Serbians and Bulgarians.[15]

Different conditions prevailed among the Greeks, whose revolutionary fervor was intense at the beginning of the nineteenth century.[16] A rebellion against Ali Pasha of Jannina was in progress in the Epirus while anti-Ottoman movements were recorded in northern Greece concurrently with the Serbian insurrection. It is believed that these movements were inflamed by appeals addressed by Karadjordje to the Chris-

74

tians of Albania, Rumelia, Bulgaria, and the Olympus. A rebellion by *armatoles* and klephts in April 1808, led by the priest Enthym Vlachavas, was also related to the events in Serbia. Greek volunteers, such as Konda of Epirus, participated in the liberation of Belgrade in 1806, and George Olympios fought in eastern Serbia. Other volunteers set up, on the initiative of Constantin Ypsilanti, a "Greek legion" in Wallachia, which numbered 1,500 Greek, Romanian, Albanian, and Bulgarian fighters. On the other side of the Balkan mountains the *armatolc* pirate Nikotzaras, working hand-in-hand with the Russian Admiral Seniavin, set up in 1807 a detachment of volunteers for the purpose of carving out a road from Olympus to the Danube.[17]

The Serbian insurgents also received help from Greek ecclesiastics and Phanariots. Thus the Hungarian-Wallachian metropolitan Dositei Filiti provided the rebels with financial aid, while the Patriarch of Constantinople and the metropolitans of Vidin and Belgrade interceded with the Porte on behalf of the insurgents in 1807 and 1808. The Greek entourage of General Marmont influenced him in favor of the insurgents, and Constantin Ypsilanti aided the rebels by serving as mediator between them, the Russians, and the Turks. During the critical period 1813–15, the insurgents received support from Count Capo d'Istria, who also provided Serbian émigrés with intelligence data during the Congress of Vienna and later. In 1816 he worked toward the establishment of a confederation of Wallachia, Moldavia, and Serbia.[18]

In the Romanian provinces, revolutionary activities manifested themselves in the form of *hajduk* and peasant insurrections.[19] These movements reflected obvious social ten-

75

sions between the masses of oppressed peasants and the ruling Phanariots and boyars. The Serbian insurrection and the Russo-Turkish war further stimulated the activities of the *hajduks*, which assumed violent expressions prior to the insurrection of 1821. Tudor Vladimirescu, the leader of that revolution, belonged to the Romanian detachment of the Russian army.[20] The first secret revolutionary organization, comprising 150 members, was established in 1816 in Wallachia for the purpose of "liberating the Principalities from the Turks." The organization had contacts with the Serbian rebels.

Over and above its significance as an internal revolutionary movement, and its relationship with revolutionary movements elsewhere in the Balkans, the Serbian revolution also affected the course of the Eastern Question. Serbia's geopolitical position and her relationship with the Southern Slavs gave the Serbian insurrection a special political significance at a time when the Napoleonic campaigns in the Peninsula expanded the scope of the Serbian question. The Russo-Turkish war also enhanced the military and strategic importance of Serbia. Thus, the Serbian insurrection, and the corollary possibility of a general Balkan uprising, played important parts in the shaping of Russian, French, and Austrian politics in Southeastern Europe.[21] However, the true significance of the Serbian insurrection can best be understood in terms of its impact on the history of the Balkan Peninsula. The uprising put in motion the process of seeking solutions to Balkan problems through national revolutionary manifestations. Until the nineteenth century, the Balkan peoples participated merely as peasant masses in the European operations directed against the Ottoman Empire. The

76

process of national and social emancipation of these peoples, and in most cases that of establishing political and state organizations of their own, began with the Serbian revolution. The Great Powers, particularly Austria and Russia, thus were obliged to consider national issues in the formulation and implementation of their Balkan policies.

The Serbian revolution of 1804, and the appearance in the nineteenth century of a Serbian national state, had indeed a profound impact on Austro-Russian relations. Slavic Russia sought, and was able to secure, support from Slavic peoples for fulfilling its ambitions in the Balkans. By way of contrast, the process of Serbian and Southern Slav emancipation, begun in 1804, was contrary to the principle of legitimacy on which the multinational Habsburg monarchy was based. Because of its identification with the principle of nationality, Serbia was to give impetus to the process of disintegration of the Habsburg Empire. In response, Austria pursued a systematic policy of containing Serbia's national aspirations throughout the nineteenth century, with a view to maintaining the status quo in both the Habsburg and Ottoman empires.

The Greek Revolution

The Greek revolution of 1821 was clearly more significant than the Serbian uprising, in that the realization of Greek independence was an achievement which profoundly affected the course of Balkan, Mediterranean, and European politics in the nineteenth century.[22] The social and economic strength of external Hellenism, particularly that of the commercial elements in Greek European and Balkan colonies,

77

gave the movement a bourgeois revolutionary character, whose mass characteristics were imparted by the activities of the *Philike Hetairia* and by the insurrection in the Romanian Principalities which marked the actual beginning of the Greek revolution in 1821.

The *Philike Hetairia* enjoyed a particular position among Balkan national organizations of the first half of the nineteenth century.[23] It was created in 1814 in Odessa by three Greek merchants: Skoufas, Xanthos, and Tzakoloff. The *Hetairia* was an expression of the aspirations of the developing bourgeoisie of the Greek colonies on the Black Sea, which sought emancipation from Ottoman rule. The *Hetairia*, first supported only by merchants and Phanariots, soon enlarged its base of support as klephts, *armatoles,* and Greek primates, as well as non-Greek Balkan insurrectionists, approved of its plans. This national and social diversity affected the activities of the organization. In the early stages of its existence, the *Hetairia,* which had the basic characteristics of a masonic Christian organization, was generally ineffectual. The Hetairists' desire to link Greek and Serbian political goals led to their establishing contacts with Karadjordje, who had settled in Bessarabia. Karadjordje joined the *Hetairia* and assumed responsibility for organizing a new insurrection in Serbia. The futility of this attempt, so contrary to the aims of Miloš Obrenovič, was evidenced in the very assassination of Karadjordje in 1817 by supporters of Miloš's policies of gradualism.

The initial ineptitude of the organization may be ascribed to conflicting views on how best to attain its goals. The conservative elements sought success through intervention by European forces, while the radical elements preached armed national revolution. After 1818, however, the *Hetairia* opted for, and actively prepared for, revolutionary action which was to be carried out in Serbia, Bulgaria, the Romanian Principalities, the islands of the Aegean, in Mane and Messenia, in Thrace and Macedonia, in Epirus and the Morea, and even in Russia. Count Capo d'Istria was asked to head the organization but, upon his repeated refusals to do so, Prince Alexander Ypsilanti, a general in the Russian army and aide-de-camp to Czar Alexander I, assumed leadership of the *Hetairia* in the spring of 1820. He reorganized the *Hetairia*'s internal structure, sought to improve relations with other Balkan revolutionary movements, and elaborated plans for revolutionary action. At a meeting of the leaders of the organization held in Ismail in October 1820, plans were devised which tied an uprising in the Peloponnesus with action in Serbia and in the rest of the Balkans. As the Ottoman forces were expected to be unable to cope with the strategic linkage, it was thought that the proposed strategy would lead to a general revolution which would result in the liberation of the peoples of the Balkans and the establishment of a Greek Balkan Empire, ruled by a descendant of the Russian imperial family.[24]

To succeed, the plans of the *Hetairia* necessitated the unconditional support of all Balkan peoples. Such appeared to be forthcoming from Moldavia and Wallachia following adhesion to the organization by the sons of the rulers of these provinces. The Balkan émigrés who had taken refuge in the Principalities after the Russo-Turkish war of 1806–12 and the debacle of the Serbian uprising in 1813 were also generally supportive of the plans of the *Hetairia*.[25] Thus, some well known Serbian insurgents—Hadji Prodan, Rade Vuč-

79

inić, Stefan Živković-Nišlija, Stefan Živković-Telemak and others—as well as members of the Bulgarian detachment of the Russian army and other Bulgarian leaders such as Hadji Mihail or Captain Kojčo, joined either the Hetairists' insurrection or that of Tudor Vladimirescu in Wallachia in 1821.

If the Serbian emigrants in the Principalities were ready to take part in the insurrection, this was not true of Miloš Obrenović and the population of Serbia proper. The Hetairists had from time to time contacted Miloš since 1817, albeit without success, since Miloš's tactics of compromise with the Porte were patently incompatible with the goals and methods advocated by the *Hetairia*.[26] The Hetairists, however, were more successful in securing support among Bulgarians.[27] This was true not only of Bulgarian emigrants in Wallachia and merchants located in the ports of the Black Sea, but also of inhabitants of Bulgarian cities, such as Sliven, Plovdiv, and Gabrovo. But that support did not result in a hoped-for insurrection on Bulgarian soil in 1821. Equally futile in that respect were the Hetairist demarches to Montenegro and, indirectly, to the tribes of northern Albania.[28] Thus, the *Hetairia*'s plans were to be realized, albeit in an unsatisfactory manner, only in the Romanian Principalities and in Greece.

The Hetairist insurrection in the Romanian provinces began with Ypsilanti's crossing of the Prut in March 1821.[29] The insurrection was the consequence of the social crisis of the Romanian peasant masses, which were overtaxed by the Porte, by the Phanariots, by the boyars, and by the church. It was also prompted by the Russo-Turkish wars of the late eighteenth and early nineteenth centuries, which were fought on Romanian soil, and which merely helped to aggravate the unfavorable socioeconomic and political conditions in the provinces; and by the rise in the political consciousness and aspirations of the nascent Romanian bourgeoisie and intellectual class.

Tudor Vladimirescu assumed leadership of the uprising in 1821 as an ally of the *Hetairia*. The Romanian uprising was joined by volunteers from other parts of the Balkans—by Serbians, Bulgarians, Macedonians, and Albanians, such as the Serbian revolutionary leader Hadji Prodan Gligorijević, the Hetairist George Olympios, Dimitrije the Macedonian, the Bulgarians Genco and Hadji Mihali, and others.

Vladimirescu called for the replacement of the Phanariots by native Romanian rulers, the convocation of a national assembly of representatives of all classes, the organization of a national army, fiscal reform, and a moratorium on tax collections in Wallachia for a period of three years. This program secured the support of the peasantry but alarmed the boyars, who sought a compromise with Vladimirescu as his military retinue, the so-called *panduri*, entered Bucharest on March 26, 1821. Meanwhile, Ypsilanti's forces were seeking to expand the scope of the modest Greek uprising in Moldavia by persuading the Moldavians and Vladimirescu's supporters that Russian participation was imminent. Vladimirescu's tentative agreement with Ypsilanti came to naught, as did his own revolution, as Czar Alexander I refused to intervene after denouncing Ypsilanti's actions and even supporting the Porte's efforts to restore order in the Principalities.[30] The congress of European sovereigns which met at Ljubljana likewise condemned all revolutions. These actions left Vladimirescu politically isolated. Without assistance from Russia, his negotiations with the boyars were doomed to failure. As the Ottoman armies marched toward Bucharest in mid-May, Vladimirescu emulated the tactics of Miloš Obrenović: he accused the Hetairists of treason against the Porte and condemned them to death on May 27. But the battle was lost for both Vladimirescu and the Hetairists.

Ypsilanti's last-ditch attempt to secure Bulgarian support for a diversionary movement on Bulgarian territory was unsuccessful. The Ottoman troops occupied Bucharest on May 29 and waged the decisive battle against Ypsilanti's forces at Drăgășani early in June. The Greek forces were decimated as Ypsilanti fled to Austria, where he was promptly imprisoned. In Wallachia, where, on Ypsilanti's orders, Vladimirescu had been assassinated late in May, a detachment of Serbs, Bulgarians, and Greeks were unable to hold back the Turkish troops at the Secu monastery, and the same fate was met by another detachment of volunteers from Ypsilanti's and Vladimirescu's armies, which sought to resist the Turkish advance in Moldavia at Sculeni, on the river Prut. Thus the revolutionary movements in the Romanian provinces collapsed at the beginning of the summer of 1821. Nevertheless, both Vladimirescu's and the *Hetairia*'s unsuccessful attempts to alter the political and social order in the Balkans were, in effect, the forerunners of the Greek revolution itself, which was to follow.

The insurrection in the Romanian Principalities was indeed an aspect of the Greek revolution of 1821. The conditions for a general insurrection in Greece proper reached their maturity in the second decade of the nineteenth century. The crisis of Ottoman feudalism had alienated the peasant masses; the Greek navy and merchant class had gained much strength during the Napoleonic wars and the Continental Blockade; the rebellion of Ali Pasha of Janina had split the military forces of the Ottoman Empire; the Hetairist rebellion had created a revolutionary leadership.

Following the summons issued by Ypsilanti and the *Hetairia*, the Greek metropolitans met at the end of January 1821 at Vostitza, in the Pelopennesus, to approve an insurrection which was to occur simultaneously with anticipated actions such as a revolution in the Romanian provinces and in Serbia, and the entry of Russian troops in Moldavia. The first skirmishes with Turkish troops began at Kalavrita shortly after mid-March. On March 21, Mane took up arms; and on March 23, Kalamata was liberated. On March 25, Metropolitan Germanos, a member of the *Hetairia*, proclaimed from the monastery of St. Lavra the start of a general uprising against the Turks. On March 28, the senate of Messenia addressed a proclamation to Europe declaring the resolution of the Greek people to fight for their independence. The Peloponnesus was aflame by April 2, and the eastern part of central Greece rose in revolt shortly thereafter. The Ottoman garrisons were immobilized on the Acropolis. By mid-April the insurrection had spread to the islands of Psara and Hydra, whose fleets were mobilized. Thessaly rose in May and Crete in June. In three months time, the insurgents had scored major successes against the Porte but their optimism soon proved to be unwarranted.[31]

The Greek revolution had three distinct phases. In its first phase, from 1821 to 1825, it scored several significant victories. During the second, from 1825 to 1827, it was almost eradicated by superior Ottoman forces. During the third, however, the intervention of the Great Powers saved the revolution and brought at least partial victory to the insurgents by 1829. At all times, the Greek revolution was the bloodiest of all Balkan uprisings. For instance, on the island of Chios alone, only some 1,800 Christians of an initial population of 113,000 survived after about one year of revolutionary action on the island. Similarly, in the same interval, some 15,000 Moslems perished in the Peloponnesus. Despite these horrendous losses recorded by April 1822, significant political changes were recorded during the first year of the uprising. Thus, in January 1822, a National Assembly, held at Epidaurus, proclaimed the independence of Greece, promulgated a constitution, and elected Alexander Mavrokordatos as the first president of the Hellenic Republic. These actions corresponded with a period of Greek military successes, during which the insurgents conquered Athens, Thebes, and Messolonghi.[32] Greek victories were recorded even later, but at a slower pace than in the early stages of the revolution. In the spring of 1822, the forces of Theodore Kolokotrones defeated the Turkish armies commanded by Mahmoud Dramali near Derenakia as the latter were staging a counteroffensive, and a similar defeat was inflicted upon the Turks in 1823. Until 1825, the combatants maintained their positions, as the Ottomans were successful in preventing the extension of the insurrection to northern Greece, while the insurgents had protected their gains in the central mountains and the Peloponnesus while safeguarding the islands with their fleet.

The position of the rebels became precarious, however, in 1825, as the Egyptian army and the fleet of Ibrahim Pasha intervened in the conflict at a time when the Greek side was badly weakened by internecine political struggles.[33] Ibrahim

84

Pasha, after crushing the insurrection in Crete, landed his forces on the Peloponnesus and started the successful and bloody reconquest of territories captured by the Greek rebels. Messolonghi was taken in April 1826, and as the resistance of Greek guerrillas began to falter in the Peloponnesus and in central Greece, the insurrection seemed doomed in a manner comparable to the Serbian uprising in 1813. The rebellion was saved, however, by the intervention of the Great Powers.

The history of that intervention is well-known.[34] The action by the Powers was determined by important military and strategic considerations, by the economic and political position of Greece in the eastern Mediterranean, and by Anglo-Russian rivalry. Moreover, the Philhellenic movement in the West rallied not only idealists, poets, national revolutionaries, and adventurers to the Greek cause but mobilized European and world opinion in favor of the revolution. The tumultuous events which swept the Balkans, such as the Russian ultimatum to the Porte in 1826 and the Battle of Navarino of the following year, forced the European powers to make prompt decisions on Balkan issues. By the Peace of Adrianople, in 1829, the Porte recognized the autonomy of Wallachia, Moldavia, and Serbia and accepted the agreements regarding the autonomy of Greece made by the Great Powers in London. Greece was declared an independent monarchy under the protection of Russia, England, and France.[35] In July 1832 the Porte recognized the independence of Greece, which was to be ruled by Prince Otho of the Bavarian dynasty.

In retrospect, and also in terms of expectations for the future, the Greek revolution had a profound impact on the course of revolutionary movements in the Balkan Peninsula. The Greek revolution mobilized all the national forces of Hellenism from the Balkans to the islands of the Ionian and Aegean seas, and to the littoral of Asia Minor. Throughout the revolution, the Greek population of the Ottoman Empire was subject to severe reprisals, starting with the hanging of the Patriarch of Constantinople in 1821 and the subsequent masacres at Smyrna, Adrianople, Salonika, Cyprus, Rhodes, Crete, and elsewhere. The Revolution had nefarious effects on Greek traders and on the Greek economy. In Constantinople, Armenians replaced Greeks in banking operations, while the Phanariots' power declined subsequent to their replacement as rulers in the Romanian Principalities. The actions of the Greeks and of the Turks had prompt reverberations in the Balkans. The revolutionaries gained the support of the Montenegrins, albeit only during the later stages of the uprising. Indicative of that support was the letter addressed by the Montenegrin Bishop Peter I to the Greek government in April 1826, in which he stated: "I am certain that the destiny of the Greek people will decide the destiny of their coreligionaries found under the Ottoman whip. The happiness of the Greeks is also the happiness of their coreligionaries."[36] The letter was, in effect, a response to the request for military assistance which an emissary of the Greek government delivered to Cetinje in 1825, and a negative response at that, since the Montenegrin Prince Bishop refused to intervene in the conflict for fear of possible action by Ottoman forces stationed in the Herzegovina, the Sandjak, and Albania. In that respect, the Montenegrin response was not too dissimilar from that of Miloš Obrenović, who did not wish to jeopardize his own negotiations with the Porte for the sake of supporting coreligionaries in Greece.[37] The Muslim Albanians, especially the feudal class, also failed to respond to Greek entreaties and, in fact, supported the Turks. On the other hand, the Slavs of Macedonia played an active pro-Greek role during the insurrection. Slav volunteers in Marco Botzaris' detachment fought well against the forces of Ali Pasha Mustafa of Scutari, and Slavs also participated effectively in the insurrection of Niaousta.[38] Similarly, Bulgarian forces especially those connected with the *Hetairia*—fought alongside Greek rebels in northern Greece, where men like Hadji Hristo of Koprivštica, Petar Moralijata of Sliven, Semko of Trnovo, and others distinguished themselves in battle.[39] The Bulgarian merchant class also provided material assistance to the rebels, and all this in the face of severe Turkish reprisals, which drove many a Bulgarian into Russia, the Romanian provinces, and Serbia. It is also noteworthy that the Albanian peasantry and the navy of the Albanian colonies of Hydra and Spetza supported the insurgents. Thus, in September 1821, an agreement was concluded in Epirus between Souliote, Albanian, and Greek companies, which called for military collaboration. Such collaboration as there was did, however, end when the Souliotes—the principal intermediaries between Greeks and Albanians—were defeated by the Turks and deported to the Ionian islands in 1822.[40]

Because of the location of Greece in the eastern Mediterranean, the Greek revolution had a major impact on the economic and political interests of the Great Powers, in that the revolution engendered a prolonged struggle over domination in the Balkan Peninsula and the Mediterranean between England, Russia, and France. Russia sought the division of the Balkan possessions of the Ottomans among the Powers, while England seemed determined to maintain its influence in the Mediterranean in the face of French and Russian

87

challenges. Therefore, the Greek Question became central to European politics between 1826 and 1830. The Greek revolution, however, led to recognition by the Powers of the fact that independent Balkan states could emerge in the Peninsula. Yet such recognition did not represent an endorsement by the Powers of the idealistic principle expounded by Balkan revolutionaries that "the Balkans belong to the Balkan peoples." It was in the interest of the Powers to exploit and even create unrest within the Peninsula, and this was particularly manifest in Greece, where intense xenophobia and severe internecine struggles among pro-British, pro-French, and pro-Russian factions continually disturbed the rule of King Otho in the thirties and beyond.[41]

In taking stock of the outcome of the Serbian and Greek revolutions, it may be concluded that both were at least partly successful in the attainment of their goals. They produced an autonomous Serbian state and an independent Greek one. In Serbia, the peasantry kept the land it had conquered, thus creating the basis for the development of a free, propertied peasant class. The success of the agrarian revolution gave Serbian society a democratic character; yet, the small rural property holders operating within the framework of an underdeveloped society facilitated the political victory of a military monarchy and the formation of a conservative state.[42] The Greek revolution represented a more complex social and political phenomenon because of the greater sophistication of the Greek society, and because of external intervention by the European powers. The Greek revolution failed to solve the agrarian problem as the more advanced social classes guided the movement and emerged as the major beneficiaries of the revolution. The Greek constitutions of 1822,

88

THE EARLY NINETEENTH CENTURY

1823, and 1827 were expressions of the ideas of the French Revolution and also reflected American constitutional principles.[43]

From a national standpoint, the two revolutions failed to attain their most optimistic goals, in that they failed to integrate all their compatriots within the framework of Greece and Serbia. The aims of the Serbian revolutionary leaders were frustrated by the passivity of Europe; and those of the Greek leaders, by the active intervention of the European powers. The restrictions imposed by the powers on both Serbia and Greece prompted continuing political actions designed to attain the ultimate goals of the leaders of Serbia and Greece throughout the nineteenth century. As these actions were to coincide with similar actions by other Balkan peoples, it seems fair to say that the process of national liberation which began with the Serbian and Greek revolutions, with the insurrection in the Romanian Principalities, and with the corollary revolutionary ferment in Bulgaria, Macedonia, Thrace, and Albania shaped the course of the history of the Balkan Peninsula until World War I.

·5·

REVOLUTIONARY MOVEMENTS
AND THE FORMATION OF
MODERN STATES, 1830–1878

*Balkan Revolutions from the Peace of Adrianople to
the Crimean War: Insurrections of the Third Decade*

Disquiet in the Ottoman Empire deepened by the third decade of the nineteenth century because of opposition by the
Ottoman feudal class to the reforms of Mahmoud II. The
resistance was particularly manifest in the peripheral regions
of the empire. The rebel movement of Mustafa Pasha of Scutari was supported by the beylicates of the Peninsula. By
1831 the rebel pashas of Albania and Rumelia took Skopje,
besieged Sofia, and were advancing toward Veles, Monastir,
and Janina. The rebels were eventually defeated, but renewed unrest was recorded in Albania in 1832 as beys and
bayraktars opposed recruitment in the regular army (*nizam*)
and performance of military service outside Albania. The military riposte of the Porte destroyed the tribal organization of
the Mirdite, in northern Albania but it was not before 1835

that forces loyal to the sultan crushed the rebellion, which by that time had spread into southern Albania.[1]

The Albanian uprising found support in the beylicate of Bosnia. Because of Bosnia's geographic location, the feudal lords of that province enjoyed unique privileges. In their quest for autonomy, the Bosnian feudatories joined the forces of Mustafa Pasha and, under the command of Captain Hussein Gradaščević, fought against the sultan's forces at Kosovo in 1831. But the Bosnian contingents were no match against the Porte's and the revolt was crushed in 1832.[2]

The Albanian and Bosnian insurrections were expressions of the conservative aspirations of those desirous of retaining feudal privileges. In Albania, they were supported by the tribal social structure, which was opposed to the strengthening of the powers of the Porte. The *çiftlik* system in the villages of Bosnia led, as elsewhere in the Balkans, to the enserfment of the peasantry and to increments in feudal taxes. Bosnia's location between the Adriatic littoral and the Danubian regions—on the so-called path of cotton, which had allowed extensive commercial traffic through Bosnia during the Napoleonic wars and the Continental Blockade—facilitated the development of a national market. The peasants wished to acquire land and the national bourgeoisie sought a free economy. The attainment of these goals seemed feasible only through the destruction of the Ottoman feudal system. The example of neighboring Serbia seemed worthy of emulation, which accounted for the establishment of closer ties between Bosnia and Serbia. In fact, a group of Bosnian refugees to Serbia, led by the priest Pavle Karano-Tvrtković, attempted to stage an insurrection in Bosnia in the fall of 1833. Other unsuccessful uprisings occurred in the

FORMATION OF MODERN STATES, 1830-1878

spring of 1834 in Derventa and somewhat later in Kraina—
the so-called Rebellion of Mašić—which resulted in severe
Ottoman reprisals and migrations of Bosnians to Serbia and
Austria.[3]

Anti-Ottoman movements were, however, not restricted
to Albania and Bosnia in the thirties. In Montenegro, for in
stance, native forces acting in concert with Mustafa Pasha
assaulted Spuž, Žabljak, and Podgorica. The Turkish counteroffensive failed as the rebels, assisted by Christian tribes of
northern Albania—such as the Klimenti, Hoti, and the
Gruda—defeated the Ottomans at Martinić in April 1832.
The Montenegrin-Ottoman confrontations continued until
1842, when the frontier of Herzegovina was redrawn to the
satisfactions of the Montenegrins.[4] The restoration of peace,
however, proved to be only transitory.

The interests of the Porte were also placed in jeopardy by
events which occurred in Serbia. In accordance with the
Hatti şerif of 1830, Miloš Obrenović sought the return of the
six districts confiscated by the Porte in 1813 and the banishment of Ottoman spahis from Serbia. Faced with opposition
from the Ottoman administrators of the disputed districts,
and with the indolent attitude of the Porte itself, Miloš decided to resort to revolutionary action to achieve his goals.[5]
Thus, the Serbians supported all movements which tended to
weaken the Ottoman Empire, including those of the beys of
Bosnia and of the restless peasants in neighboring territories,
particularly in the coveted areas. The influence of Serbia and
the restlessness of the masses caused the outbreak of an insurrection in the district of Kruševac in April 1833, which
rapidly spread into the regions of Svrljig, Crna Reka, Banja,
and Ključ. The 12,000 to 15,000 peasants who took part in

93

the uprising were armed entirely by Serbia. Miloš sent his own military units, comprising some 6,500 men, to disputed areas on the Timok and Danube. On May 24, 1833 the Porte conceded defeat by accepting the fait accompli and recognized the new frontiers of Serbia, whereby the size of autonomous Serbia was expanded by nearly one-third.[6]

The successful resolution of the Greek revolution and of Serbia's territorial aspirations increased the level of unrest among the peasants of regions adjoining eastern Serbia, as well as in northern Bulgaria. Thus, insurrections broke out in Niš in 1833, 1835, and 1841; in Bulgarian lands at Pirot and Belogradčik in 1836; and at Berkovica in 1836 and 1837. These uprisings, however, proved to be unsuccessful largely because Miloš, for political reasons of his own, failed to provide the combatants with adequate support. Nevertheless, the tumultuous events of the late twenties and early thirties did lead to increased agitation by advocates of the Bulgarian liberation movement, both on and outside Bulgarian soil, for revolutionary action which would lead to Bulgaria's liberation from the Turks.[7]

In 1828–29, Miloš indeed encouraged the establishment of ties with Bulgarians in Vidin, Gabrovo, Koprivštica Šumen, Sliven, and Plovdiv. He even sought Russian military support for Serbian action against Vidin and for the staging of an uprising in the pashaliks of Vidin, Niš, and Sofia.[8] Bulgarian merchants established in Bucharest likewise addressed a memorandum to the Russians, in September 1828, demanding an identical status for Bulgaria with that enjoyed by Serbia, the Romanian Principalities, and Greece. But insurrectionary plans failed to materialize as the Turks uncovered a revolutionary committee set up at Sliven and the Russians failed to respond to the appeals of the would-be rebels.[9] Bulgarian disappointment with the Treaty of Adrianople was profound. Georgi Mamarčev of Kopel, one of the leaders of the Bulgarian volunteers in Greece, although despondent over Russia's lack of support for his revolutionary plans at the end of the Russo-Turkish war, planned in 1835-36 another insurrection to be staged at Trnovo. Mamarčev's conspiracy was readily discovered by the Ottoman authorities and came to naught. Still, that conspiracy was the first of many plots organized by Bulgarian merchants, usually with external support from Russia, the Romanian Principalities, Serbia, and Greece.[10]

The Eastern Crisis of 1839-1841 and Its Aftermath: Insurrections of the Fourth Decade

A new crisis disturbed the Ottoman Empire in the fourth decade of the nineteenth century. It was caused by the rebellion of Mohammed Ali of Egypt and the internal reforms of Sultan Abdul Mejid. The Egyptian insurrection precipitated action by the Great Powers, while the reforms antagonized the feudal ruling classes and facilitated the development of liberation movements in the Balkans.

On the southern frontier of Serbia, in the Niš region, one of the more significant peasant insurrections of this period broke out in April 1841.[11] It was the result of accumulated pressures exerted by Ottoman feudal lords, who were opposed to the reforms promulgated by the *Hatti şerif* of 1839, and of direct encouragement by Miloš Obrenović in

95

his quest to regain the throne from his exile in Wallachia. The Serbian government failed to support the rebels, which allowed the Turks to crush the uprising in short order.

This period was also characterized by the establishment of secret insurrectionist organizations which had networks throughout the Balkan Peninsula. The membership of these organizations was recruited from official circles in Greece and Serbia, from merchant groups, and from émigré Balkan intellectuals. In the first phase of their activities, until the early 1870s, these organizations had two common characteristics: they were predominantly bourgeois in social origin and their revolutionary purpose was to stage a general Balkan insurrection which would result in the attainment of specific national goals. The activities of the secret organizations were most profuse in the Romanian Principalities, where conditions were propitious for revolutionary planning. Young Romanian intellectuals who had studied in the West created in 1833 the Philharmonic Society, whose radical left wing sought national unification, constitutionalism, and democratic liberties—ideas which found their full expression in 1848.[12] In 1839 a group of boyars and members of the bourgeoisie engaged in a conspiracy in Moldavia, directed against Prince Sturdza and the Russian protectorate, whose aim was to establish a Danubian confederation. Three revolutionary manifestations took shape at Brăila in 1841, 1842, and 1843, with close Serbian, Bulgarian, and Greek cooperation. Their goal was to provoke a general insurrection in Bulgaria and the Ottoman Empire.[13] Miloš Obrenović supported the first movement, which, in his view, had to be coordinated with the insurrection of Niš. His agent, M. Stanisavljević (alias Tadić), was particularly active among Bulgarian,

Greek, and Serbian émigrés and an émigré detachment was actually assigned the task of taking Brăila. The plot was uncovered, however, by the Romanian authorities and the revolutionary plans came to naught. A second attempt, in 1842, was marshaled by the Bulgarian George Rakovski and had a Greco-Bulgarian character. In 1841 Rakovski was in contact with young Greek revolutionaries and together they concocted projects, within the so-called Macedonian Society, designed to stage insurrections in Macedonia, Bulgaria, Crete, and Thessaly. In Brăila proper, Rakovski collaborated with a Greek captain, Stavra, who had been delegated by the revolutionary committee of Thessaly and Epirus, in enlisting Balkan émigrés for military action in Bulgaria. The conspirators were apprehended by the police in February 1842. Still, a third attempt was made in 1843 by the Bulgarian Vasil Hadjivelkov, who sought to raise a detachment for the same purpose. That attempt too was frustrated by the Romanian authorities.

Revolutionary agitation was also rampant in Greek lands.[14] The Greek liberation movement encouraged internal resistance to foreign rule in Greece proper, as well as revolutionary activities in Greek territories still under Ottoman rule. The internal dissatisfaction with Bavarian governance culminated in rebellions, albeit of limited accomplishment, between 1833 and 1843. The Eastern Crisis of 1839–41, provoked by the war directed by the Porte against Mohammed Ali, also contributed to unrest among Greeks by awakening Hellenistic sentiments throughout the eastern Mediterranean. As Mohammed Ali tried to capture Albania and the Epirus, Greek forces retorted by moving into Thessaly, the Epirus, and southern Macedonia. The Greek commander Ve-

97

lentzas operated in Thessaly; Caratassos, the son of an old rebel leader of the Greek revolution of the twenties, worked in the Salonika area; the priest Hilarion meanwhile was preparing an insurrection at Mount Athos. The island of Samos requested that it be annexed by Greece. The culminating point of the crisis was the insurrection on Crete, in 1841, which was to be the first of many insurrections on that island during the nineteenth century.[15] Although Greek volunteers rallied to their struggle, the Cretan insurgents were unable to withstand the British forces, which, as protectors of the Ionian islands, put down the rebellion in short order.

The revolutionary atmosphere among Greeks was also inflamed by the activities of secret national societies which were established on Greek territory. The old rebel leader Kolokotrones, for instance, organized such a secret organization, Phoenix, whose aim was to stage insurrections in Epirus, Thessaly, and Macedonia. Another secret organization, the Philorthodox Hetairia, which represented a mixture of national and orthodox theological purposes, was created in 1839 with a similar objective. At the time of the Cretan insurrection, yet another such organization, the Athens-based Central Committee of Cretans, was active in securing aid for the rebels.[16]

Developments in Greece were paralleled elsewhere in the Balkans. The relatively calm period following 1815 made for economic prosperity in Serbia as a result of the growth of the national economy and of trade with Central Europe. Greek maritime commerce became the link between the eastern Mediterranean and Europe as a result of the economic development of liberated Greece and of increased Greek trade in the Ottoman Empire itself after the *Tanzimat* of 1839.

Similarly, economic development was experienced in other parts of the Empire. The urban population of Bulgaria, doubled in size after the settlement of new colonists from the Balkan mountains and from Rhodope, took advantage of trade opportunities on the Danube and the Black Sea. Trading organizations were also set up in Macedonia, with a resultant increase in the size of cities.

The economic changes had social and political consequences. The new capitalist formations gradually destroyed the social structure focusing on the patriarchal village, while the expansion of capitalism stimulated the creation of a Balkan national bourgeoisie. It is under these circumstances that the bases of the modern Balkan societies of the nineteenth century were established in the liberated parts of the Peninsula. Social change also ushered in a rise in political consciousness and activities. The liberal ideas of nineteenth century Europe first manifested themselves in Southern Slav territories in the form of the Croatian national rebirth. The Illyrian movement (1830–48) was an expression of a national idea aiming at the cultural unification of the Croatians and the rest of the Southern Slavs. In Serbia, the cultural unification goals of the younger generation collided with the absolutism of Prince Miloš, a conflict which led to Miloš's abdication in 1839. In Greece, the liberal bourgeoisie, taking advantage of the general discontent provoked by foreign rule, staged a successful military coup against the monarch in 1843 and instituted a system of constitutional and parliamentary government.[17]

The formation of the national society and the building of free Balkan states was reflected in the development of national movements. In the 1840s, these movements assumed two primary characteristics—nationalism and expansionism. The expansionist ideas of Balkan societies were at the core of Balkan nationalism. The ideological bases of these national ideas were laid in history as nationalists sought the restoration of the historic empires of Byzantium, of Simeon, and of Dushan. The new Balkan societies, deprived as they were of a national tradition under Ottoman domination, now sought to legitimize their existence through resuscitation of the historic past; thus, the medieval Balkan states provided roots and support for the realization of the new political aspirations. But this historicism, which played such a crucial role in the process of emancipation of the Balkan peoples, was a two-edged sword: it was progressive when it stimulated emancipation; yet regressive when it engendered internecine Balkan conflicts. And this was true throughout the Peninsula.

The formulation of the Serbian national program was closely related to the activities of the Polish émigrés in the Balkans. After the failure of the 1830 insurrection in Poland, the Polish emigration—in quest of support for the restoration of Poland—extended its activities also into the Balkan Peninsula, as the Balkans were regarded as a potential base of action against Austria and Russia.[18] The Polish émigrés, having failed in their attempt to establish a viable state of their own, "*Holmia,*" on Serbian and Montenegrin territory, became persuaded that they could best realize their plans regarding the Balkans only with the aid of Serbia. In 1841, Prince Czartoryski set up an agency in Belgrade, which, as of 1843, entertained close contacts with the Polish political mission for the Near East, which was functioning in Constantinople. Czartoryski provided a blueprint for action, "Advice on the source of action to be followed by Serbia," which he sent to his agent in Belgrade, Franja Zach, in January 1843. Serbia, he wrote, had to expand territorially at the expense of Turkey with the support of France and England, the two powers which, unlike Russia and Austria, had no specific interests in the Balkans. Serbia also had to demand the withdrawal of Turkish garrisons from its cities, had to unite with Montenegro, and secure an outlet to the Adriatic in order to exert influence on Slavs under Austrian and Ottoman domination.[19] After consultation with the Serbian politician Ilija Garašanin, Zach drew up a "Plan of Slav politics for Serbia," which was based on Czartoryski's ideas. The new plan envisaged expansion of Serbian activities to encompass Bosnia, Herzegovina, Montenegro, and northern Albania, as well as the Illyrian movement and Croatia. Garašanin added two elements of his own to Zach's plan: he softened Serbia's anti-Russian positions and assigned priority to the resolution of the Serbian national question. The end product, the *"Načertanie"* (Project) of I. Garašanin, contained the following thoughts: to guard its own independence and to bring about the unification of all Serbian people, Serbia should restore its medieval Balkan empire through liberation of Bosnia and Herzegovina, union with Montenegro, and securing of an outlet on the Adriatic. Since Austria was opposed to such schemes, Serbia was to seek the support of the Western European powers. The ideas summarized in the *Načertanie* in 1844 were to guide the national policy of Serbia until 1918.[20]

The national program was an expression of the state of mind in Serbia in the 1840s, which was supportive of schemes such as Zach's or Garašanin's. The Ragusian Matija Ban, who was in contact with the Polish revolutionaries, created in Belgrade a Panslav democratic secret society whose members included Serbs, Croats, Bulgarians, Czechs, and Slovaks.[21] The Illyrian movement in Croatia reached its height in 1840. When transformed into a political movement in 1841, it came into conflict with Vienna and had to turn toward Belgrade. The leader of the movement, Ljudevit Gaj, who had been in close contact with Zach, came to Belgrade in 1846 and elaborated there a third national plan which envisaged a Greco-Slav alliance and an insurrection whose goal was the establishment of a Balkan confederation.[22] Meanwhile, Garašanin, paralleling the initiative of private groups in Serbia, undertook an ambitious plan for national action beyond Serbia's frontiers. His agents traveled through Slav territories south of Serbia with a view to establishing political contacts and spreading Serbian propaganda. In this manner, bonds were established with Bosnia, Herzegovina, Old Serbia (Kosovo), and northwestern Macedonia. In 1846 Garašanin's activities reached the Christian tribes of northern Albania. Contacts on Bulgarian territory were supported by Bulgarian émigrés settled in Serbia. It was also in these years that the secret Serbian organization which was to be active in the national movements of 1848–49, and which was to prepare the Balkan insurrections of the sixties and seventies, was established.[23]

During the 1840s, too, the national movement gained strength in Greece, particularly after the coup of 1843 and the promulgation of the democratic constitution of 1844.[24] The elaboration of a national program was affected largely by the geographic division of the Greek nation and the relative strengths of the economic forces of internal and external Hellenism. The Greek ethnic element formed a compact body in liberated Greece, much of the Epirus and Thessaly, and certain parts of Macedonia, and was an important segment of the urban population of many cities of Macedonia, Thrace, and southern Bulgaria. Greeks were also located in the Ionian and Aegean islands, and on the littoral of Asia Minor, while numerous Greek colonies were widespread on the littoral of the Black Sea, in Central Europe, Italy, southern France, and North Africa. This peripheral Hellenism was economically a much stronger force than that of free Greece. Indeed, throughout the nineteenth century, the Greek economic capital was Constantinople rather than Athens. External Hellenism was a focus of attraction and of influence for, and on, the national society of liberated Greece. The economic and financial difficulties connected with the building of the Greek state, together with the quest for national liberation and emancipation of all Greeks, directed Greek national action toward territorial expansion at the expense of the Ottoman Empire. The intertwining of internal and external factors, of the affirmation of the liberation movement in Greece and of the economic superiority of the Diaspora, led to the formulation of the *Megali Idea* (Great Idea), the ideological cornerstone of Greek national politics until recent times.[25]

The *Megali Idea* was based on historicism: the resurrection of the glory and power of the Byzantine Empire, whose roots were formed in the brilliant ancient past, when Greek culture, art, and science were the essential elements of European and world civilization. The *Megali Idea* carried the political heritage of Byzantium, the cultural heritage of antiquity, and the ecclesiastical heritage of the Orthodox Patriarch of Constantinople. It traced the frontiers of Hellenism from the Balkan mountains in the north as far south as Cape Matapan; from the Adriatic Sea in the west to the Black Sea in the east. On January 15, 1844, Colettis, the Greek premier, explained the program of integral Hellenism to the Athens Assembly. According to him, there were two great centers of Greek peoples—Athens and Constantinople. The former was the capital of Greece, the latter that of Hellenism. The Kingdom of Greece may, in fact, comprise only the poorest peoples of the Greek nation, but that nation includes also the inhabitants of Jannina, Seres, Salonika, Adrianople, Crete, Samos, and Constantinople.

Political activity directed toward the realization of the *Megali Idea* found its fullest expression during the premiership of Colettis (1844-47), who enjoyed the confidence and support of both Russia and France.[26] That activity manifested itself through secret national societies and revolutionary propaganda disseminated in Epirus, Thessaly, southern Macedonia, and Thrace. These activities by Greek agents, supported by Russian consular representatives, aroused Ottoman protests and counteractions such as banning of the Greek press, occasional expulsions of Greek consuls from Turkey, and barring Greek ships from anchoring in Turkish ports. The Porte was particularly opposed to the activities of the Greek secret society Grand Fraternity, an updated version of the *Philike Hetairia*. According to a report of an Ottoman agent in Greece, three conspiracies were organized against the Ottoman Empire in 1844-45 alone.[27] Colettis himself was accused of preparing a general Balkan insurrection against the Ottomans, designed to liberate Epirus, Thessaly, Macedonia, and Constantinople, with the assistance of Serbs and Bulgarians. An organization consisting of inhabitants of Thessaly, Macedonia, and Epirus, was ostensibly also readying insurrections in those regions. The report of the agent contained 53 names. Lastly, a third conspiracy was a Bulgarian one led by Simeon Semkov, who organized in Greece a volunteer Slav company, which was to sail to the Bulgarian littoral on the Black Sea and raise the flag of a Bulgarian insurrection at the Rila Monastery Semkov was presumably a member of the "Thraco-Bulgarian-Serbian Society" (or Macedonian Society) which, under Hadji Hristo's leadership, was engaged in spreading revolutionary propaganda in the Ottoman Empire. These multiple activities, insignificant as they were in general, were symptomatic of changing conditions in the Peninsula and, as such, related to the revolutionary manifestations of 1848–49.

The Revolutions of 1848–1849

The economic and social changes which had taken place between 1815 and 1848 in Europe provoked the revolutionary events of 1848–49. The "February Days" in Paris and the proclamation of the Republic, the March demonstrations in Vienna and the destruction of the absolutism of Metternich, the Frankfurt program for the unification of Germany, the insurrections in Italy and in Hungary put in motion the revolutionary wave in Europe. It immersed the Balkans, the Southern Slav territories in the Habsburg monarchy, the Romanian Principalities, and reached as far as the Ionian archipelago and Greece. The revolutions of 1848–49 in Europe brought victory to the forces of economic liberalism and affirmed the principles of nationality and democracy. Balkan society, an offspring of the economic and political developments of the first half of the nineteenth century, came to accept the revolutionary ideas of 1848, albeit at a slower pace, in the course of the following decades. Economic liberalism and democratic politics answered the needs of the young Balkan bourgeoisie, while the principle of nationality was generic to all Balkan national movements in the nineteenth century.

The social and political revolutions in the multinational Habsburg Empire, which engulfed the territories ranging from Trieste to the Voivodina, were in effect national revolutions. The revolutionaries of 1848 demanded the union of Croatia with Dalmatia, Rijeka, and the Croatian littoral; the elimination of serfdom; and the democratization of the political process. All these demands were based on the principles of nationality and of historic rights. A community of interests linked the Croat movement to that of the Serbs in the Voivodina, whose inhabitants had developed, by 1848, a sense of national consciousness.[28] Inspired by Serbian bourgeois economic progress, and by peasant resistance to feudalism and opposition to the bureaucratic apparatus, the revolt of the Serbs in southern Hungary began as an agrarian movement. It soon became political, seeking recognition of national rights and political autonomy. Kossuth, the leader of the Hungarian revolution, shied away from carrying out the proclaimed revolutionary goals of 1848—agrarian reform, resolution of national questions on the basis of the principle of territorial self-determination—at least as far as the Southern Slavs were concerned. The Hungarian thesis of the existence of a single historical nation in Hungary, in which resided the idea of Hungarian hegemony over the other nationalities, was unacceptable to the Serbs and the Croats, who, following their rapprochement with Vienna, joined the forces of the counterrevolution. The proclamation of the Voivodina Serbs,

106

issued at Karlovci at the Assembly of the Serbs of Hungary and of Croatia, meeting on May 1–May 3, 1848, as well as their subsequent alliance with Croatia, Slavonia, and Dalmatia, resulted in a Serbo-Hungarian civil war.[29] That struggle aroused strong emotions in Serbia. Volunteers assembled as the Serbian government sent its delegates to the assembly at Karlovci. Stevan Knićanin and his 8,000 volunteers then joined in the military operations of the Voivodina Serbs. Aid and donations were sent to the insurgents from the Serbs of Dalmatia, Trieste, and Vienna. Although supportive of the movement in the Voivodina, the Serbian government resolutely prevented dissemination of the demands of the Society of Serbian Youth for political reforms, and of the National Assembly for administrative autonomy in Serbia proper.

The revolutions of 1848–49 left significant legacies in Croatia and in Serbia. In Croatia, the revolution gave impetus to the "national rebirth," which in turn led to economic, social, and political emancipation. In Serbia, the legacy of 1848 was the creation of a new generation committed to the implementation of the ideas of the revolutionary period. Moreover, the bases for Serbo-Croat cooperation were established. Croatian envoys came to Belgrade as Serbian representatives went to Zagreb. Ties were also established between Serbia and Montenegro, and even a union of Serbs and Bulgarians was contemplated by some extremists.[30]

The crisis of the Habsburg monarchy, the national movements of the Italians, Hungarians, and Southern Slavs, stimulated new revolutionary activities in Serbia, designed to bring about an insurrection in Southern Slav territories under Ottoman domination. Garašanin continued his work, begun in 1844, by drafting in March 1849 a plan for national

107

and revolutionary action, the "Constitution of political propaganda to take place in Slavo-Ottoman lands."[31] That propaganda was to affect the territories immediately adjoining the Croatian-Slavonian borders; Bosnia, Herzegovina, Dalmatia, Montenegro, the Sandjak, northern Albania, Macedonia, and southwestern Bulgaria. The leaders of the organization which was to organize these activities were Garašanin himself and his closest collaborator, Jovan Marinović. The tasks of the organization were soon expanded to comprise recruitment of adherents, collection of weapons, and covert setting up of military detachments, which, upon receiving word from Serbia, would begin an insurrection. That insurrection would start simultaneously in all regions: the Mirdites of northern Albania, with the aid of Montenegro, would conquer Scutari and would then pursue their activities in the Sandjak and in Kosovo, from whence the insurrection would spread to Macedonia. At the same time, forces from Dalmatia and the Croatian littoral would join with those of Bosnia and Herzegovina, while Serbian forces would move toward Kosovo and Bulgaria, which, by then, would already be in a state of insurrection.

Garašanin's organization functioned between 1849 and 1853, when it came into conflict with Russia. It was strongest until 1851, when the relaxation of international conflicts and the ensuing period of reaction in Europe blunted its ill-conceived revolutionary schemes.

Nevertheless, the revolutionary ferment of the period had, by 1850, stimulated the outbreak of national resistance movements in many areas of the Balkan Peninsula, from Bosnia to Bulgaria. The bitter struggle of the beylicates against the Porte became exacerbated in Bosnia, with nefarious results for the enserfed peasant masses.[32] Influenced by by the events of 1848, the peasants of Bosnia and Herzegovina politicized their agrarian reform program along more clearly definable national lines at a time when the Porte sought to reestablish its shaky authority in the beylicates. Order was temporarily reestablished by the Turkish forces commanded by Omer Pasha Latas in 1850, but Omer Pasha was unable to disarm the population and thus had to cope with a revolt in Herzegovina, which enjoyed the support of Montenegro. The insurrection in eastern Herzegovina, led by Luka Vukalović in 1852, brought the intervention of the Montenegrin prince Danilo and led to open warfare against the Ottomans. At the beginning of 1853, Omer Pasha attacked Montenegro with superior military forces, and the Montenegrins were saved from annihilation only by the intervention of the Great Powers.

In Bulgaria, the peasant masses were restless after the insurrections of the 1830s and 1840s; in fact, the participants in the Niš rebellion continued their anti-Ottoman activities in the regions of Pirot, Vidin, and Sofia.[33] A new peasant uprising occurred in 1847 in the region of Kula. Agitation also simmered in Northern Bulgaria as a result of knowledge of the actions of the Wallachian peasantry in 1848. By 1849 peasant unrest was evident in the region of Vidin and, by 1850, the unrest was translated into a major peasant insurrection. The leaders asked aid from Serbia and weapons were delivered to the rebels. In June 1850, the insurrection spread beyond Vidin to the regions of Kula, Belogradčik, and Lom, but the rebels were defeated by superior Ottoman forces, as they failed to obtain overt military support from Serbia at a time when Belgrade was not inclined to go to war against the

Porte. Ottoman reprisals against the rebels were severe, especially in Belogradčik and Lom. Despite the calamitous defeat of the revolutionary forces the Bulgarian Question assumed greater significance in Balkan and European politics after 1850.

Equally unsuccessful were revolutionary attempts among Greeks.[34] The revolutionary ideas of 1848 reached the Ionian Islands and Greece proper via Italy. The national and liberation movements in the islands were aimed at the British and sought union with Greece. Under the pressures of 1848, the English administration initiated a program of belated reforms which were, however, insufficient to stem the insurrection which broke out in Cephalonia in September 1848. The British carried out arrests and attempted to revive the Constitution of 1817. These actions did not restore peace, and a new uprising broke out in 1849. That insurrection was readily crushed. Resistance to British rule thereafter assumed the form of political action in favor of democratization of political life and of union with Greece. The immediate result was the dissolution of Parliament in 1851.

The ideas of 1848 also found an echo in Greek society among young liberal intellectuals and students who found inspiration in Mazzini's Young Italy and the activities of Italian revolutionaries of the Risorgimento. In March 1848, the provisional republican government of Venice addressed a message to the Greeks stating that "finally Greece and Italy would meet on the path of liberty."[35] After the collapse of their revolutionary efforts a large number of émigrés found refuge in Greece. Hungarians, Italians, and Poles elaborated a project for the unification of Slavs and Greeks and the formation of federal republics of emancipated peoples. Greek

Hetairists, whose activities paralleled those of the "Grand Fraternity" and of the Philorthodox, even prepared an uprising in Thessaly. All these actions and plans, however, came to naught in the face of British opposition, which culminated in the naval blockade of Greece in 1850. Still, the ideas of 1848 were to play an important role in the political life of Greece in the years to come.

The revolutionary ideas of 1848 had a much greater impact on the events in the Romanian Principalities.[36] These ideas were prevalent among the young Romanian intelligentsia well before that year. They manifested themselves in the activities of literary and secret political societies, such as the Brotherhood of Justice (*Dreptate-Frăție*), which, in its program, advocated the union of Moldavia and Wallachia, the establishment of a free and independent state, the abolition of feudal privileges, the democratization of the country, and the creation of a national army. The ideas of democratic revolution were expounded by Romanian students in France, organized in the "Society of Romanian Students" with headquarters in Paris, who in the first days of the revolution of 1848 raised the Romanian national flag on the Hôtel de Ville. The Romanian revolutionary movement could rely on citizen associations and, to a certain extent, also on the cooperation of those boyars who were engaged in trade or business. The bulk of the revolutionary armies assembled by the "Forty-eighters" consisted, however, of the landless and restless Romanian peasantry.

The narrow political platform of the leaders of the revolution, which essentially sought to secure extended political rights for the bourgeoisie and lesser aristocracy alienated the peasantry. This was particularly true in Moldavia, where the

III

primary goal of the revolutionary bourgeoisie and aristocracy was the abolition of the autocratic rule of Mihai Sturdza. The ineffectiveness of the Moldavian action was evident as the revolutionary coup staged at Iassy in April 1848 was readily crushed. In Wallachia, however, the revolution which broke out in June 1848 took a different course. It was prepared more carefully than that in Moldavia and included promises of liberation of the peasantry, attainment of national independence, constitutional rule, and political, religious, and national equality for all. Thus the leaders were able to secure the support of the masses at least during its initial stages. Thousands of peasants joined the aristocrats, intellectuals, merchants, and artisans in the revolution which began on June 11; however, as opposition by the boyars to emancipation of the peasantry increased, and the revolutionary leaders themselves split on that essential issue, the support given to the movement by the peasantry began to wane. The weakened revolutionary forces were unable to resist the ensuing intervention by Russian and Turkish forces which brought an end to the revolution in short order.

The revolution in Transylvania had yet another character than those in the Romanian Principalities proper.[37] It started as an agrarian movement directed against the great Magyar landowners but soon assumed the character of a Romanian national movement. At the Great Assembly which took place at Blaj in mid-May 1848, some 40,000 peasants approved the revolutionary demands of the Romanian bourgeoisie and intellectuals while demanding the abolition of serfdom. The negative response of the leaders of the Hungarian revolution to the Romanian demands drove many a Romanian revolutionary into the arms of the counterrevolutionary Habsburgs, in the expectation that Vienna would recognize the Romanians' national autonomy. The radical wing of the Romanian movement preferred, however, to seek a compromise between the Romanian revolutionary aims and those of the Hungarians, with a view to rallying all revolutionary forces into a vast movement for independence of the peoples of Eastern Europe based on Slavo-Romanian-Hungarian cooperation. It is noteworthy that the Wallachian revolutionary leader Nicolae Bălcescu shared the views of the Transylvanian radicals in the first meaningful display of cooperation among Romanian revolutionaries on both sides of the Carpathians. However, all revolutionary plans and activities were frustrated by internecine conflicts within the revolutionary leadership of the various movements in the Habsburg Empire, by the failure of the revolutions in the Romanian provinces, and by the ultimate military intervention by the forces of Czar Nicholas I.

The Aftermath of 1848: Revolutionary Plans and Actions in the Fifties and Sixties

The legacy of 1848 was, however, far-reaching. The immediate repercussions were strongly felt in the Eastern Crisis of 1853–56. The revolutionary events of 1848–49 aroused worries among the ruling circles of the Habsburg monarchy as they perceived the dangers of unification of the Southern Slav movements, and of the possibility of a major Balkan revolution erupting during the Russo-Turkish war which commenced in the fall of 1853. The Austrian policy was aimed at preventing the spreading of the war to the Balkans, and at maintaining the status quo. Austria was prepared to take mil-

113

itary action against Bosnia, Montenegro, and Albania, and to occupy Serbia, should any unrest occur in the Balkans concurrently with the Crimean War. Vienna's goals were secured by the Peace of Paris, in 1856, when its influence in Serbia increased to the detriment of that of the defeated Russians. However, during the war years, Russia had encouraged revolutionary activities directed against the Turks. The Russians stimulated peasant insurrections in Wallachia and Moldavia, and formed Bulgarian detachments in the Russian army.[38] Moreover, the military occupation of Wallachia and Moldavia, and the subsequent crossing of the Danube by Russian forces in March 1854, encouraged subversive activities by Bulgarian émigrés and *hajduks* in Bulgarian territories. Early in 1854, a Bulgarian Committee was established in Bucharest, with Russian support, to represent Bulgarian interests and organize detachments of volunteers. At the same time, the Bulgarian revolutionary George Rakovski set up a secret society in Constantinople, which had branches in several Bulgarian towns. Pursued by Ottoman authorities, Rakovski had to flee to Stara Planina and, toward the end of 1855, to Wallachia. An attempt was also made by Nikola Filipov, a participant in the revolutionary events of 1848 in the Romanian provinces, to organize a revolution in Trnovo. That attempt, like all other subversive plans directed against the Porte, was frustrated by Turkish vigilance and the withdrawal of the Russian forces from the Romanian Principalities.

Equally unsuccessful were the revolutionary activities recorded among the Greeks.[39] The crossing of the Prut River by the Russian armed forces in July 1853 was regarded by Greek nationalists as the signal for the invasion of Epirus and

Thessaly by Greek forces bent on liberating those territories from Turkish rule and realizing the goals of the *Megali Idea*. The chances of success seemed favorable, as the Turks had moved their forces to the Danube, leaving behind only Albanian garrisons. Athens and other Greek cities assembled volunteers, to be led by officers of the regular Greek army, and sent, during the winter of 1853–54, some 7,000 men into Epirus and Thessaly. National societies operating in the Ionian Islands also sent volunteers to Epirus. The insurrection itself broke out at the end of January 1854 in the Arta region. Hadji Petros and a company of volunteers raided Thessaly near Lamia, as the forces of Karatassos raided Macedonia, and those of Philaretos were active in the region of Pindus. The insurrectionists' flag bore the noteworthy emblem E.O.ΘM. (Epirus-Thessaly-Macedonia). The Porte, supported by the anti-Russian powers, sent an ultimatum to Athens in March 1854, demanding the immediate withdrawal of the military companies from those territories. Diplomatic relations between Turkey and Greece were severed, and by mid-April the Porte started to expel Greeks from Ottoman territories. These actions were preliminary to the collapse of the insurrection in Epirus and Thessaly. The better-armed and more professionally organized Turkish troops sent to cope with the situation defeated volunteer forces at Peta and at Domoko. Meanwhile, a French cruiser sank a vessel carrying weapons to Karatassos' forces, which were operating in the Salonika region. These actions resulted in the abandonment of military activities by the Greek volunteers, who, after four month of warfare in Epirus and Thessaly, recrossed the frontier into Greece. The corollary activities of a "Greek Legion," which operated in the Crimea alongside Serbian, Bulgarian, and even Albanian volunteers, were equally obnoxious to the anti-Russian coalition. Fearing the possibility of a Greek-Turkish war at the time of the Crimean conflict, the allies—and particularly England—put extreme pressure on the Athens regime—which culminated in the British military occupation of Piraeus—to insure Greek neutrality in the Crimean War. The final humiliation of the efforts of Greek nationalists was recorded in the Treaty of Paris, when the Great Powers guaranteed the integrity of the Ottoman Empire and thus thwarted the Greek plans for liberation and annexation of Epirus and Thessaly.

These setbacks for Balkan revolutionary leaders and nationalist politicians who would use force for the attainment of their goals did not, however, discourage the renewal of plotting and planning after the Crimean War. The 1860s, in particular, were notorious in that respect. It was in the sixties that nationalism reached its height in Europe. The Franco-Austrian war of 1859 led to the unification of much of Italy. Prussia's victory over Austria in 1866 precipitated the political activities of the Southern Slavs, which threatened the integrity of the Austro-Hungarian Monarchy. National insurrections were recorded from Poland to Crete.[40] An in-insurrection in Herzegovina led to war between Montenegro and the Porte. The bombardment of Belgrade by Turkish forces precipitated the final removal of Ottoman garrisons and officials from Serbian towns. Serbian secret organizations were active in the northern and central parts of the Balkan Peninsula, as were the Greek Hetairists in the southern regions and Bulgarian committees in the eastern regions of the Balkans. The Ionian Islands were united with Greece in 1864 and a major insurrection broke out in Crete in 1866.

The union of Moldavia and Wallachia was consolidated in the sixties also. The first Balkan agreements, based on the principle of nationality, were concluded between 1866 and 1868, and, throughout these years, Polish, Hungarian, and Italian revolutionaries inflamed the spirits of revolutionary-oriented leaders in the Balkans. The intensive subversive activities recorded throughout the Peninsula naturally caused concern to all forces committed to the maintenance of the integrity of the Ottoman Empire, as well as to those anxious to maintain the status quo in Eastern Europe as such. In a way, the creation of new centers of revolutionary agitation and activity exacerbated the fears of conservatives and elevated the hopes of Balkan leaders committed to promotion of instability in the Peninsula.

In the 1850s, Herzegovina became one of the main "hot spots" in the Balkans.[41] The reforms undertaken by Constantinople, designed to pacify the province, did not alter the fundamentally bad situation of a peasantry subject to exploitation by feudal lords and to political propaganda originating in Serbia and Montenegro. The Herzegovinian tribal chiefs, led by Luka Vukalović and supported by Montenegro, decided to stage an insurrection toward the end of 1857. After initial successes were recorded by the rebels at Orahovica in December 1857, the revolt spread to the tribes adjoining the Montenegrin frontier. Despite Austrian attempts to pacify the area by closing its borders, the revolt continued as the rebels, aided by Montenegrin volunteers, repulsed Turkish attacks in January 1858. The attempt by the Porte to inflict a decisive military defeat on Montenegro, and thus crush the insurrection altogether, came to naught as the Turkish army was defeated by the Montenegrins at Grahovo late in April 1858.

117

Only action by the Great Powers, which redrew the Montenegrin-Ottoman borders and granted recognition to Montenegro's independence, led to pacification of Herzegovina.

The insurrection in Herzegovina was followed by uprisings in the Bosnian regions of Sava and Kraina.[42] These had
started during the Crimean war as the peasants refused to
abide by their feudal obligations. By the beginning of 1858,
armed revolts were recorded in the regions of Gradačac, Bosanski Šamac, and in the Trebava mountains. The peasants,
led by Serbian priests, attacked the property of the beys but
they were promptly repulsed by Turkish forces. In the
Kraina, *hajduks* were active in the regions of Sava, Una,
Sana, and along the Austrian frontier. By 1858 the number of
insurgents reached 4,000. The insurgency, however, was
overcome by the Ottoman army for Banja Luka, as reinforced
by troops stationed in Herzegovina in July 1858. This was not
the end of unrest in the region. In fact, the events in Italy;
the activities of Italian, Hungarian, and Polish revolutionaries
in the Balkans; the work of the Russian Slavophiles; the encouragement received from Serbia and Montenegro; and the
continuing unrest caused by strained feudal relationships,
led to a new rebellion in Herzegovina. This insurrection, led
by Luka Vukalović, had from its inception the support of
Montenegro and quickly spread beyond the Montenegrin-
Herzegovinian frontier as far as Popovo Polje, near Dubrovnik, and to the area of Mostar. The Great Powers intervened
with the Porte and formed a commission for the pacification
of the areas in turmoil. By the beginning of 1862, Ottoman
military intervention and internecine discord threatened the
success of the insurrection. At that time, Prince Nikola of
Montenegro formally joined the conflict against the Turks,

only to be defeated within three months by superior Ottoman forces. Following the fall of Crnojevica Rijeka and the ensuing threat posed to the capital, Cetinje, Nikola accepted the ultimatum issued by Omer Pasha Latas in September 1862.[43] The military failure of Montenegro was symbolic of the weariness of the Herzegovinian movement. Luka Vukalović tried to rekindle the insurrection in 1864, but by 1865 he was obliged to seek refuge in Russia. Another insurrection broke out in Austrian territory, in the Boka Kotorska, at Krivošije in 1869.[44] This rebellion was caused by opposition to Austro-Hungarian measures seeking to abolish ancient privileges and tribal autonomy. The mountain communities, objecting to these measures, which included also the performance of military service outside the Boka Kotorska, rebelled with the aid of Herzegovina and Montenegro, but the insurrection was readily contained by Austrian forces. These failures did not, however, discourage the schemes of other planners of revolution in the Balkans, who were operating primarily in Serbia, the rapidly rising center for coordination of anti-Ottoman agitation and revolutionary activities.

The Balkan Peninsula, in the sixties, was the center of activity for Italian, Hungarian, and Polish revolutionaries, as it was for exponents of Russian Panslavism.[45] These groups, as well as Italian, French, and Prussian diplomats, promoted plans for the attainment of Balkan national aims, hoping to create diversions which would facilitate the attainment of their own political goals. Action in the Balkans depended on the renewal of Slavic-Hungarian contacts. Kossuth, for one, realized that the Slavs were indispensable allies in the Hungarian struggle against Austria. He therefore elaborated a scheme for the creation of a Danubian Confederation and,

119

in 1859, began negotiations with Prince Michael of Serbia to secure Serbian support for his plans. Concurrently, Cavour opened Sardinian consulates in Belgrade and Bucharest. The Hungarian émigré General Stefan Türr, who collaborated with Garibaldi, was instructed in the fall of 1860 to seek Serbian cooperation for a general insurrection in Serbia, Croatia, Dalmatia, and Hungary. Envoys of Garibaldi even visited Prince Nikola of Montenegro. The new king of Greece, through the intermediacy of the Committee of the Ionian Islands, worked with the Garibaldians toward the staging of a revolution in Epirus, and in Albania in cooperation with Montenegro. According to this scheme, Garibaldi was to land in Dalmatia, in the spring of 1862, while General Türr would land concurrently at Durazzo and at Bari. Moreover, Montenegro would attack Albania and the Sandjak and join forces with Serbia, while Greece was to use the Hetairists for staging the insurrection in Epirus. Italy, of course, was to declare war on Austria. This utopian scheme could never be realized but other such schemes were concocted under the impact of the Polish uprising of 1863. Thus, the Hungarian committee of émigrés at Turin proposed to the Serbian government in 1863 the conclusion of an agreement which would commit the partners to war against the Turks and diversionary military action against Austria. The outbreak of the Austro-Prussian war of 1866 rekindled plans for a Balkan insurrection, which would facilitate the unification of Italy and of Germany, as well as the resolution of the Hungarian question. In April 1866, at the suggestion of the Italians, Garibaldi's Adriatic Plan for a Yugoslav-Hungarian insurrection within the framework of Italian operations against Austria was presented to Bismarck. On Bismarck's orders the adviser to the

Prussian minister to Madrid, von Pfuel, and General Türr were sent to Belgrade to work toward the unleashing of an insurrection in Hungary and in the Croatian littoral.[46]

Panslavist propaganda from Russia evolved in the Balkans concurrently with these revolutionaries entreaties from the West.[47] The propaganda became more intense after the establishment of the Slavophile Committee of Friends of Moscow in 1858. The Panslav ideas related to the creation of a greater Slavic state were freely circulated in Serbia by Serbian students returning from Russia. Similar activities were stimulated by the visit, in 1860, of Ivan Aksakov to Croatia, Montenegro, Dalmatia, and Serbia. The Panslavs provided significant assistance to the rebels in Bosnia and Herzegovina, as well as to the military forces of Montenegro in 1862; and they were also very active in supporting subversive activities by planners of the liberation of Bulgaria. Still, all in all, Serbia, was the focal point for all activities in the sixties.[48]

The policies of Serbia were directed toward preparation of a general Balkan revolution against the Turks, and appropriate planning was done at both official and unofficial levels. Serbia was closely involved in the Bosnian revolutionary movement. After the uprising of 1858-59, Bosnian refugees came to Serbia, where they organized *hajduk* companies to be used in a future insurrection. The Serbo-Bosnian Committee, generally known as the Central Committee, was established in 1860 on the initiative of these refugees. Matija Ban was the head of the Committee, Metropolitan Mihailo was the honorary president, and Ivan Aksakov was an honorary member. The Committee worked for an insurrection in the Ottoman Empire, in collaboration with Italian and Hungarian revolutionaries, and with the financial support of the

Russian Panslavs. The Committee organized 17 agencies in Serbia, Dalmatia, Croatia, and Slovenia; sent protests and petitions from Bosnia and Kosovo to the Great Powers and to the Porte; and welcomed refugees from Bosnia, who were actively engaged in planning and readying revolutionary activities. The Committee, however, became defunct in the spring of 1861 when, for reasons of their own, the Serbian government and the Panslavs withdrew their support.

The activities of the organization directed by Garašanin in 1844 and in 1849, however, were revived in that very year. By the beginning of 1862, the so-called Serbian Committee was established in Belgrade, with the announced goal of disseminating national propaganda and preparing a revolution in the Ottoman Empire. The Committee elaborated several projects for insurrection in Bosnia and Bulgaria. To attain that end, a detachment of 200 Southern Slav volunteers was set up in Valjevo. The Committee also financed the Bulgarian Legion, composed of Bulgarian refugees, as well as the Bulgarian Provisional Chancellory (*Privremeno bugarsko načelstvo*), which Rakovski had set up in Serbia in June 1862, and which became the office of the Bulgarian Provisional Government. According to the Committee's plans the task of the Bulgarian Legion was to stage an insurrection in Bulgaria; and that of the Southern Slav volunteers, one in Bosnia, which would prompt Serbian military intervention in support of the revolutions. Indeed, the problem of Bosnia became particularly acute during the Austro-Prussian war and the Cretan insurrection in 1866. A committee whose task was to coordinate the activities of an insurrectionary network in Bosnia was established in Sarajevo, and its leaders were sent to Serbia for training. In 1867, the emissary of the Serbian government, Oreškovic, prepared a project for a new Bosnian insurrection, which would be assisted militarily by companies dispatched from Serbia, Slavonia, Dalmatia, Montenegro, and even from Italy and Corfu. These utopian plans were, however, frustrated by a show of force and clever use of propaganda by Vienna. Nevertheless, all these plans and activities envisaging participation in one form or another by Southern Slavs caused concern to the international forces committed to the maintenance of the status quo.[49]

The 1860s were indeed very important for the ideological development of the Southern Slavs. Social and economic progress, largely resulting from the crisis of absolutism which was manifest in the Habsburg Empire, and from the corollary influences exerted by the Italian and German unification movements, was recorded in Croatia in those years. The successors of the Illyrians gathered around the National Party of Strossmayer and Rački, which expounded a broad Southern Slav program. Their activities focused on the development of closer cultural and political ties among the Southern Slavs and corollary federative reorganization of the Habsburg Empire. The Party of the Right, headed by Starčevic, went even further in asking for total national and political individuality, based on historical rights, for Croatia. A period of national rebirth also occurred in Dalmatia, under the stimulus exerted by the urban population, by the events in Croatia, and by those in Italy. The Dalmatians professed a Greater Slav ideology, seeking ties with all the Slavs of the Monarchy, opposing the centralism of Vienna, and demanding unification with Croatia. Serbia encouraged the Dalmatians. At the end of 1860, a Serbo-Croatian agreement was drafted, whereby Yugoslavia would be a common federative state consisting of the three branches of the Southern Slavs: the Serbs, the Croats, and the Bulgarians. It is noteworthy that the term Yugoslavia, rather than Illyria, was used at this time.

The Serbian government also took the initiative in the summer of 1866 toward formalizing Serbo-Croatian contacts. Garašanin, in collaboration with Bishop Strossmayer, recommended that closer arrangements be made between Serbs and Croats with a view to establishing a common Yugoslav state "independent of Austria and of the Ottomans." In September 1866, the scope of this collaboration was expanded to include efforts toward the achievement of liberation of all Slavs from Ottoman and Austrian domination, the creation of a Yugoslav state, and the conclusion of alliances with neighboring Balkan peoples. Garašanin presented this program to Strossmayer in March 1867. Inasmuch as Serbia possessed a government, an army, and a foreign policy of its own, it was to assume responsibility for the conduct of diplomatic and military activities. The "liberation movement" was to be started in Bosnia, in the summer of 1867, by means of an insurrection. The insurgents were to establish a government, convoke an Assembly, and proclaim union with Serbia. A Central Committee, to be created in Zagreb, was to direct Croat participation. The "Circular of the Belgrade Central Committee for the Unification of the Southern Slavs Addressed to Committees Abroad," issued in March 1867, indicated the extent of the common Southern Slav state: it was to include Serbia, Bosnia, Herzegovina, Montenegro, northern Albania, Macedonia, Bulgaria, a large part of Thrace, Croatia, Srem, Dalmatia, Istria, Carniola, and the northern parts of Styria and of Karst. It is interesting to note that the leaders of the Croatian National Party accepted the Belgrade plan and set up, in May 1867, in Zagreb, the Central Committee, which was led by Mrazović, one of Strossmayer's collaborators. The Croatian leaders even recognized "the identity and equality of rights" of the Serbian people in Croatia.

The federal plans of the Southern Slav movement were related to a series of projects dealing with federation and confederation of Danubian and Balkan peoples, which were drawn up by Hungarian, Polish, and Romanian émigrés, as well as by Italian revolutionaries. Garašanin himself explained the need for liberation of the Balkan peoples in a memorandum drafted in September 1866 for the use of Napoleon III. Garašanin, in anticipation of the decline of the Habsburg Empire, proposed the creation of a vast confederation of some 44,000,000 people, which would extend from the Black Sea to the Adriatic, and which would serve as a buffer zone between Germany and Russia.

This utopian scheme, like most other schemes devised by Serbs, envisaged active participation by Bulgarians as a guarantee of success. The Serbian view was shared by leaders of the Bulgarian liberation movement.[50] Thus, Rakovski was in constant touch with Novi Sad and Belgrade. The first Bulgarian paper, *Dunavski lebed* (The Swan of the Danube), appeared in 1860 in Belgrade and was financed by the Serbian government. Bulgarian refugees studied at the Serbian Military Academy and other schools, while Bulgarian *hajduk* companies took refuge in Serbia. Toward the end of 1861, Rakovski drew up the Plan for the Liberation of Bulgaria and the Statute of the Bulgarian Provisional Administration. In 1862, the Bulgarian Legion was created.

The Serbian government's reluctance to go to war

125

against the Turks in 1862, following the bombardment of Belgrade, disappointed the Bulgarian émigrés in Serbia and resulted in their going to Bucharest, to the detriment of existing Serbo-Bulgarian relations. Serbia considered the Bulgarian movement as part of the Southern Slav—however, subordinated to Serbian political and state interests. The Bulgarian circles, in turn, were fearful that the politically backward Bulgarian population would necessarily fall under the political influence of Serbia. In the ensuing period of rapprochement resulting from the events of 1866 the Bulgarian Committee in Bucharest (*Dobrodeteljnata družina*—Benevolence Committee), on the initiative of the Russian ambassador to Constantinople Count Ignatiev, proposed to the Serbian government at the beginning of 1867 a "program of Bulgarian-Serbian political relations," which envisaged the creation of a Serbo-Bulgarian state, with a common capital, to be ruled by Prince Michael. The Bulgarian proposal was accepted in principle by Belgrade and a protocol was drawn up, in which the regions which would comprise the "Yugoslav Empire" were enumerated: Serbia, Bulgaria, Thrace, and Macedonia.

Other plans for altering the status quo in the Peninsula were also drawn up in the 1860s. One of these envisaged a Balkan insurrection which was to start in Albania.[51] The would-be Albanian rebels were to be supported by the Serbs with the Catholic abbot Don Krasnik, the Slovene priest Franz Mauri, and the chief of the Mirdites Bib Doda acting as intermediaries between Albanians and Serbians. At the beginning of 1868, contacts were in fact made—however through the intermediacy of Count Ignatiev—with the Albanian Djelal Pasha, who was imprisoned in Constantinople;

and, in the spring of 1868, an uprising occurred among the Ghegs. The revolt was quickly crushed by the Turks.

Preparations for a Balkan revolution were an essential complement to the political agreements of the sixties. All Serbian "revolutionary" organizations of this period had similar structures and identical working methods.[52] They were all supported by a network of committees and by agents who travelled through Serbian, Ottoman, and Austrian territories—advocating insurrection, unification, and the formation of a large state. None, however, worked out any meaningful social and economic programs that would appeal to the masses, and their essentially amateurish and conspiratorial character could not guarantee successful attainment of their basically unrealistic goals.

Of greater significance for the sixties was the development of the Bulgarian national movement, which was to reach its climax in the following decade. The Bulgarian movement began in earnest in the years immediately preceding the liberation of Bulgaria and was largely a function of conditions within the Ottoman Empire and Bulgaria, as conditioned by general factors affecting Balkan and European developments.[53]

The Ottoman Empire, subsequent to the conclusion of commercial treaties with the Great Powers in 1839 and 1862, to the construction of railroads, and to the development of customs and communications system, opened its ports to economic penetration by foreign interests. As a result, the crisis of the Ottoman system became more acute, as evidenced by the further depreciation of the currency and decline in feudal tax revenues. Economic difficulties, most evident after the Crimean War, affected Bulgaria, in particular,

127

with resultant large-scale emigration of its population; a significant business crisis caused by external industrial competition; and rapid social differentiation of the Bulgarian rural population and the developing middle class. While rich non-Muslim office holders, the so-called *čorbadjis,* had economic ties with the Turks and, consequently, were opposed to the liberation movement, the petite and middle bourgeoisie, especially that segment which had emigrated to neighboring Balkan countries and had adopted Western liberal ideas, became the champions of the Bulgarian liberation movement. Intellectual and cultural emancipation was regarded as a prerequisite for national liberation. Recognition of nationality was, in the Ottoman Empire, a function of recognition of a national church. This is why the struggle for Bulgarian national liberation was linked to the struggle for the independence of the Bulgarian church, which, in turn, provoked a major conflict with the Orthodox Patriarch in Constantinople, the champion of Hellenism in the Balkans. The conflict between the Bulgarian bourgeoisie and the Greek clergy became evident by the 1830s and was only to be aggravated by the *Hatti şerif* of 1839. The quest for Bulgarian ecclesiastical emancipation was initially directed by the colony of Bulgarian merchants in Constantinople. In the 1840s, the struggle was led by Neofit Bozveli and Ilarion Makariopolski and transcended Bulgarian territory as such as it spread into Macedonia and addressed itself also to the numerous Bulgarian émigrés in the Romanian provinces and Russia.

There were two conflicting currents in that ecclesiastical struggle—the conservative and the liberal—both of which, however, demanded support from the Porte for its successful resolution. The proclamation of independence, made by Ilarion Makriopolski in April 1860, created the crisis which attracted the attention of external forces. Russian diplomats in general, and Ignatiev in particular, supported the Bulgarians, as did the Serbs for that matter. The Bulgarian ecclesiastical question, in the process of becoming an instrument of Balkan and European diplomacy, was also affected by political developments in the Balkans. At the time of the insurrection in Crete, in 1866, Patriarch Gregory IV sought to further the Greek cause through Greco-Bulgarian cooperation. He therefore recognized the autonomy of the Bulgarian Church (the Exarchate) in 1867. The Porte, in its determination to hinder favorable development of Greco-Bulgarian relations and to placate Russia, in turn recognized the independence of the Bulgarian church in February 1870. In retaliation, the Patriarch denounced the Exarchate as schismatic in 1872. The recognition of the Bulgarian Exarchate ended three decades of struggle. It was a momentous achievement in that it expedited the process of Bulgarian national and cultural affirmation and served as a vehicle for Bulgarian expansion into Macedonia toward the end of the nineteenth century.[54]

In any event, the Bulgarian liberation movement assumed major proportions in the 1860s with the activities of Bulgarian committees established in Serbia and in the Romanian Principalities, and of insurrectionist organizations operating in Bulgarian territories as such. National elements were infused by the liberation committees abroad and were affected by the social and political tendencies manifest among Bulgarian émigrés, as well as by political conditions and influences present in the countries wherein the committees were located. Four men were in the forefront of the liberation movement in the sixties—Rakovski, Karavelov, Levski, and Botev.

The Bulgarian activists in Serbia were in close contact with the Serbian organizations which were preparing an insurrection in the Balkans. Rakovski was the head of the Bulgarian movement in Serbia. He published the *Dunavski lebed* and worked out a plan for the liberation of Bulgaria which entailed forming a provisional government, organizing the Bulgarian Legion, and developing extensive propaganda activities. His great merit rested in his original plan for staging an internal revolution in Bulgaria itself. He organized companies and committees to that end, and, in fact, one of these committees, led by Hadji Stavra, was sent from Serbia to attempt an insurrection in Bulgaria. The attempted insurrection, however, failed miserably.[55]

The center of the Bulgarian movement was soon transferred to the Romanian Principalities, where in 1862 the Benevolence Society was set up. After the ouster of Prince Alexandru Ion Cuza in 1866, the Romanian "liberals" supported the Bulgarian movement. The Bulgarian Secret Central Committee was thus created, with Romanian assistance, in 1866, and was active until 1868.[56] Influenced by the Austro-Hungarian dualist system, its members favored Bulgarian-Ottoman duality. Toward the end of 1866, Rakovski formed in Romania the Secret Supreme National Commission of Bulgarian Citizens, whose task was to raise companies for an insurrection in Bulgaria. In 1867, the "Provisional Law for the Year 1867 of National Mountain Companies" elaborated a plan for military action by these companies. Two companies did, in fact, cross the Danube in April and May 1867 in the regions of Sliven and Kotel, under the command of P. Hitov and F. Totiu. They were promptly defeated and their failure was roundly condemned by less adventurous commercial émigrés in Romania. A new attempt to create a second Bulgarian Legion, made in 1867 in Serbia, was unsuccessful, as the Serbs, having secured the cities abandoned by the Ottomans by peaceful means, were in no mood for confrontation with the Porte. Thereupon the legionaries went to Romania where they created, after the death of Rakovski in 1867, a new committee—the Bulgarian Society. Hadji Dimitur and Stefan Karadja crossed into Bulgaria with a new company in June 1868 on the Stara Planina but were readily defeated by the Turks.

After Rakovski's death, the Bulgarian movement split into two factions: that of the liberal democrats and that of the revolutionaries. Liuben Karavelov, an ideologue, publicist, and ardent supporter of Southern Slav and Balkan federation schemes—particularly, Serbian-Bulgarian collaboration—expressed the liberal democratic position in arguing that the liberation of Bulgaria was possible only within the framework of general Balkan collaboration. By contrast, Vasil Levski, the ideologist of the Bulgarian revolution, argued that the liberation of Bulgaria should occur through a revolution of the Bulgarian masses. Levski desired to free the Bulgarian movement of dependency on foreign forces and undertook, in 1869, the creation of an internal revolutionary organization on Bulgarian territory. The diversity of views was reconciled in the spring of 1872 through a compromise resulting in the creation of the Bulgarian Revolutionary Central Committee (B.R.C.K.). Its program sought the liberation of Bulgaria through moral and armed revolution. Levski entered Bulgaria in the summer of 1872 to continue his revolutionary activities, but he was captured by the Turks and executed in Sofia in February 1873. Levski's death was a severe blow to the liberation movement, which was plagued by internal dissent. The internecine conflicts were at least papered over at the meeting of the B.R.C.K. held in Bucharest in May 1873, when Hristo Botev emerged as its new leader and champion of the principles of national and social revolution for the attainment of the ultimate goal of the Bulgarian liberation movement.[57]

The activities of the Bulgarians did not overshadow the significance of contemporary events in Greece, the Ionian Islands, and Crete.[58] The furthering of the economic and political union of Greece with Greek elements of the Diaspora assumed major proportions in the 1850s and 1860s. In 1850 ties between Athens and the Patriarch in Constantinople were tightened in matters related to the administration of the Greek Church, in a manner which increased the degree of political influence exerted by Athens in the affairs of the Orthodox Church in general. The Greco-Turkish commercial treaty, concluded in 1855, aided the development of Greek trade in Ottoman territories. After the ouster of the Bavarian dynasty in 1862, the new National Assembly demonstrated the unity of Hellenism by granting representation in parliament to all Greeks residing outside the territorial limits of Greece proper. This economic and political process, paralleling the tumultous European and Balkan events of the period, rekindled plans for the realization of the *Megali Idea*. Events in Italy affected Greece in that plans devised by Italian, Polish, and Hungarian revolutionaries, by Garibaldi and by the Venetian Canini, called for a "general synchronized revolution" against the Turks and for a "Holy Alliance of Slavo-Hellenes." Some 20,000 volunteers were to be readied, according to these schemes, in Greece for the purpose of staging an insurrection in Epirus and Thessaly.

The unification of Italy affected the Ionian Islands in particular. Corfu had close contacts with Italian revolu tionaries and many an Ionian radical was in touch with Garibaldi. The Ionian parliament declared unequivocally in 1857, and again in 1859, in favor of union with Greece in the face of contrary "reform projects" advocated by England. The struggle of the Greek population of the Islands, and Britain's own determination to check the spread of Russian influence in Greece and safeguard its interests through the election of a suitable Greek sovereign, were responsible for England's decision to cede the Ionian Islands to Greece in December 1862. While the signatory powers of the Treaty of Vienna of 1815 sought to protect their respective interests, the Ionian parliament voted in October 1863 in favor of total and prompt union with Greece. In March 1864, the British troops left the islands, and on June 6 King George disembarked at Corfu. On July 31 of that year, 84 Ionian deputies became members of the Parliament in Athens. The Ionian lessons were not lost on other Greeks.

After a period of relative calm, following the insurrection of 1841, a new revolt broke out in Crete in the spring of 1866.[59] It was prompted by the inadequacies of the fiscal reform of 1858, by the national and liberation activities supported by Greece, and by Turkish military pressures. On September 2, 1866 the national parliament of Crete proclaimed unilaterally the island's union with Greece. The Cretan insurrection caused excitement in Greece and throughout the Bal-

133

kans. Committees were formed in Athens, and in other Greek cities, for the purpose of assembling volunteers and gathering arms for the insurgents. Officers of the Greek army went to Crete as General Kalergis assumed command of military activities. The Greek navy transported military supplies to the rebels. The Athens government remained officially neutral but allowed popular demonstrations in favor of the Cretan uprising. Athens tried to avoid armed confrontation with the Porte but did not shy away from provoking an insurrection in Epirus, Thessaly, and Macedonia, which would draw in Ottoman forces and thus ease pressure on the Cretan insurgents. The Committee of Epirotes in Athens, the Ionian *Hetairia,* and Riciotti Garibaldi and his officers, were all planning an insurrection in Epirus, which was to break out in September 1866. Meanwhile, Serbia was consulted about joining the Greek action. The rebellion did in fact break out in Epirus in the fall of 1866 and promptly spread into Thessaly. An attempt was even made by L. Bulgaris, as head of a small company operating at Seres, to spread the insurrection into southern Macedonia as well. All these movements were related to the uprising which had been staged in southwestern Macedonia by Spiro Djerov. At the same time, the insurrection in Crete proper met with varying success. In the spring of 1867, a provisional government was established which ostensibly acted in the name of King George of Greece. However, after a protracted struggle, the uprising failed to attain its goals. Crete was devastated as more than 600 villages were destroyed by fire and some 50,000 refugees fled to Greece. The Ottoman counterinsurgency forces led by Omer Pasha Latas also lost some 20,000 men. Several actions taken by the Porte, including the promulgation of a new

Organic Statute for the island and the breaking of diplomatic relations with Greece, doomed the uprising, as the Great Powers were also opposed to the liberation of Crete and its union with Greece. Under the circumstances, the Greek government in Athens agreed in February 1869 to refrain from sending military formations into Ottoman territories, which led to the final collapse of the insurrection. The lack of success of Greek efforts was not paralleled in the Romanian provinces, however, where internal activities and Great Power rivalries brought a happier ending to the resolution of political aspirations.

The affirmation of the principle of nationality recorded its greatest success in the Balkans in the unification of the Romanian Principalities.[60] Danubian navigation, the beginning of railroad construction, and the growth of internal economic activity consequent to the penetration of Western capitalism, led to the economic integration of Moldavia and Wallachia. The Romanian peasants, however, caught between the traditional feudal and the new economic relations constituted a potentially revolutionary mass, a fact which did not escape certain segments of the unionist movement.

The unionist movement of the Romanian nationalists was the expression of the ideas of 1848, which were embraced by Romanian émigrés and by the liberal intelligentsia of the two provinces. The activities of the "left" of the emigration, led by Nicolae Bălcescu, were patterned on those of similar national and revolutionary movements, such as those of Hungarian and Polish émigrés established in the major European political centers, those of Italian revolutionaries, and those of the Bulgarian liberation forces. The émigrés advocated the unification of Romania as the Belgium of the

135

Balkans, a form which they thought would be acceptable to the Powers.

The Crimean War brought successive occupations of the Principalities, first by Russia and then by Austria. The conflicting interests of the European Powers, so evident at the Congress of Paris in 1856, could not be reconciled to insure the fulfillment of the desiderata of the unionists. The negative attitude of the Powers persuaded the Romanians that unification could be achieved only through a fait accompli. The unionist movement was organized politically in 1856–57. The Electoral Committee of Union, working in Moldavia, established contacts with the unionist forces in Wallachia. In March 1857 a proclamation, issued in the name of the unionists, was posted in Bucharest. It called for unification of the two provinces. The elections of September 1857 gave the unionists a clear majority; and on October 19 of that year, the union of the Principalities, under Ottoman suzerainty and the rule of a foreign prince, was proclaimed at Jassy. The Powers, however, decided against acceptance of the Romanian decision. Nevertheless, the process of unification, once begun, could not be arrested. The representatives of Moldavia and Wallachia elected early in 1859 the same person, Alexandru Ion Cuza, as ruler of both provinces. This action, which amounted to de facto unification of the Principalities, became official on December 23, 1861.

The unification of the Romanian provinces, which had met with significant opposition from Austria and the Porte and with only limited support from England, could not by itself further the cause of militant nationalism in the Balkan Peninsula. The Romanian and other Balkan leaders had to reckon with the essential determination of the European

136

Powers not to allow significant alterations in the status quo. To counteract the position of the Powers, the political leaders of the Peninsula decided to conclude a system of political agreements—which was, in fact, realized between 1866 and 1868—among representatives of Serbia, Greece, Montenegro, and of the Bulgarian national movement

At the core of the Balkan alliance system were the agreements between Greece and Serbia.[61] Greece initiated the negotiations in 1860, and the overture was accepted by Belgrade on Garašanin's advice. Formal negotiations began in Constantinople in April 1861, but it soon became evident that the two sides could not reconcile their conflicting territorial ambitions. The Greek demands, reflective of the goals of the *Megali Idea,* encompassed regions as far as the Šar-Planina and the Balkan mountains, including all of Macedonia and substantial portions of Bulgarian territory. The Serbian government, anxious to create a greater Southern Slav state, sought to expand Serbia's borders to the east also at the expense of the Bulgarians. Nevertheless, the negotiators in Constantinople tried to reach an agreement which would include two major documents. The first, the Greco-Serbian convention that summarized their respective obligations in an offensive and defensive alliance, had to offer a plan for the division of Balkan territory. The second, a "declaration of rights" of the Balkan states, tended to disavow the interference by the Great Powers in Balkan affairs and envisaged expansion of the Greco-Serbian agreement through adherence thereto by Romania and Montenegro. Acceptance by Greece of the eventual establishment of Bulgaria did not entail Serbian support for Athens' proposed compensation of acquisition of Macedonia and Thrace with its three million Slavic inhabitants. Therefore, instead of signing a formal treaty, Belgrade merely advised Athens that it was prepared to collaborate fully with Greece in matters related to the preparation of uprisings in the Ottoman Empire and to common diplomatic moves designed to prevent interference by the Powers in Balkan affairs.

The bombardment of Belgrade in 1862 and the prospect of war against the Turks prompted the Serbian government to seek renewal of negotiations with Greece. However, this was impossible because of the internal dynastic crisis in Greece, which prevented further contacts at that time. Negotiations were renewed, however, in 1863 and 1864, in an atmosphere strained by Greco-Romanian conflicts over the secularization of religious properties in Romania and by Greco-Bulgarian disputes over the independence of the Bulgarian church. On the Greek side, at least, the securing of the Ionian Islands, and the ensuing Anglophile current, made agreement with pro-Russian Balkan Slavs less desirable than a few years earlier.

The Cretan insurrection and the Austro-Prussian war caused yet another shift in Balkan negotiations. The Greek opposition circles began their own direct *pourparlers* with the Serbian representatives in Constantinople in January 1866. Agreement was readily reached on twelve points related to the eventual rise to power of the opposition in Greece, to the conclusion of an alliance between Serbia and Greece on the basis of the negotiations of 1861, and to military conventions on preparations for a Balkan-wide revolution and direct military confrontation between Serbia and Greece, on the one hand, and the Ottomans on the other. The accession to power of the leader of the opposition, Alexander Kumunduros, in December 1866 paved the way to further Greco-Serbian negotiations. However, disagreements over territorial questions were still apparent as the new negotiations began in Constantinople in January 1867. An agreement, in principle, was reached in Vienna, where the negotiations were completed to avoid the arousing of Ottoman suspicions, in August of that year. The delicate territorial issues were resolved through delineation of maximal and minimal requirements. The minima for Greece were Epirus and Thessaly; and for Serbia, Bosnia and Herzegovina. The maxima were to be determined after military victory over the Turks and in agreement with the wishes of the liberated Balkan peoples. The formal treaty of alliance between Serbia and Greece was signed at Voeslau, near Vienna, on August 26, 1867 and was ratified by Belgrade on October 5, 1867 and by Athens on January 22, 1868.[62] Among its most notable provisions were the delineation of a Greek sphere of military operations in Epirus and Thessaly, of a Serbian one in Bosnia and Herzegovina, and of a joint area of cooperation on Albanian and Macedonian territories. Moreover, the Serbian government assumed responsibility for the staging of the revolution in Bulgaria, while the two contracting parties were jointly to prepare the uprising in Albania and to form guerilla detachments, comprising 5,000 men, which would precipitate a general insurrection on Ottoman soil preliminary to the proposed war against the Porte.

Negotiations between Serbia and Montenegro proved to be more difficult, largely because of the struggle between Belgrade and Cetinje over the question of leadership of the Serbian national movement.[63] Relations between Serbia and Montenegro since the time of the mission of Vuk Karadjić to

Cetinje, in 1860, were generally cool because of Serbia's indecisiveness during the Montenegrin-Ottoman war of 1862. Some improvement was, however, noticeable by 1865 as the Serbian government purchased weapons for the Montenegrins from Germany. The relations between the two states became decisively friendlier as a result of the crisis caused in the Habsburg Empire after the Austro-Prussian war. Yet it was the insurrection in Crete which hastened the conclusion of the Serbian-Montenegrin alliance, which was signed in Cetinje in October 1866. The parties agreed to prepare an insurrection in the Ottoman Empire and coordinate their military efforts for war against the Porte. Moreover, the Prince of Montenegro agreed to the union of Montenegro with a Greater Serbian state which would be ruled by Prince Michael of Serbia, with the proviso that the Montenegrin ruler would retain the rank of "Prince of the ruling family." [64]

Romania alone remained outside the system of Serbian alliances. Although the two countries exchanged diplomatic representatives in 1863, the Romanians—because of internal conflicts caused by the struggle between Cuza and parliament over the disputed agrarian reform of 1864, and also because of Great Power interference in Romanian internal affairs—were in no position to adhere to the Serbian system of Balkan alliances. It was only in 1866, following the accession of Carol of Hohenzollern to the Romanian throne, that the Romanians drew closer to Serbia. A Romanian proposal for a defensive alliance against the Porte was submitted to Belgrade, but Garašanin's fall from power, coupled with Serbia's rejection of Romanian territorial demands affecting northeastern Bulgaria, limited the scope of potential collaboration. Thus, only a treaty of "friendship and economic cooperation" was signed in Bucharest in February 1868, which, however, assured Serbia of Romania's benevolent neutrality in the event of war against the Porte.[65] In any event, all these initiatives, alliances, and anti-Ottoman plans and preparations of the sixties assumed genuine importance only in the revolutionary seventies, the fateful years of the Balkan revolutionary tradition.

The Revolutionary Seventies and the Eastern Crisis of 1875–1878

The unification of Italy and Germany, the death of Prince Michael in Serbia, and the tension in Greece at the time of the Cretan insurrection, all led to a period of relative calm in the Balkans. But the quiescence was at best superficial, as the factors leading to the Eastern Crisis of 1875-78 soon became evident. An Austro-Russian conflict in the Balkans was brewing as the Habsburgs, ousted from Italy and Germany, turned toward the Balkans as the Russians, following removal in 1870 of the restrictions imposed upon them by the Treaty of Paris, reactivated their Balkan policies. The coalescence of internal and external conditions provoked the insurrections in Bosnia and Herzegovina in 1875, in Bulgaria in 1876, in Thessaly in 1877–78; the war between Serbia and Montenegro directed against the Porte in 1876; the armed intervention of Russia in 1877, and the diplomatic entaglement of Europe in 1878. The internal Balkan factors loomed larger in the seventies than ever before.

Indeed, the Balkans, in the process of development of modern societies and under the influence of the ideas of young intellectuals who had studied abroad, generally be-

141

came familiar with the ideas of Western European liberalism and with those of Russian reformers and radicals. Such ideas precipitated the fall from power of Prince Alexander in Serbia in 1858, and of King Otho in Greece in 1862.

Among the key exponents of external political thought was the Union of Young Serbs, constituted, at its inception, by Serbian students in Vienna and Budapest.[66] The Union was patterned on the German *Tugenbund,* the Italian *Carbonari,* Young Italy, and the Greek *Hetairia.* Created, in 1866, at Novi Sad, it was first known as Alliance of Young Serbs (Omladina). Its doctrine was that of a liberal, national, democratic, and cultural movement. The Omladina preached the ideas of 1848: self-determination, national sovereignty, constitutionalism, and parliamentarianism, all for the purpose of liberating and unifying the Serbian people. These ideas, transmitted by students, young intellectuals, merchants, and artists, quickly gained acceptance in the Voivodina and then in Serbia, Bosnia, Herzegovina, Montenegro, and on the Adriatic littoral. The activities of the organization took two distinct forms: in Serbia, those of a liberal and political movement; and beyond Serbia, those of a national and revolutionary one. In Serbia, these goals collided with those of Prince Michael. Outside Serbia, the movement continued the tradition of the existing revolutionary organizations.

The activities of the alliance of Young Serbs were further continued by the Serbian Society of Liberation and Unification founded, in 1871, in Cetinje.[67] That society had the distinctive character of a secret revolutionary organization. It emphasized in its statute the goal of "organization of conspiratorial action with a view to liberation and unification of the Serbian people" and of "harmony with all those who will join the struggle as Serbian people." It established a Central Committee, representative of regional and local committees, which was empowered to carry out preparations for revolution in Bosnia and Herzegovina. These activities were endorsed also by the first Serbian socialists, Svetozar Marković and Vasa Pelagić, and their effectiveness was manifest at the time of the insurrection in Herzegovina in 1875.

The liberalism of the 1860s and 1870s had its impact on the formulation of ideas on inter-Balkan relations also. All these ideas shared the tendency to relate the liberation movements to external political factors. As early as 1862, the Voivodinian politician Mihailo Polit Desančić outlined in his *Die orientalische Frage und ihre organische Lösung* a project for a Balkan confederation, united by the bond of nationality, which would replace the Ottoman Empire and transform the Balkans into an "Eastern Switzerland." The leader of the Serbian National Party in the Voivodina, Svetozar Miletić, developed the same thesis in his work *Die Orientfrage* in 1877. But whereas Desančić was looking for support in Europe in an attempt to coordinate Balkan with European interests, Miletić emphasized the paramount significance of Balkan liberation forces as consonant with the "natural rights" of peoples struggling for liberty. The conceptions of Desančić were expressions of liberalism; those of Miletić, of radicalism.[68]

The relationship between the Balkans and the Eastern Question also preoccupied the ideologue of the Omladina and one of the leaders of the Liberal Party in Serbia, Vladimir Jovanović. Under the strong influence of Mazzini and Young Italy, his ideas were expressions of West European national romanticism and liberalism. Jovanović favored an alliance of Balkan states based on the principle of "the Balkans to the

143

Balkan peoples." In contrast to Jovanović's liberalism, his companion in the Omladina and one of the leaders of the Bulgarian liberation movement, Ljuben Karavelov, favored a federation of "free Balkan countries," patterned on the United States of America.[69]

The new ideas of socialism were manifest in the Balkans in the seventies. They developed as a consequence of the Paris Commune, of the new West European imperialism, of the internal crisis of Russian czarism, and of the discontent generated in the Balkans by internal social and political developments. This discontent gave rise to realism, positivism, and utopian socialism and assumed the form of sharp critiques of the entire social system. It was most evident among young Serbians and Bulgarians, who were influenced by the political, social, and philosophical ideas of such Russian radicals as Chernyshevsky, Dobroliubov, and Pisarev.

The Serbian Svetozar Marković and the Bulgarian Hristo Botev were representative of Balkan socialist thought. Marković, in his political, economic, social, and literary treatises, condemned all Serbian political ideas including the romanticism of the Omladina, the opportunism of the liberals, and the modus operandi of the monarchy and of the bureaucracy. For him, the basis for a new society had to be found in the democratic patriarchism of the village, in the alliance of free and autonomous communes, in the community of municipal lands, and in organized cooperative production. Marković believed that the process of national liberation of the Serbian people, and of the other Balkan peoples, had to entail revolutionary action and had to gain coherence through social and national freedom, attained within a Balkan federation based on the principle of individual liberty. The only issue facing the Serbian people was that of revolution against the two petrified empires—the Habsburg and the Ottoman—which hindered liberation. Thus Marković, starting from a revolutionary solution of Serbian and Bulgarian problems, connected the social and national issues; for him, the national revolution could be successful only if it were linked organically to the social.[70]

The principal exponent of revolutionary ideology in the Bulgarian liberation movement was Vasil Levski, whose revolutionary goal was the destruction of "despotic tyranny," the establishment of a "democratic" republic and of the community of equal Balkan peoples. However, radical socialist ideas as such were expressed most lucidly by the revolutionary writer, poet, publicist, and leader of the Bulgarian national movement, Hristo Botev.[71] Botev saw the liberation of Bulgaria as an insurrection en masse, which, as both a national and social revolution, would be directed not only against the Turks but also against the čorbadjis. It was to be a revolution which would "cleanse the Balkans not only of the Ottomans but of everything that hindered the liberty of man." The ensuing organization of the free Bulgarian state was to be based on the rural commune, had to be republican, and was to be incorporated into a framework of Southern Slav republics.

Marković and Botev were very close ideologically. This similarity may be traced to the common influence exerted upon them by Russian radicals and by utopian socialists, as well as by the common social milieu within which they developed. Radicalism and utopian socialism in the Balkan liberation movement assumed the form of deviations from European patterns, of which the most significant was that of omission of the stage of capitalism and the adoption of the principle of direct "leaping" from feudalism into socialism. The ideas of Marković and Botev were nevertheless important for the development of Balkan revolutionary movements because of their linking social and national revolutionary manifestations into an integral revolutionary whole.

Independently of revolutionary ideology, however, the territories of Bosnia and Herzegovina were in a state of constant agitation as a consequence of peasant opposition to feudal exactions in their own quest to gain possession of the land, of the demands of the bourgeoisie for political and economic freedom, and of political propaganda emanating from Serbia and Montenergo.[72] Bosnian and Herzegovinian unrest manifested itself in the seventies by an increase in the number of *hajduks;* by the sending of delegations to Vienna, Constantinople, and Saint Petersburg, which sought support against abuses committed by Ottoman authorities; and by demands for assistance in the preparation of revolutionary actions against the Porte, addressed to Serbia and Montenegro.

Already, by 1868, the Regency of Prince Milan resumed pro-Bosnian activities by supporting a "committee" consisting of the archimadrite Nićifor Dučić; the old Herzegovinian insurgent Mića Ljubibratić; and the former member of the Garašanin's Serbian Committee, the Bosnian merchant Nika Okan. This committee cooperated with, and strengthened, the secret agencies which were in existence at Kotor, Brod, Sarajevo, Bihać, Dubrovnik, Trieste, Novi Sad, Lom Palanka, and Banja Luka, and which were planning to stage a revolution in Bosnia. According to the plan devised in 1868 by Okan, the insurrection was to start in Herzegovina and then spread to Bosnia. A provisional government was to be formed in Bosnia as Serbia and Montenegro would joint the hostilities and assume responsibility for the conduct of military operations against the Turks. Further contributions to revolutionary planning were made by Captain Orešković and Father Grga Škarić, the latter being most active among the Catholic clergy in western Herzegovia.[73] Meanwhile, the Serbian government was seeking the assumption of administrative powers in Bosnia through negotiations with the Porte, while the Serbian Committee was active in spreading nationalist and cultural propaganda in Bosnia, Herzegovina, and Kosovo. In 1872 the Committee's work was in full force and the Omladina was also active in preparatory work for a revolution in Bosnia and Herzegovina. The Omladina operating independently of the Serbian government, had sought to create The Society for the Assembling of Popular Artistic Works in Sarajevo, in 1866; and, by 1871, was advocating the establishment of a "great independent state in the Balkans composed of Montenegro, Bosnia, Herzegovina, Serbia, and Bulgaria," whose birth would be marked through the insurrection which was going to break out first in Herzegovina and then in Bosnia in the Fall of 1871. The work of the Omladina was also carried out by the Serbian Society of Unification and Liberation, which was active in Novi Sad, Belgrade, and Cetinje. Lacking official Serbian support, however, the Society was unable to act effectively. This was also true of the socialists who, under the aegis of the Serbian Revolutionary Party, began preparations for the launching of a national and social revolution in territories under Ottoman control. The Party, led by Svetozar Marković, entertained relations with the Slavic Section of the First International and with Russian revolutionaries. In 1872, at Novi Sad, Marković established the Revolutionary Liberation Committee, which became part of Miletić's and Descančić's National Party. Similar committees were created in Belgrade, Kragujevac, and Cetinje. The socialists, émigrés from Turkey, and the National Party of Voivodina all participated in these activities and even tried to establish contacts with the National Party of Croatia.[74]

Insurrectionist preparations occurred also on Herzegovinian territory.[75] While Bosnia sought support from Serbia, Herzegovina had contacts with Montenegro. After the insurrection of the sixties, the Herzegovinian tribes on the Montenegrin frontier gained a degree of semiautonomy which was then sought by other tribes as well. Unrest was manifest in Nevesinje, Stoce, and Bilece, regions inhabited by Serbians raising cattle. Herzegovinian émigrés met in Belgrade in 1872 and agreed to stage an insurrection in 1873 with Montenegrin support. The conspirators were in contact with Bulgarian voevods, such as Panajot Hitov, who were preparing a Bulgarian insurrection from Serbia. Upset by the news concerning the alleged Austro-Hungarian plans for occupation of Herzegovina, the tribal chiefs decided in February 1874 to rebel. The massacre of Montenegrins by Ottoman forces over a conflict in Podgorica, in October 1874, further aggravated the tense political situation. Would-be revolutionary leaders, however, were forced to flee into Montenegrin territory by the Turks. In the summer of 1875, however, the Montenegrin ruler assured them of support. By that time, the Herzegovinian insurrection was already in full swing.[76]

The rebellion in Herzegovina broke out on July 9, 1875 near Nevesinje. The nearby tribes joined the insurgents and

148

rallied the serfs, thus spreading the revolution to Bosnia. The number of insurgents increased, as Montenegrins joined in, to 10,000 to 20,000 men. By the spring of 1876, the rebel forces in Bosnia alone numbered 15,000 and the total insurgent forces consisted of some 25,000 men. The Ottomans sent 30,000 men to crush the rebellion.

The decisive event in the insurrection was the Montenegrin decision to support the insurgents, which was taken in August 1875. Voevod Petar Vuković, the leader of the Montenegrin insurgents, operated from within Montenegro, while the Montenegrin forces in Herzegovina proper were active under the command of Voevod Peko Pavlović. At the insurgent Assembly, held on August 27, 1875 at Vranjska, a plan for military action was drawn up and a proclamation to the Herzegovinian people was issued. In the first two months of the uprising, the rebels isolated Ottoman garrisons in Herzegovina and destroyed the lines of communication between Podgorica, Nikšić, and Mostar. At the end of August, the insurgents attacked Nevesinje. They conquered the town but not the fortress. The insurgents also scored several additional victories under the leadership of national tribal chiefs and voevods such as Bogdan Zimonjić, Maksim Baćević, and Peko Pavlović. They defeated Ottoman reinforcements sent from Constantinople, cut the Nikšić-Gacko line of communication, and expanded the insurrection to the valleys of the Lim and from the Piva toward Sarajevo. During the winter of 1875-76 most of the rebels moved into southern Herzegovina, where climatic conditions were more favorable. The revolution resumed with full fury in the spring of 1876. Most of the bloody battles were fought at Nikšić, as the Turks tried to lift the siege which had been set by the insurgents. Guerilla warfare was being carried out elsewhere in Herzegovinian territory as well at the time when Serbia and Montenegro declared war on the Porte in June 1876.

Meanwhile, the revolution in Bosnia was also in full swing.[77] The Bosnian revolution was originally planned for August 18, 1875, but it started a few days earlier along the Austrian frontier as rebels occupied the territory stretching from Banja Luka to Bosanka Gradiška. In contrast to the insurrection in Herzegovina, where Catholics and Croats took part in the military operations, participation in the Bosnian uprising was limited almost entirely to Serbs. The Muslim areas of central and northeastern Bosnia remained loyal to the Porte. There were no continuous battles in Bosnia; rather, the uprising consisted of a series of diversionary actions led by Ostoja Kormanoš and Petar Petrović-Pecija, in the north, and by Golub Babić and others in the southwest. The insurgents operated from the inaccessible Bosnian mountains, which were de facto immune to Ottoman counterinsurgency actions.

Serbia exercised much influence on the development of the Bosnian insurrection, especially in the northern parts of the province.[78] The Committee to Aid the Insurgents was formed in Belgrade in August 1875 under the leadership of Metropolitan Mihailo and with financial support from the Serbian government. In fact, the Committee directed the insurrection, as it gathered, equipped, and sent volunteers, money, arms, and supplies to the rebels; took care of refugees; and disseminated propaganda. Moreover, the Serbian government sent General R. Alimpić to the Bosnian frontier to welcome refugees and organize the passage of troops. The Principal Committee of the Insurrection for the Liberation of

Bosnia, formed at Nova Gradiška by the Bosnian insurgents themselves, directed the revolt in northern Bosnia. Along the Austrian frontier, committees were set up, unbeknown to Austrian authorities, at Vučjak, Montajica, Kozara, Gremeč, and other places. The socialist ideas of Vasa Pelagić, a member of the Committee and successor to Svetozar Marković, found expression in the "Insurrectionist Proclamation of National Rights," which stated that parallel to the national and political liberation of Bosnia, it was necessary to secure also communal autonomy and distribution of the land to the peasantry. The Committee organized the Revolutionary Assembly, held at Jamnica in December 1875 under the presidency of I. Guteša, where the rebels rejected the promised Ottoman reforms, addressed a petition to the Powers, and decided on the formation of a provisional government. Military operations ceased during the winter of 1875–76 and resumed in the spring of 1876, especially in the southwest, where Babić liberated Uvac and set up headquarters there, wherefrom he pursued activities directed toward Glamoč and Livno.

The events in Bosnia and Herzegovina had a profound impact on the Balkans and on Europe. Committees supportive of the insurgents were established in London, Paris, Geneva, and in Germany and Italy. The Russian Panslavs sent aid and volunteers. Committees for the organization of aid were active in Southern Slav territories: in Croatia, Dalmatia, Dubrovnik, Boka Kotorska, and in Slovenia. Most significant, perhaps, was the fact that the conditions created by the revolts in Bosnia and Herzegovina, as well as by the prospect of military confrontation between Serbia, Montenegro and Greece, on the one hand, and the Porte, on the other, fa cilitated the spreading of revolutionary activities in the Peninsula, most notably in Bulgaria.

By the spring of 1875, Botev and Stambolov, sought to unify the activities of Bulgarian émigrés in Romania.[79] In August 1875, new leaders were chosen for the Bulgarian Revolutionary Committee, which was to be headed by Botev himself. At that time, the decision was made to stage an insurrection in Bulgaria and agitators were sent there. The preparations were hurriedly completed and the revolt broke out at the end of September in the region of Stara Zagora. Limited movements followed in the regions of Rusen and Šumen but a general uprising did not occur. The Trnovo Committee withheld participation from all action and the Ottoman authorities made a number of arrests. The peasants, disappointed, returned home. Internecine conflicts among the Bulgarian émigrés led to Botev's resignation from the Committee.

A new attempt to organize an insurrection in Bulgaria was then made by Botev's supporters. The revolution was to occur in May 1876. The members of the conspiracy crossed the Danube at Djurdjevo in January 1876 to put their plans into effect. The general conditions appeared favorable in the spring of 1876 as the Bosnian and Herzegovinian insurrections were renewed after the winter lull and the Ottomans sent their troops toward Serbia and Montenegro in the expectation of war. At a meeting of 57 representatives of the insurrectionist committees, it was decided, on April 14, to start a general uprising. The revolution broke out on April 20 at Koprivštica wherefrom it spread to Panadjuriste and the town of Klisura, and from there toward the south. but it did not reach Plovdiv and Pazardjik where large Ottoman contingents were stationed. George Benkovski, a participant in the ill-fated Stara Zagora uprising, took command of the insurrection. Other revolutionary forces were badly informed of developments, failed to receive support from Bulgarian towns, and were short of supplies. The Ottoman authorities reacted harshly, counterattacking with basibozuks, regular army troops, and the Circasian cavalry. Bitter encounters occurred between the end of April and early May near Strelča, Petrič, Panadjurište, Peruštica, and Bracigovo. The Turks burned Panadjurište as Benkovski retired to Stara Planina before being killed in battle. Despite continuing stubborn resistance by the rebels, particularly in monasteries such as St. Archangel, Drianovo, and Gabrovo, the Turks were able to crush the uprising by the end of May. A last, desperate attempt was made by Botev as he boarded with some 200 men the Austrian ship *Radetzky* at Djurdjevo on May 16. The ship was commandeered and forced to land in northern Bulgaria. The Ottoman army immediately pursued Botev's company and on June 1 Botev was killed by a stray bullet. The survivors took refuge in Serbia and Romania.

The failure of the Bulgarian uprising should be ascribed to the unfavorable conditions under which it occurred.[80] The Turks were determined to protect the integrity of the most sensitive part of the Ottoman Empire. Moreover, a significant segment of Bulgaria's population was Turco-Islamic and supportive of Ottoman rule. Finally, the *čorbadjis,* the wealthiest of the Bulgarian bourgeoisie, were unsupportive of revolutionary ventures.

The Turks dealt harshly with the Bulgarians as 80 villages were burned, 200 villages were plundered, and 30,000 people died either in battle or at the hand of Turkish authorities. Nevertheless, the insurrection proved to be decisive in the struggle for Bulgarian liberation as the echoes of the revolt brought the Eastern crisis to a head and awakened the Bulgarian people to the realities of Turkish rule. In fact, the resolution of the revolutionary crisis in the Balkans by action of the Great Powers was also precipitated by the military conflict between the Porte and Serbia and Montenegro which also broke out in 1876.

The insurrection in Bosnia and Herzegovina increased pressures for military intervention by Serbia and Montenegro. The accession of the "War Cabinet" to power in Serbia, in August 1875, reflected the bellicose atmosphere. A Serbian-Montenegrin war against the Ottomans could have transformed a local insurrection in Bosnia and Herzegovina into a major Eastern crisis. Thus, the powers comprising the Three Emperors' League sought to hinder military action by Serbia and Montenegro, although Russian officials and Panslav circles urged liberation of the Balkan Slavs. The Porte, meanwhile, stationed some 160,000 soldiers at the Serbian frontier. Thereupon, a political crisis ensued in Serbia with conservative political forces seeking avoidance of military conflict with the Porte as the year 1875 was nearing its end. However, as the insurrection in Bosnia and Herzegovina was resumed in the spring of 1876, and the April uprising occurred in Bulgaria, Serbian public opinion and the Serbian army were clamoring for war.

In June 1876, Serbian and Montenegrin forces began military operations, but a powerful Ottoman counteroffensive resulted in an invasion of Serbia by the Turks. The Serbian army was able to contain the Turks at Šumatovac, on August 23, yet the Ottoman advance could not be arrested altogether. Meanwhile, the Montenegrins fought the Ottomans to a standstill at Fundina and in the vicinity of Vučji Do. The Serbian and Montenegrin plans were hampered by the inaction of other Balkan states, which refused to participate in the conflict. However, the Herzegovinian insurgents supported the Montenegrin army, and Serbia's entry into the war helped the Bosnian insurgents to capture Sjenica, Skucani Vakuf, and Kamen-grad in July. But other Serbian-supported military operations in Bosnia were unsuccessful. Serbian plans for Bulgaria also came to naught in the wake of the failure of the April uprising.

To save Serbia and Montenegro from defeat, Russia concluded the Reichstadt agreement with Austro-Hungary in July 1876, which, for the Serbs, meant abandonment of plans for the unification of Bosnia and Serbia. Toward the end of August, on the intervention of the Powers, Serbian military operations against the Porte were suspended. The rejection by the Serbian military command of a proposed armistice prolonged the war until the fall of 1876, when Serbia was saved from total defeat only by a Russian ultimatum to the Porte. The humiliation of Serbia in the war of 1876 was inevitable, given Ottoman military superiority and the lack of support for military action from Romania, Greece, and any of the Great Powers. In March 1877, the Serbian government, largely because of its inability to maintain a large standing army for any length of time, decided, on Russia's advice, to conclude peace with the Porte on the basis of the *status quo ante bellum.*[81] The Serbs were obliged to disband all Serbian organizations which had been engaged in the preparation of revolutionary actions directed against the Ottomans. Meanwhile, while preparing for war against the Turks, the Russians agreed to Austrian occupation of Bosnia and Herzegovina in return for Vienna's neutrality in the anticipated Russo-Ottoman conflict.

The actual outbreak of the Russo-Turkish war, on April 24, 1877, brought the Eastern crisis to a boil. The Serbian government, which had to contain an attempted military rebellion by dissatisfied army officers after the humiliation of 1876, decided to join the Russians in December 1877. The Serbian offensive was aimed at Niš, and, toward the end of December, Serbian forces freed Palanka, Pirot, and Niš, as well as Gnjilane, Toplica, Kosanica, and Jablanica. Montenegro had entered the war in June 1877 and scored a victory at Krstac while directing its operations toward the littoral, Bar and Ulcinj, and Scutari in northern Albania. The Montenegrin army, supported by Herzegovinian insurgents, also captured Nikšić. In Bosnia, insurrectionist activities assumed the form of guerrila warfare in the Kozara, Prosara, and Vučjak mountains, and could not be ended by a massive Ottoman offensive launched in April 1877.[82]

The Russo-Ottoman war, however, had its greatest impact in Bulgaria.[83] The Central Bulgarian Beneficial Committee addressed an appeal for insurrection to the Bulgarian people, while Russian Panslav committees and the Bulgarian Committee set up, in Kishinev in April 1877, a "Bulgarian regiment" which was to fight with the Russians. The Russian offensive, which had been arrested by the Turkish forces on the Danube for over six months prior to the fall of Plevna in December 1877, finally gained momentum in January 1878 when Plovidiv and Adrianople were conquered. The ensuing Peace of San Stefano recognized the creation of a Greater Bulgaria but did not mark the end of the Eastern crisis, which was deferred at least until the Congress of Berlin later that year. One reason for the continuing crisis was the revolutionary unrest in Epirus, Thessaly, and Crete.

Russia's support of the Bulgarian quest for an independent church, together with Panslav assistance to the revolutionary movements of Slavic peoples in the Peninsula, ran counter to England's policy of supporting the integrity of the Ottoman Empire. These opposing positions worked to the disadvantage of Greece.[84] In fact, the fear of Panslavism was the principal. factor which determined Greece's neutrality during the Eastern crisis. The official governmental position was, however, incompatible with that of extreme Greek nationalists, who sought to exploit the Bosnian, Herzegovinian, and Bulgarian events to Greece's advantage. Thus, an insurrection committee was established in Athens under the leadership of L. Bulgaris. Delegates from Epirus, Thessaly, and Crete sought support for revolutionary plans of their own as Greek officers landed secretly in Crete, as arms were gathered in Corfu destined for Epirus, and as Greek volunteers enlisted in the Serbian army. The entry of Russia into the war against the Turks exacerbated internecine conflicts in Greece, as a Russian victory was regarded as threatening to Greek interests in Macedonia, Epirus, and Thessaly. To prevent such dire consequences, Athens advised St. Petersburg, on August 1, 1877, that Greece was prepared to organize an anti-Turkish insurrection in Greek regions ruled by the Porte. Indeed, Greek agents were making preparations in Epirus and Thessaly and by mid-August Greek military units began to cross the frontier. The Porte, however, responded by mobilizing Muslim Albanians, bashibazouks proclaiming a state of siege.

157

The fall of Plevna caused alarm in Athens. The leaders of previous Cretan insurrections landed on the island while L. Bulgaris' forces crossed into Thessaly, and the leaders of the Epirote movement were hailed to Athens. The government called up the reserves and sent General Soutzo to the frontier to help the insurgents. As the Russian forces marched on to Constantinople the insurrection in Epirus, Thessaly and southern Macedonia gained momentum.[85] A provisional government was formed in Thessaly, which proclaimed the union of Thessaly to Greece. A similar government was formed also in Epirus, and, on February 2, 1878, the Greek government ordered its troops to cross the frontier. But Greek action came too late, since, on February 1, Russia concluded an armistice with the Porte, and Greece became isolated and exposed to Ottoman military action. Athens, thereupon, ordered its armies to recross the border immediately. The insurgents addressed an appeal to Europe on February 8 as the insurrection faltered because of the withdrawal of the Greek forces. In May 1878 the revolts had formally ended.

An insurrection had also broken out in Crete in 1876, when the leadership asked the Porte for autonomy.[86] In 1877 the leaders of Crete emigrated to Athens to seek support for their revolutionary program. The uprising gained momentum in 1878 as Greek troops entered Thessaly. A provisional Cretan government, which sought complete autonomy for the island, continued the fight until the end of May when an ill-kept armistice was concluded between rebel and Ottoman forces. For all intents and purposes, however, the armistice recorded the temporary end of the revolutionary wave which engulfed the Balkans in the seventies.

The Eastern crisis of 1875-78 was caused by Balkan in-

158

surrections and was ended by the intervention of the Great European Powers. The crisis could not be solved without such intervention, because only such action by the Powers saved Serbia, Montenegro, and Greece from defeat by the Ottoman armies. The Habsburg Monarchy was committed to the repression of liberation movements in the Balkans and prevention of the formation of a greater Southern Slav state. The occupation of Bosnia and Herzegovina, however, brought the aspirations of the Southern Slavs into open conflict with those of Austro-Hungary. Russian policy was to support Balkan movements which would undermine the Ottoman Empire and threaten the Habsburg Empire. But the lending of support to insurrectionists was essentially conditioned by Russia's own interests. As Bulgaria became the pivotal point in Russia's schemes, St. Petersburg was willing to ignore the aspirations and activities of other national movements. The Greater Bulgaria set up by Russia at San Stefano satisfied the goals of the Bulgarian Society but frustrated those of the Serbians, Greeks, and above all, those of the Romanians who fought bravely alongside Russian forces in 1877–78, only to be deprived of parts of Bessarabia by their Russian allies at the end of the war.[87] England's Balkan policies were determined by factors European and Mediterranean, Ottoman and Balkan. From the European, derived the struggle of the great colonial powers for supremacy in the Mediterranean, in Africa, and on the routes to India; from the Balkan, came the conflict with Russia and the corollary support of Turkey. It is for these reasons that England was opposed to all national movements which could undermine the stability of the Ottoman Empire in a manner beneficial to Russian interests.

The Eastern crisis of 1875–78 had its epilogue at the

Congress of Berlin, which replaced Russian hegemony in the Balkans with that of an Austria-Hungary supported by Germany. An Austro-German threat to Salonika was substituted for a Russian threat to Constantinople. The Balkan peoples did not participate in the determination of their destinies. The Bulgaria of San Stefano was replaced by a smaller autonomous Bulgaria. Serbia's ambitions were reoriented toward the south, toward Kosovo and Macedonia. Montenegro doubled the size of its territory but Romania gave up southern Bessarabia in return for the Dobrudja. Independence was granted to Serbia, Montenegro, and Romania. Greece was to negotiate for three years before obtaining Thessaly and a part of Epirus in 1881. Macedonia remained under Ottoman domination.

The Balkan peoples, by 1875-78, were prepared to divide the Ottoman Empire according to the principles of nationality. However, the Balkan revolutions which occurred between 1848 and 1878 were unsuccessful, as they could not succeed without the support of the European Powers. The consequence of the policies of the Powers became apparent after 1878—the policies were to lead, in conjunction with those of the Balkan nations and nationalists, to World War I.

·6·

REVOLUTIONS AND WARS,
1878–1914

*The "Fin du Siècle"—Old Wine in New Bottles:
Macedonian Uprisings in the Eighties*

Interrelated geopolitical, economic, and social factors determined the development of the Macedonian region. The region included part of the central Balkans: the areas from Lake Ochrida in the west to the Shar Mountain in the north, and from the Rhodopian mountains in the east to the Aegean Sea in the south. Macedonia was divided into three vilayets, those of Salonika, Monastir, and Uskub. Macedonia's location made it important from a strategic point of view, especially along the Vardar valley. The Macedonian society reflected Ottoman social structures and was based on a clear division between Moslem landlords and Christian peasants. The city consisted of the Turkish garrison and the typical Balkan *carçi*, the cosmopolitan urban grouping of Greeks, Jews, Armenians, Tsintsars, and other commercial elements. The ethnic structure of the city did change, however, during the nineteenth century, as a result of resettlement and coloniza-

161

tion by Moslems and the development of a local Macedonian middle class. Moreover, the peasants began to migrate to the city and immediately adjoining neighborhoods. The ethnic origins and national feelings of the Macedonian population continue to be a source of controversy in modern Balkan historiography. Macedonia was inhabited primarily by Macedonian Slavs, Greeks, Albanians, Vlachs (Kutso-Vlachs and Aromuns), and Turks. The Greeks had a predominant influence over urban life and culture in Macedonia, as well as over the southern part of the littoral and the Aegean coast. Until the formation of the Bulgarian Exarchate in the 1870s, the Greek element and language were also predominant in the Church. The Macedonian Slavs were related by linguistic similarities, common traditions, and national identification with the neighboring Balkan and Slavic peoples, primarily the Bulgarians and also the Serbs. National identification was, however, ambiguous, as one could be a Macedonian and a Bulgarian at the same time, with the accent on either depending on the historical moment, on geographic location, on personal affinities, on family ties, and on similar considerations. National identification, however, reflected the development of Balkan nationalism and was stimulated by the actions of neighboring Balkan states and by internal changes occurring in Macedonia itself. External pressures stimulated the reaction of regional "Macedonianism." One may, in fact, speak of Macedonian nationalism only since the eighties, when Macedonia became a peripheral region of the Ottoman Empire, and the railroads, as well as other means of communication, allowed the establishment of closer economic, social, and political contacts among the peoples of the Balkan Peninsula. All this taken together created a very complex configuration of nationalities in Macedonia. Bulgarian affiliation was strongly supported by the Exarchate. Greek sentiments were based on centuries of domination by the Greek Church and Greek culture. Serbian propaganda activities, initiated during the 1860s, advanced the Serbian national cause. Macedonian nationalism emanated from the Macedonian intelligentsia and middle class; the majority of the Slav peasantry remained, nationally, an ill-defined mass affected by localism and regionalism, speaking varying dialects, and being subject to varying external influences.

The Eastern Crisis of 1875–78 was reflected in Macedonia by four uprisings connected with general unrest among the peasantry. Peasant revolts occurred in Razlog in 1876, in the regions of Kumanovo and Palanka in 1878, in Kresna in 1878–79, and in western Macedonia in 1880. The first echoed the April 1876 uprising in Bulgaria; the others, inspired by the Bulgarian and Serbian examples, expressed the disappointment of the population with the decisions of the Congress of Berlin.[1]

Dimitrije Pop-Georgijević-Berovski, the leader of the organizers of the Razlog Insurrection, devised a plan for revolution from as early as 1875, according to which the insurrection was to occur in eastern Macedonia, in the regions of Strumica, Radoviste, Štip, Kočane, Maleševo, and Melnik. In fact, the rebellion broke out on May 2, 1876 in Razlog, with an assault directed against the local authorities and the burning of fiscal and cadastral registers. Toward the end of May, Ottoman troops from Strumica, Melnik, and Gornja Džumaja cut off the rebel villages. The insurgents retreated to the

163

REVOLUTIONS AND WARS, 1878-1914

mountains of Plačkavica and continued to fight as guerrilas until a new insurrection broke out in Kresna in the fall of 1878.[2]

The Serbo-Ottoman wars of 1876–77 triggered off revolutionary activities by the population of northern Macedonia, where proximity to the Serbian frontier made it easy for the *hajduks* located in the regions of Djerman and Kozjak to engage in militant activities. The *hajduk* companies participated in the Serbian operations during the second war of 1877, fighting behind the Ottoman lines. The insurgents received 2,000 guns from the Serbian military commander at Vranje, which allowed them to expand the scope of their activities in the Kumanovo region as far as Pčinja, Ovče Polje, and the Bulgarian frontier. While the Ottoman authorities were anxious to avoid expansion of the activities of the *hajduks* after the Treaty of San Stefano, the Serbian government encouraged such activities as a means for undermining the provisions of that treaty. The Central Committee of Serbians for Non-Liberated Regions was created in Belgrade, with the task of coordinating the political activities of emigrants from Ottoman territories, and of sending petitions to the Great Powers in favor of the incorporation of those territories into Serbia. The Porte, however, decided to crush the insurrection and, in May 1879, troops were sent from Priština against the rebels. The insurgents were defeated in the battle of Čelopek and took refuge in Serbia.[3]

The insurrection of Kumanovo was related to Serbian interests, but the insurrection of Kresna, in eastern Macedonia, was an expression of Bulgarian opposition to recognition and consolidation of Ottoman power in Macedonia. The negation of the articles of San Stefano at Berlin prompted a two-pronged reaction in Sofia, directed at seeking reversal of the decisions of Berlin and at preparing an insurrection in Macedonia. Revolutionary committees were thus set up in Sofia, Ćustendil, and Gornja Džumaja, and, in August 1878, the Unity committee was formed in Trnovo and assumed the task of coordinating insurrectionist activities in Macedonia and Eastern Rumelia. As a result, the number of *hajduk* actions increased in the regions of Bitolj, Veles, and eastern Macedonia.

The first attempt of the Bulgarian committees to send military companies into Macedonia, under the joint command of the Russian officer A. I. Kalmikov and the Pole Voitkević, was unsuccessful, as the Turks repulsed the armed forces as they crossed the frontier. Meanwhile, the leaders of the Macedonian companies, who met at the Rila Monastery, decided to organize an insurrection on the left bank of the Pčinja, at the foot of the Pirin mountain. That insurrection broke out in the village of Kresna on October 5, 1878 and spread rapidly to about thirty neighboring villages, including some on the right side of the Struma river. The Turkish armies staged an offensive at the end of October and, despite fierce resistance, captured Kresna on November 11. New attempts to arouse the population to revolutionary action were unsuccessful. The insurrection was completely crushed in April 1879. About ten villages were burned and some 25,000 inhabitants were forced to emigrate to Bulgaria.[4]

The last insurrection of this period broke out in October 1880, in western Macedonia, in the region of Demir-Hisar, Kičevo, and Poreč, as a consequence of increased Ottoman-Islamic colonization from the regions lost in 1878. Four expe-

165

rienced leaders, I. Delija, R. Kostadinović, M. Krstić, and A. Tanasović, headed this so-called *Brsjačka buna*. The uprising was, however, crushed as the rebels, deprived of support from neighboring Balkan states, were unable to resist the superior Ottoman forces located in central Macedonia.[5]

Macedonia was not the only center of agitation in the early eighties for, in fact, the agitation was widespread and encompassed even the hitherto isolated regions of Albania, where the first tangible signs of a movement for national emancipation were recorded.

National Emancipation in Albania: The Early Stages

The national emancipation of Albania took place under peculiar external and internal conditions.[6] Albanian development was a function of Ottoman feudalism, of the slow penetration of capitalism, of regional and religious differences, and of specific relations with neighboring Balkan peoples in border regions. The complexity of the structure of feudal Albanian society reflected these factors; the society was more developed in the south than in the tribal and patriarchal north. The Ottoman-supported colonization by hillsmen of the fertile plains lasted many years and resulted in the formation of ethnic Albanian groups in Kosovo, Macedonia, and Epirus. Externally, Albania was affected by the community of interests of the feudal class and the ruling circles of the Ottoman Empire and, toward the end of the nineteenth century, also by the economic and political imperialism of Austria-Hungary and Italy.

The development of Albanian society gained momentum by the middle of the nineteenth century. Albanian cities were then formed. Following the inclusion of Turkey into the European body economic, and the concurrent establishment of commercial contact with Italy, a new class of merchants and of urban-oriented wealthy peasants grew in Scutari, Berat, and Elbasan. This group gave Albania its first intellectuals—teachers, functionaries, and soldiers. However, the absence of economic unity between northern and southern Albania seriously hindered the development of nationalism. The peculiar social structure was reflected in conflicting political and action programs: pro-Ottomanism, antifeudal peasant movements, and autonomy-oriented tribal struggles. Albania was wrecked by bloody insurrections since the 1830s, some aimed at protecting the integrity of the Ottoman Empire threatened by Balkan movements, and others opposing Ottoman centralism in the name of safeguarding feudal privileges and tribal customs.

The first manifestation of an organized Albanian movement for autonomy was the League of Prizren.[7] At the instigation of the Porte, Albanian chiefs, tribal *bairaktars,* merchants, and representatives of the intelligentsia assembled at Prizren at the time of the Congress of Berlin. The League addressed a memorandum to the Great Powers, on June 15, 1878, demanding "the integrity of Albanian territory" and thus posing for the first time the Albanian Question to an international forum. The League, however, lacked unified organization and it promptly split into northern and southern wings, with respective headquarters at Prizren and Djinocastro. In the first phase of its activity, the League opposed the alienation of territories in the regions of Plav and Gusinje made at the Congress of Berlin in favor of Montenegro. The League also objected to Greek claims to Janina and Arta in the Epirus. In fact, the League fought the Montenegrins from December 1879 to January 1880 to prevent acquisition of the contested territories as Abdul Frasheri led 30,000 men into southern Albania to prevent Greek moves into Epirus. In September 1880, however, the Porte was obliged to accede to the decisions of the Powers to surrender Dulcigno to Montenegro and make territorial concessions to Greece in Epirus. The League's continuing opposition to these concessions marked the start of its conflict with Constantinople and pursuit of its autonomist aspirations. The first program of the League called for Albanian assumption of such functions as recruitment and assessment of taxes. The program was expanded in October 1879 when the League sought the unification of the four vilayets—Janina, Monastir, Uskub, and Scutari—into an administrative unit under Albanian functionaires and with Albanian as the official language.

The League's heterogeneous social composition precipitated its split, in the autumn of 1880, into two branches of which one sought autonomy within the framework of the Ottoman Empire and the other merely advocated a program of reforms. Thus, in October 1880, two resolutions were addressed to the Porte—one autonomist, the other reformist. Because of Turkish inaction and corollary escalation of opposition by various groups—feudal beylicates, intellectuals, and peasants—to the centralistic policies of the Porte, a rebellion broke out in January 1881 at Prizren and rapidly spread to Pristina and the regions of Skopje and Debar. In March 1881 the Turks readied 20,000 soldiers at Skopje, and that force defeated the rebels, arrested their leaders, and occupied Kosovo and southern Albania.

In the last two decades of the nineteenth century, Albania was subject to rival influences from Austria-Hungary and Italy. Austria-Hungary sought access to the Vardar valley, a goal contrary to that of Italy, which sought control over the entire eastern littoral of the Adriatic. Albania thus became a focal point in both Austrian and Italian imperialism. Strictly Balkan influences were also operative in Albania, which helped to raise the level of antagonism between Moslem Albanians and their Christian neighbors, with resultant emigration by Albanians into the Christian Balkans, western Europe, Africa, and even the United States of America. The émigrés played an important role in Albania's national rebirth. In the last decades of the nineteenth century, they established cultural and political societies which created the Albanian alphabet, literary language, the idea of autonomy, and finally that of independence. Of all Albanian colonies, those in Italy were the most active. In fact, it was from Italy that the two principal currents of the Albanian movement emerged: one, identified with G. Shiro, which sought close collaboration between Albania and Italy; and the other, identified with A. Lorrechio, which sought outright autonomy for Albania.

In Albania proper, the Assembly of Albanian Chiefs addressed a petition to the Porte, in 1896, reiterating its prior demands for autonomy. These demands were repeated, in 1897, to the British ambassador to Constantinople by members of the National Albanian Society in Italy and, the following year, to the Sultan himself. By 1904, the aspirations of Albanian militants had escalated as the Albanian Congress, which convened in Bucharest in 1904, demanded actual independence for Albania.

Local insurrections, directed either against neighboring

Balkan countries or against the Turks, continued to occur sporadically late in the nineteenth century.[8] In 1883, the Kastriote, Hoti, Gruda, and Skerli tribes waged a local war against Montenegrins. Unrest was also manifest in the region of Prizren as a result of fiscal pressures. However, southern Albania sided with the Porte during the Turko-Greek war of 1897. The number of raids staged by Albanian companies on Serbian territory, in the regions of the Sanjak and Kosovo, increased at the turn of the century. The Mirdite rebelled in 1903 and blocked the route from Scutari to Prizren. As a protest movement directed against the Mürz-steg reform program of the Powers, Vucitrn was occupied in Kosovo in 1903, and an armed attack was launched against the Ottoman garrison at Mitrovica.

By the beginning of the twentieth century, the idea of autonomy within the imperial framework, and even that of total independence, had taken root in the more developed southern regions of Albania, particularly among the intellectuals who belonged to Albanian colonies in Europe. However, even tribal organizations in northern Albania demanded autonomy to safeguard their customary rights and patriarchal institutions. By way of contrast, the beylicate of central Albania and the feudal lords of Kosovo were determined to preserve the existing social and economic structures, based on the *Seriat* and feudal institutions.

Unrest, in the eighties, was not limited to areas subordinated to the Porte. It was manifest also in areas subordinated to Austria, as evidenced by the insurrection which occurred in Herzegovina in 1882.

The Insurrection in Herzegovina of 1882

The Congress of Berlin gave Austria-Hungary the mandate to occupy Bosnia and Herzegovina. The Austro-Hungarian occupation brought an unexpected rapprochement between Moslems and Serbians, who decided to collaborate in resisting the Austrians. The resistance was strongest among the Moslem masses, which feared for the safety of the official Islamic religion and of their Turco-Oriental culture and civilization. The resistance was organized in June 1878, with the creation of a body of national representatives, who assumed power on July 28. The new domestic government expelled the Ottoman vizier and Austrian representatives from Bosnia, whereupon the Austrian armies entered Bosnia. By the beginning of August, the presence of the Austrian armed forces brought on a military confrontation with the Moslems of central Bosnia, who were supported by the Serbian population. After a two-day battle, near Tuzla, the Austrian armed forces, headed by General Sapari, decided to withdraw. The Bosnian region along the Sava also rebelled and succeeded in driving the Austrian garrisons out of Gradačac and Šamac. Moslem companies from Krajina also advanced toward Banja Luka. Unrest was manifest in Herzegovina, too. However, the rebels were no match for the reinforced Austrian forces, which entered Sarajevo on August 19. Even though Bosnian resistance assumed the form of guerrila warfare, the Austrians ultimately prevailed, and the total occupation of Bosnia was accomplished by October 20, 1878.[9]

The events in Bosnia proved to be a prelude to those which led to the Herzegovinian uprising of 1882.[10] The Habsburgs failed to resolve the agrarian and national prob-

171

lems of Bosnia-Herzegovina. By order of the occupying authorities (October 1878), the Ottoman legislation remained in force. Agrarian servitude was retained in the villages as the new authorities increased the burden of taxation and custom duties. The natural resources of Bosnia were now exploited for the benefit of the Austrians, who established a bureaucracy alien to the people, consisting largely of functionaries and adventurers who came to Bosnia for financial reasons alone. The autonomy of religious institutions was weakened as the Orthodox Church was separated from the Patriarch, and the Moslem religious organizations from Constantinople. Secular organizations of the Catholic Church were, however, granted certain privileges. The uncertain international status of Bosnia-Herzegovina, the agrarian problem, and the policies of denationalization were the causes of renewed discontent, which soon assumed the form of an armed insurrection.

The first signs of restlessness occurred in 1879 among former Herzegovinian insurgents, who formed and mobilized units of *pandurs*. The *pandurs* of Nevesinje rebelled in August, burning the barracks of the police. On September 12 they clashed with the army, but martial law was established and the rebellion was localized. A second confrontation occurred at Mostar, the Serbian center of Herzegovina, over issues related to religious autonomy and instruction. A revolt of Boka Kotorska followed in June 1881, in response to the enforcement of the *Landwehr* law. The rebellion then spread to Krivošije, where the rebels expelled the Austrian authorities in November 1881. Martial law was proclaimed on November 4, 1881, and this action provoked the insurrection of 1882.

The insurrection broke out on January 11, 1882 and spread, at first, to the regions along the frontier with Montenegro and, later, toward southern Bosnia.[11] It reached its height by the end of January and the beginning of February. The first efforts of the Austro-Hungarian military authorities, which urgently demanded reinforcements, did not produce noticeable results in the battles on the Neretva and at Glavatičevo. The insurgents, having crossed the Drina, moved toward the Sanjak. After conquering Tjentište, they attacked Foča, only to be repulsed by the Austro-Hungarian artillery. The rebel force of 3,000 men then turned in the direction of Sarajevo. The insurrectionary forces were poorly organized; yet a number of popular leaders gained distinction during the insurrection. Moslems like Salko Forta and Ibrahim Čengić bey Kutalija; Serbians like Stojan Kovačević, Pero Tunguz, the voevode Radović; and members of the supreme command (Medžlis), who numbered seven Moslems and six Serbians, displayed courage but were unable to resist the superior Austrian forces. The Bosnian government at Sarajevo proclaimed the end of the insurection and pardoned the participants on April 22, 1882, but the rebellion lingered on in eastern Herzegovina until November 1882.

The insurrection of 1882 was handled deftly by the Austrians, who were determined to maintain control in Bosnia-Herzegovina at a time of Russian weakness. Under the circumstances, the efforts of Russian Slavophiles and of a secret revolutionary committee, created at Šabac for aiding the "liberation" of Bosnia-Herzegovina, were frustrated by official Russian inaction, and by Serbia's own unwillingness to confront the Austrians in 1882. Similar considerations also af-

173

fected events in Bulgaria, which, in the eighties, led to at least a partial achievement of the national goals which were frustrated by the decisions of the Congress of Berlin in 1878.

The Unification of Bulgaria

The political life of Bulgaria after 1878 focused on two problems: the conflict between liberals and conservatives regarding the formation of the state, and opposition to the Treaty of Berlin. The external activities were directed primarily toward the incorporation of Eastern Rumelia and, secondarily, toward the annexation of Macedonia with pro-Austrian, respectively pro-Russian sympathies in the background. Eastern Rumelia was an autonomous region under the suzerainty of the Sultan but with a Christian governor-general. Its legislative organ was the regional Assembly, composed of elected and appointed members. In the first election of deputies to the Assembly, which occurred in October 1879, the Bulgarians won 40 out of 56 seats. The Bulgarian conservatives supported the Unionists, while the liberals supported the governor-general; both sides, however, agreed on union with Bulgaria.[12]

The decision of the Congress of Berlin to separate Eastern Rumelia resulted in violent demonstrations in the towns of southern Bulgaria. Petitions were sent to the Great Powers. Paramilitary organizations were established, which enjoyed the support of the revolutionary network of the pre-1878 period. The newly created "societies of physical culture" were armed by Russian military warehouses and concentrated on the mobilization of young Bulgarians. On the initiative of political parties in Bulgaria and Eastern Rumelia, a secret Central Bulgarian Committee, whose program was the revival of the greater Bulgaria of San Stefano, was created in 1880. In May 1880 the National Central Committee was established at Sliven. The activities of the National Committee assumed major significance only by the beginning of 1885, when Z. Stoianov, a participant with Levski, Karavelov, and Botev in earlier revolutionary movements, drew up a new statute and action program. On the anniversary of Botev's death, on May 19, 1885, the Committee organized violent demonstrations in favor of union. Similar manifestations, organized by committees at Stara Zagora, Pazardžik, Sliven, Čirpan, Jambol, and Plovdiv, occurred during the summer of 1885. Toward the end of July, the newly elected Central Committee of the organization decided on unification by means of a coup which would face the Turks with a fait accompli. Agitation was rampant throughout the summer as the Committee reached an agreement with Prince Battenberg in Bulgaria and with D. Nikolaev, the commander of the military forces in Eastern Rumelia, on the staging of the coup. The coup began as an insurrection on September 17. The insurgents moved toward Plovdiv and arrested the governor-general, while a new provisional government proclaimed the union of Eastern Rumelia to Bulgaria on September 18. According to the script, Battenberg recognized the union on September 20.[13]

The unification of Bulgaria brought on new conflicts among the European Powers and led to the Serbo-Bulgarian war of 1885. King Milan and the conservatives, fearful of the possibly adverse political consequences of the ongoing collaboration between Serbian radical émigrés and Bulgarian liberals, and also of the reestablishment of the Bulgaria of San Stefano, sought to prevent the unification of Bulgaria by force. With the support of Austria-Hungary, King Milan declared war on Bulgaria—a war which was, however, to end in a humiliating defeat.[14] The Serbian reaction to unification was consonant with that of Greece, which mobilized its own forces with a view to joining Serbia. Pressure from England prevented Greek participation in the war, but it did not alleviate the opposition of Athens to Bulgarian expansionism. The strained relations between Bulgaria and her neighbors were soon to reach the breaking point over the Macedonian question.

The Liberation Movement in Macedonia

Macedonia, during the last two decades of the nineteenth century, became the focal point of conflict among the states of the Balkan Peninsula.[15] The conflicts on Macedonian territory were the result of the intermingling of internal and external factors—Balkan nationalism, Great Power imperialism, and political problems generic to Macedonia itself.

After the Congress of Berlin, Austria-Hungary became the dominant power in the Balkans through its links with Serbia, forged by the secret convention of 1881; with Romania, forged by the alliance of 1883; and through its influence in Bulgaria and Albania. Russia thought to counteract this by encouraging Serbian and Bulgarian opposition forces, including the Panslavs, and by agreeing to the maintenance of the status quo in the Balkans by its compromise agreement with Vienna of 1897. Serbia felt particularly threatened by these actions and also by the corollary Bulgarian policies aimed at unifying Bulgaria and Macedonia. Belgrade's fears were not allayed by the liberation of Thessaly and part of the

Epirus in 1881, which expanded the frontiers of Greece as far as Macedonia and enhanced Athens' determination to refocus its own foreign policies and territorial ambitions on Macedonia.

The interests of the three Balkan states, however, ran counter to those of the native Macedonian movement, which evolved during the last decade of the nineteenth century.[16] The activities of the Balkan states concentrated, at first, on the dissemination of cultural propaganda in Macedonia. The Exarchate, with the support of Ottoman authorities, was the bearer of Bulgarian culture and nationalism in the province. The Exarchate created a cultural and propaganda network, which transmitted Bulgarian linguistic, cultural, and nationalist propaganda. Greek nationalism was, in turn, transmitted by the Orthodox Patriarch and the wealthy bourgeoisie of the Macedonian cities. In 1871, the Greeks created the Propaganda Association of Hellenistic Letters in Athens, with the task of coordinating the spread of Greek influence from societies located in Constantinople, Salonika, and Seres to other Macedonian towns. The Greeks also established cultural societies in Monastir, Kruševo, Melnik Strumica, and other towns.

Without the support of an ecclesiastical organization, the propaganda and cultural activities of Serbia were limited to those which could be carried out through schools established in Kosovo and in northwestern Macedonia. In 1886 the Serbs created, on Bulgarian and Greek prototypes, the Society of St. Sava, whose purpose was to open schools in designated areas of Macedonia. Serbian activities expanded considerably after the opening of Serbian consulates in Skopje and Salonika in 1887, in Monastir, in 1888, and in Priština in 1889. From

REVOLUTIONS AND WARS, 1878-1914

1886 to 1890, Serbian propaganda supported a Macedonian movement with resultant creation of "Serbo-Macedonian ecclesiastical communes" at Monastir, Poreč, Kumanovo, Tetovo, Prilep, Kičevo, Ohrid, Gostivar, Debar, Štip, and other towns. The Slavo-Macedonian Committee of Ancient Serbia was set up in Vranje in 1887, with the purpose of preparing an insurrection in Macedonia. The Society of Serbo-Macedonians was established in Constantinople in 1886, and by 1890 Serbian propaganda was also carried out by the Fraternity of Serbo-Macedonians and of Serbs of Ancient Serbia.[17]

The internal Macedonian forces seeking political emancipation started their activities in the province in the 1870s, and shifted from cultural to revolutionary activities in the early 1880s. In 1881 the Turks discovered a secret organization at Ohrid. Similar groups soon appeared in the Monastir region, and by 1885 a revolutionary committee of 45 members was set up at Štip. Locally organized *čete* also operated on Macedonian territory. An all Macedonian revolutionary organization was contemplated by 1888, and by 1892 committees were actually created at Prilep, Monastir, and in several other towns. The Internal Macedonian Revolutionary Organization (IMRO) was finally established one year later in Salonika.[18]

The new revolutionary organization reflected specific local interests and Macedonian separatism, which demanded autonomy for Macedonia. The movement for autonomy originated among the young Macedonian intelligentsia and was primarily urban-oriented. The intelligentsia preached liberation and an equalitarian social order. The peasantry, which joined the movement in the following years, acted in re-

178

sponse to intolerable abuses committed by Ottoman authorities, rather than to nationalistic entreaties. Although the IMRO expressed Macedonian separatism and opposed Bulgarian integral nationalism, close ties existed between the Macedonian organization and Sofia. Nevertheless, as a reaction to IMRO's separatism, the Macedonian émigrés in Bulgaria established a rival organization, the so-called Supreme Committee (*Vrhovist* Committee), in Bulgaria proper in 1894. This Committee, although primarily an instrument of Bulgaria's official circles, exerted considerable influence in Macedonia proper. The two wings of the Macedonian movement were not adverse to either clashing or collaborating with one another, depending on circumstances. By 1899, the External organization, led by Boris Sarafov, actually sought to unify the efforts of both organizations by preaching common action against the Turks and avoiding references to the inclusion of liberated Macedonia into Bulgaria.

In accordance with its plans, the IMRO organized regional revolutionary committees composed of both urban and rural inhabitants. The first military units were of the *hajduk* variety but they were reorganized on a territorial basis in 1898 for greater efficiency. After 1898, clashes between Macedonian *čete* and Ottoman forces in Macedonia began in earnest and continued with ever-increasing frequency until the time of the Ilinden insurrection of 1903. At the same time, the *Vrhovists* organized their own *čete*, which were led by Bulgarian officers, and which were to carry out military diversionary actions in Macedonia. They even attempted to stage an insurrection in the region of Melnik. These activities provoked Ottoman reprisals, which precipitated the dissolution of the Supreme Committee and of the Revolutionary Fra-

179

ternity of Salonika in 1900, and the resultant joining of the IMRO by former members. Meanwhile, however, two additional Greek societies were set up on Macedonian territory, Hellenism and the Macedonian Society, which joined in 1902 to form the Macedonian Committee. Furthermore, Ion Dragoumis, the secretary of the Greek consulate in Bitolj, established the Defense Society, whose military character was to affect the future of the Macedonian Question early in the twentieth century. All these activities compounded the unrest in Macedonia and, as far as the Greeks were concerned, were also closely related to the Cretan insurrection and to the unsuccessful Greco-Turkish war of the late 1890s.[19]

The island of Crete was in turmoil in the 1880s and 1890s. In 1886 the Cretans demanded union with Greece; violent confrontations between Turks and Greeks broke out in 1889 and continued until 1890; in June 1894 the Cretans demanded fiscal reform and a Christian governor. The appointment of Alexander Karatheodori Pasha as vali of Crete, in 1895, infuriated the Ottoman inhabitants of the island and resulted in the murder of several Greeks.

The tense internal relations led to an insurrection by the Greek population, which began in May 1896 as the insurgents blockaded the garrison at Vamos, and street fighting occurred in the streets of Canea. The Cretan committees in Greece failed to secure direct Greek intervention in the conflict; however, after the burning of the Greek section of Canea by the Turks in February 1897, and the ensuing renewal of the insurrection on the island, a reluctant government in Athens decided to send warships to Crete. As Prince George, the head of a fleet of torpedo boats, sought to prevent the landing of Turkish reinforcements on the Island, Colonel Vassos was ordered to occupy Crete in the name of the King of Greece. However, the Great Powers intervened by occupying Canea, and by bombarding the insurgent positions near Acroteri, thus forcing the Greek expeditionary forces to withdraw. A blockade of the island followed as the Powers proclaimed the autonomy of Crete under Ottoman suzerainty and European protection on March 20. But the insurrection continued.

Inflamed by nationalist sentiment, Greek volunteers called for renewed action against the Turks in Crete. As Prince Constantine was designated commander-to-be, the National Society was preparing a concurrent insurrection in Macedonia. The Porte responded by declaring war on Greece. The Turkish armies entered Thessaly, occupied Larissa on April 25, and advanced toward Volos. The Greek forces, led by Colonel Smolenski, offered resistance at Meluno and Velestino but were defeated in the battle of Domoko on May 17. In Epirus, too, the Greek forces suffered defeats at the hands of the Turks. Only the intervention of the Great Powers saved Greece from total defeat, and the status quo was reestablished by the Peace of Constantinople of December 4, 1897. The Cretan question was also resolved by the Powers when, following continuous confrontations between Greek and Turkish inhabitants, the post of governor was given to Prince George of Greece late in the fall of 1898. Union with Greece, the principal aim of the Cretan nationalists, was however frustrated through this dictated solution.[20]

The suspended stage of animation, reflective of the inability of Balkan revolutionary and military forces to upset Ottoman interests by unilateral military action, was short-lived, as new crises—largely generated by, and reflective of, the interests of the Balkan nations and of the Great Powers themselves—were to destabilize the precarious status quo during the first decade of the twentieth century.

Balkan Crises and Revolutionary Activities, 1903–1908

By the beginning of the twentieth century, the Balkan Peninsula became the major theater of conflicts involving the Great Powers and the new Balkan states. The opposing interests of the Powers were further exacerbated in the decade preceding World War I by the struggle for domination of the commercial and financial markets of the Balkan states and of the Ottoman Empire, and for securing the strategic road to the Near and Middle East by the rival Triple Alliance and Triple Entente. Parallel to the aggravation of external pressures, the Balkan peoples were making rapid strides in the process of economic, social, and national development. The ensuing confrontations, internal and external, created a potentially explosive political dynamism throughout the Peninsula.

The changed relations of the Powers altered traditional policies and undermined the principle of the status quo that had prevailed as a balancing force during most of the nineteenth century. The Russo-Japanese war of 1904–5 and the Russian Revolution of 1905 altered the Austro-Russian equilibrium in the Balkans in Vienna's favor. Germany revealed her plans for penetration of the East, through the Balkans, by means of the Bagdad railway. German and French capitalists were engaged in fierce competition in Turkey. As a result of

Germany's penetration into the Ottoman Empire, the British altered their traditional pro-Turkish policies. The Anglo-French and Anglo-Russian agreements of 1904 and 1907, respectively, achieved the separation of the world into two great political blocs. Italy too began a policy of penetration into the Balkans to the chagrin of Austria-Hungary.

Within the Peninsula, Serbia became integrated into the economic system of Central Europe, thus securing a basis for economic and political emancipation from the Habsburg markets. Because of its position on the Black Sea, and its close ties to the Turkish economy of the Middle East, Bulgaria established meaningful economic relations with Turkey, England, France, Germany, Belgium, and Austria-Hungary. Greece had, at the beginning of the twentieth century, a merchant marine of 400,000 tons, which was active in trans-oceanic navigation and a major factor in commercial traffic between Europe and the eastern Mediterranean. The Balkan states were also developing industrially. Foreign capital investment grew, and the general economic progress was reflected in the increased traffic of the ports of Salonika and Piraeus, as well as in the exportation of cereals on the Danube, which increased eightfold between 1867 and 1911. The Balkan regions still under Ottoman rule were also affected by the process of economic change, and this was particularly true in Macedonian and Albanian territories. The general economic growth reinforced the Balkan nations' search for total independence in the economic and political spheres. Thus, the customs wars between Austria-Hungary and Romania, waged between 1886 and 1893; Austria-Hungary and Serbia, waged between 1906 and 1911; and Bulgaria and Turkey, which occurred in 1908, all lessened the economic

183

ties between the Balkans and Austria-Hungary and increased economic and political tensions.

Tensions were also increased because of the arms build up in the Peninsula. Bulgaria had concluded treaties for the acquisition of artillery from France and munitions from Germany in 1904. Greece obtained rifles in Austria in 1905 and sought cannons from France. In Turkey, a bitter struggle developed between France and Germany over Turkish military acquisitions. In Serbia, after the coup of 1903, the strengthening of the army became the major political issue of the day. Serbia's seeking military equipment from France resulted in violent anti-Serbian reactions in Vienna, which included the launching of the celebrated customs war, with corresponding delays in the implementation of Serbia's armament program.

Crises also occurred in railway policies. Austria-Hungary's plans to extend the Sarajevo-Uvac rail project as far as Salonika ran counter to Serbia's intended Adriatic Railroad project, which was designed to secure independent access to the Adriatic. The Valona-Monastir rail line, planned by Italy, threatened Ottoman interests in Albania, just as the Bulgarian Custendil-Kumanovo and the Greek Larissa-Monastir projects exacerbated the perennial Macedonian crises. Still, at the beginning of the twentieth century, the most inflamatory crisis involved Austria-Hungary and Serbia as it focused on the Southern Slav movement.[21]

Austria, Serbia, and the Southern Slav Movement at the Beginning of the Twentieth Century

The expansion of Serbian goals to encompass the Southern Slav program transformed the Serbian Question into a Central European Question, which affected the internal and external policies of the Habsburg Monarchy. As Austria-Hungary was opposed to the emancipation of the Southern Slavs, the checking of Serbian ambitions became of paramount importance to Vienna.

The crisis of Austro-Hungarian dualism, born of the Hungarian struggle for independence, threatened the foundations of the Monarchy. This was manifested by the Hungarian demands for a separate army, a customs regime, and a National Bank. The struggle for independence provoked a violent crisis in Hungary in 1904, which resulted in the establishment of the dictatorship of General Fejervary. In its opposition to Austria, Budapest sought support in the Balkans. It was believed that Hungarian independence could be secured if a Danubian confederation of independent Balkan states, headed by Hungary, were to be formed on the basis of common opposition to Austro-Russian hegemony. Serbia was regarded as the greatest potential beneficiary of the Hungarian struggle for independence, since the Hungarian political crisis precluded Austrian advances in the Balkans at the very moment that Russia was engaged in a war in the Far East. Hungary thus became a "natural ally" of Serbia in the struggle against Vienna.[22]

This community of interests was first expressed at the commercial level. In May, August, and October 1904, the first exchanges of visiting merchants and journalists occurred. Contacts were expanded in 1905 subsequent to the aggravation of the Austro-Hungarian crisis and Serbia's determination to accelerate the process of emancipation of Southern Slavs. They reached their highest level in 1906, during the Austro-Serbian customs war, as the Hungarians

185

supported the Serbo-Bulgarian customs union and condemned Vienna's aggressive Balkan policies. Serbo-
Hungarian relations, however, were superficial, as the two
countries had fundamentally different interests. The split between Belgrade and Budapest soon became apparent in the
political sphere as the dualism of the Monarchy assured the
supremacy of the Hungarian elite over the non-Magyar peoples subject to the crown of Saint Stephen. The advent of the
united opposition to power, in April 1906, signified the abandonment of the anti-Austrian policies of Budapest. The railway project in Croatia, initiated in 1907, and the anti-Serbian
attitude displayed by Hungary at the time of the annexation
of Bosnia-Herzegovina in 1908 made further political collaboration between Belgrade and Budapest all but impossible.

Difficulties were also evident in the economic field. Serbian agricultural exports threatened the well-being of the
Hungarian peasantry, while the industrialization of Hungary
hampered the development of Serbia's industry. The emancipation of the Serbian economy and the securing of her political independence could be achieved only through emancipation from economic and political ties with Central
Europe, which indeed negated the possibility of fruitful
Serbo-Hungarian relations. Thus, from the standpoint of Belgrade, the attainment of Serbia's political goals could not be
realized through collaboration with Budapest. The easier, and
more direct venue, remained through exploitation and encouragement of the desiderata of the Southern Slavs of the
Monarchy.

Indeed, the internal crisis of the Habsburg Monarchy facilitated the development of the Southern Slav movement in
Croatia and Dalmatia.[23] It found its expression in the policy

of the "new current" which manifested itself toward the end of the 1890s among the Southern Slav youth. It was based on the Serbo-Croat entente, on the need for social reforms and for democratization of political life. The movement became politicized at the time of the Rijeka Resolution of October 1905, by which Croatian representatives supported the Hungarian demands for independence, and by the Zadar Resolution of the same month, by which the Serbian parties of the Monarchy also endorsed the Croatian and Hungarian positions. The coalition of the Croatian and Serbian parties was an expression of common aspirations for the national emancipation of the Southern Slavs in Austria-Hungary. Moving from the limited program of Croatian "legitimate rights" to the broader one encompassing Serbo-Croatian and Southern Slav interests, the coalition paved the way to the eventual union of Southern Slav territories of the Habsburg Monarchy with Serbia in 1918. This "new current policy" was readily accepted in Serbia, and gradually it became a framework for a coordinated Southern Slav movement, which even gained the partial support of Hungary and Bulgaria.

The Serbo-Croatian rapprochement had its greatest impact in Bosnia-Herzegovina.[24] Serbia encouraged pro-Serbo-Croatian activities there by providing financial assistance for national and cultural propaganda, and by supporting demands for religious and cultural autonomy in Bosnia. In 1907 demands were voiced for complete autonomy, an independent judiciary, and the right to secret ballot in that province.

Between 1904 and 1906, several meetings, congresses, mutual visits, and agreements were recorded throughout the Southern Slav regions of the Balkans with Slovene, Croatian, Serbian, and Bulgarian participation. A group of young intellectuals and students established in Belgrade, in 1904, the society *Slovenski Jug,* which stressed the unity of the four Southern Slav peoples—Serbs, Croats, Slovenes, and Bulgarians.[25] In the summer and fall of 1904, the coronation of King Peter I and the celebration of the centenary of the 1804 insurrection took place in Belgrade. Delegates from Southern Slav regions attended the coronation. In May 1904 approximately 200 Bulgarian students visited Belgrade, while in September of the same year the First Congress of Young Southern Slavs was held in the Serbian capital. More than 100 representatives from Bulgaria, Serbia, Croatia, and Slovenia were present at the congress. The Congress of Southern Slav Authors took place in November 1905 and adopted resolutions on the necessity of maintaining mutual contacts and cultural exchanges. A second such congress took place in Sofia in August 1906. In August 1906 the Serbian Society of Teachers also organized a congress in Belgrade, which was attended by more than 800 teachers from Bosnia-Herzegovina, Macedonia, Dalmatia, the Voivodina, Slovenia, Croatia, and Montenegro. In the fall of the same year, the Congress of Serbian and Bulgarian Professors, attended by 150 Serbian professors, was held in Sofia. The Resolution of the congress stated that "the Serbian and Bulgarian instructors are so impressed by the idea that the destiny of the two neighboring peoples of the same race has been so closely related in the past and present that it is impossible to imagine the existence of these two peoples without close political and economic ties." Therefore, the professors of the two countries decided "to put the youth on the path of complete spiritual and political union of the Serbian and Bulgarian peoples."[26]

The University of Belgrade made, at the beginning of the

twentieth century, a major contribution to the success of the Southern Slav movement by transforming the *Velika Škola* into a university which was to be active in the propagation of national goals. A significant number of young Croats studied at the University of Belgrade. When the University of Sofia was closed in 1907, following demonstrations directed against Prince Ferdinand, Bulgarian students went to Belgrade where they were able to continue their studies. All in all, the Southern Slav movement gained in intensity by the beginning of the twentieth century, a fact which did not escape the attention of politicians, such as M. Milovanovič, who remarked that the "final phase was drawing near." This realization was not unique to Serbian political leaders; it was also understood by Vienna, which reacted with vigor as early as 1906.

The Serbian armament question, Belgrade's contacts with Hungarian opponents of Vienna, the political activities of the Southern Slav movement in Croatia and Serbia, the Serbo-Bulgarian entente, opposition by Austro-Hungarian landowners to renewing export concessions to Serbia were all basic to the unleashing of the Austro-Serbian customs war in 1906. The conflict was ultimately an expression of the collision between Austro-Hungarian imperialism and Serbian nationalism. It was the prelude to the annexation of Bosnia-Herzegovina in 1908. The fact that Serbia won the customs war and, in the process, strenghtened its ties with the Southern Slav movement, bode ill for the future of Austro-Serbian relations and for the maintenance of peace in the Balkans. In fact, by 1906 the Balkans were in turmoil over the Macedonian Question.

The Ilinden Uprising and the Macedonian Question, 1903-1908

The quest for national emancipation in the Balkans and the corollary crisis in the Ottoman Empire were the root cause of the insurrection of Ilinden, which occurred on Macedonian territory in 1903.[27] The decision to stage an insurrection in Macedonia was initially that of the Bulgarian *Vrhovists,* who saw in revolution the means for attracting European attention to Macedonia and its eventual annexation to Bulgaria. The *Vrhovist* scheme was opposed by some leaders of the IMRO, who preferred independent action at a time of their own choosing. Despite opposition within IMRO, the *Vrhovists* were able to secure the consent of the Macedonian organization, following the death of its leader G. Delčev, for revolutionary action in 1903. The uprising, scheduled to start on August 2, began in the region of Veles-Debar. Attempts to liberate Kičevo were unsuccessful, but the insurgents conquered Kruševo, which became the center of the revolution. Six men, headed by the socialist Nikola Karev, assumed command of the movement, and the first popular Macedonian republic was formally established at Kruševo. The insurrection then spread to other regions, notably to eastern Macedonia, where J. Sandanski was most active; as well as to the southwest, in the areas of Prespa, Ohrid, and Monastir, where conflicts with the Ottoman army were recorded. However, a general insurrection which would have entailed armed intervention by Bulgaria did not occur, because the two powers most concerned with Balkan affairs, Austria-Hungary and Russia, favored the maintenance on the status quo. Left to their own devices, the revolutionaries were unable to resist the Ottoman forces and in October the unsuccessful leaders withdrew into Bulgaria.

It is estimated that 26,000 people participated in the uprising. It is, however, noteworthy that the majority of town dwellers scorned the revolution. Turkish reprisals, as usual, were drastic. More than 9,000 houses were burned and some 30,000 people were forced to leave Macedonia altogether. Yet, although unsuccessful, the Ilinden uprising was not totally ineffectual. The brutality displayed by the Turks in crushing the insurrection brought the Macedonian issue to the fore in the Balkans, Western Europe, and even the United States. Committees for Macedonian aid were established in London, New York, Philadelphia, Boston, Paris, in Italy, and in the Balkan countries. Political reverberations were most evident in Southern Slav lands, where the press and students, in particular, vocally supported the Macedonian cause. The Serbian social-democratic party also advocated Macedonian students, in particular, vocally supported the Macedonian autonomy within the framework of a Balkan confederation.

The Macedonian events provoked intervention by the Great Powers and resulted in the Austro-Russian program of reforms adopted at Mürzsteg in October 1903. The program, reluctantly accepted by the Porte in November, was inconclusive because of international rivalries; sabotage of reform plans by military units sent into Macedonia by Greece, Bulgaria, and Serbia; failure of the Porte to implement its commitments; and the generally chaotic conditions prevailing in Macedonia prior to the Young Turk revolution of 1908, which terminated de facto the reform program altogether.

The failure of the Ilinden uprising dealt a near fatal blow

191

to the IMRO. In 1904 the organization split into right and left wings. The former, represented by *Vrhovists* and supported by Bulgaria, favored centralization of power and external intervention, while the latter advocated decentralization and continuing preparations for a general insurrection by Macedonians only. The split between the left and the right wings of the organization sharpened after 1905 as the left gained in strength. In general, the left proved more successful as it condemned external intervention in Macedonian affairs. But internecine conflicts were exacerbated after 1905 and assassination plots and other manifestations of violence gained momentum as factionalism continued to grow within the movement and within Macedonia proper.

One element of unrest was the constant infiltration into Macedonia of armed *čete* from Bulgaria, Serbia, Greece, and even Romania.[28] The Bulgarian incursions, organized by *Vrhovists* and the right wing of the IMRO, were supported by Bulgarian military circles and Prince Ferdinand himself. The Macedonian committees in Bulgaria constituted, in fact, a state within a state, whose purpose was to insure the realization of Bulgarian aspirations in Macedonia at the expense of all rival claimants. Bulgaria's activities were countered by armed intervention in Macedonia by Greece and Serbia. Greek companies started incursions into Macedonia as early as 1903 and were actively supported by Macedonian committees in Greece, and by the Greek government itself. The Greek consulate in Salonika, staffed mainly by Greek army officers, was de facto a general staff for directing the activities of Greek *čete* in Macedonia. A secret Greek organization, modeled on the IMRO, was established under the leadership of A. Souliotis, an army officer. In 1907, Ion Dragoumis published his "Blood of Martyrs and Heroes" asking for greater Greek involvement in Macedonian affairs. Long before that, however, in fact as early as 1904, the Macedonian Committee in Athens sent five companies of armed *andartes* into Macedonia and the number of armed companies increased in the following years. Direct military confrontation between Bulgarian and Greek armed men in Macedonia created crises in Greco-Bulgarian relations to the detriment of the Macedonian population. Serbia was also militarily involved in Macedonia. Increased Austro Hungarian influence in northern Albania and Kosovo, together with the expansion of Bulgarian military activities in Macedonia proper, caused Serbian intervention, particularly after 1905. The first Serbian committee seeking armed action in Macedonia was set up in 1902. The first *čete* were formed in 1904 both in Serbia and in Macedonia. As the Macedonian crisis intensified, the Serbian government began to support the activities of the rapidly growing number of Macedonian committees which were active in Serbia and, particularly, the *"Srpska odbrana"* (Serbian Defense) organization, which was operating in the regions of Skopje and Monastir. Military companies destined for action in Macedonia were equipped in Belgrade, Vranje, Leskovac, and Niš, and were commanded by military personnel of the Serbian army. The companies operated primarily in the Kosovo area and on the right bank of the Vardar. Between 1905 and 1908, direct confrontations occurred between Serbian and Bulgarian units with nefarious consequences for Serbo-Bulgarian relations. The Macedonian Committee in Belgrade was disbanded in 1907 under pressure from the Great Powers but its activities continued, in fact, until the Young Turk revolution. By contrast, the activities of Romanian *čete* in

193

Macedonia were very limited, but their actions helped cause tensions in Greco-Romanian relations. Altogether, according to Ottoman statistics, 110 Bulgarian, 80 Greek, 30 Serbian, and 8 Romanian companies were active in Macedonia in 1907. Thus, on the eve of the Young Turk revolution, and the corollary and ensuing Balkan crises, the Macedonian question, perhaps even more so than the Southern Slav question, was potentially the most explosive issue in Balkan politics. The Young Turk revolution and the Bosnian crisis merely added fuel to open the smoldering fires.

The Crises of 1908: The Young Turk Revolution, the Annexation of Bosnia-Herzegovina, and their Aftermath

The Young Turk movement sought to renovate the structure and spirit of the ailing Ottoman Empire.[29] The movement was the creation of the Turkish intelligentsia, which lived in Western Europe during the 1860s, particularly in Paris and Geneva. Representatives of subject peoples—Armenians, Macedonians, Arabs, and Albanians—were present at the congresses organized by the Young Turks in Paris in 1902 and 1905. In 1906 the Young Turks moved to European Turkey, and a number of committees were set up in Macedonia and Albania—in places such as Skopje, Ohrid, Monastir, Scutari, and Kosovo—which were in contact with Balkan revolutionary movements. The transfer of the activities of the Young Turks also altered the social base of the movement away from the economically and socially retarded Turkish bourgeoisie toward the army. The adherence of the army insured the success of the Young Turk revolution but, in the process, the Young Turk movement lost its democratic character.

The Young Turk revolution broke out at Resan at the beginning of July 1908, with the support of the entire Third Army. Upon securing Salonika, the rebels reinstated the 1876 Constitution of Midhat Pasha. As troops from Asia Minor joined the rebel garrisons of Macedonia, the Sultan capitulated; and the Young Turks proclaimed the beginning of a new era.

The population in Macedonia welcomed the proclamation of the new constitutional era, as did the left wing of the IMRO, which promptly organized itself into the National Federative Party. At its congress, held on August 13, 1908, its delegates adopted a program favoring the extension of political liberties, the freeing of the peasantry from feudal constraints, the right of all peoples to self-determination, and the formation of a free Balkan federation. Three Macedonian representatives, led by D. Vlahov, fought in the Ottoman Parliament for strict observance of Macedonian cultural and national rights. However, in 1910, as the Young Turk movement veered away from its original goals, members of the National Federative Party rallied to the young socialist movement.

The *Vrhovists,* who together with Exarchate adherents formed the Alliance of Bulgarian Constitutional Clubs in Turkey, also operated legally as of September 1908, albeit with financial support furnished by Sofia. The Bulgarian clubs, however, stressed military preparedness in anticipation of a Bulgarian-Ottoman conflict. The Greek organizations also created political clubs, such as the Greek Club of Monastir, and the National League at Melnik. At the beginning of

195

1908, the Greek army officer I. Dragoumis, established a committee in Constantinople which supported the Young Turk movement. The Serbian organizations created the Serbian Democratic League. Its Provisional Central Committee organized a Serbo-Turkish meeting in February 1909, at which time a program seeking expansion of privileges enjoyed by ecclesiastical communities, reform of the fiscal system, and amelioration of the status of the peasantry was proposed.

Constitutionalism and liberal politics, however, were short-lived in the Ottoman Empire. The Young Turk regime quickly displayed tendencies toward military dictatorship, with corollary Ottomanization, Panturanianism, and Islamization. This process, which began in 1909, found its fullest expression by 1910 when political organizations set up by nationalities under Ottoman rule were banned. Thereupon Balkan military units started to reassemble and, by 1911, Macedonia was in a state of revolutionary turmoil directed against the Young Turk regime.[30] In the meanwhile, the Bosnian crisis and its immediate aftermath exacerbated the prevailing unrest in the Peninsula.

Austro-Hungarian interests in the Balkans were to be achieved through three successive actions—the customs war, the rail project of Novi Bazar, and the annexation of Bosnia-Herzegovina. The failure of the customs war, the diplomatic conflict provoked by the proposed railroad, the Young Turk revolution, and the failure of the Mürzsteg program were the prelude to the new Balkan and European conflict, which resulted from the annexation of Bosnia-Herzegovina in 1908. The annexation, designed to preclude the achievement of the goals of the Southern Slav movement, provoked violent political resistance from Serbia, whose national aspirations were in fact frustrated by the Austro-Hungarian action. The annexation crisis revealed the vulnerability of the Balkans to Great Power imperialism and the need for unified action. If the crisis paved the way to the creation of the Balkan alliance of 1912, it also precipitated the exportation of revolutionary propaganda from Serbia into the Southern Slav territories of the Habsburg Monarchy and corollary terrorist manifestations, which paved the way for the ultimate confrontation in 1914.

In response to the annexation, the Serbs created on October 21, 1908 the Central Committee for National Defense, whose purpose was the arousing of the Serbian national consciousness, the uniting of all forces of the country, and the organizing of volunteer units for action against Austria-Hungary. The agitation subsided by March 1909, when the Serbian government was forced to recognize the validity of the annexation and to dissolve the volunteer units. The Committee for National Defense was reorganized in July 1909 to assume national and cultural functions. The Committee, largely because of its extensive propaganda work, had by this time gained significant recognition among Southern Slav groups in the Habsburg Monarchy, as well as under Ottoman rule. In fact, the Committee soon became the rallying point of actual and potential revolutionaries. Its activities became even more significant after 1911 when the secret organization Union or Death, created by army officers, conducted its own activities under the aegis of the Committee for National Defense.[31]

The Committee for National Defense deployed its activities among youth and nationalists, who were charged with propagating the Serbian and Southern Slav ideologies among

197

the masses. Toward this end, it used the physical educa-
tion Sokol and the cultural society *Prosvjeta* in Bosnia-Herzegovina, the society *Privrednik* in Zagreb, and members of
the Orthodox clergy, young merchants, and wealthier peasants whenever possible. Agents of the Committee for National Defense were used by the Serbian military information
service after 1911. The Serbian government, however, did
not fully endorse the activities of the Committee for National
Defense, as it was in conflict with the officer-conspirators
who had taken hold of the reins of the organization in 1911.
The national policy of the Serbian government was clearly
more restrained and pragmatic than that of the nationalist
circles. The government had to cope with such realities as
Croatia's tacit acceptance of the annexation as potentially ad-
vantageous to the Southern Slav cause in the Monarchy. In
fact, the Croatians demanded the annexation of Bosnia to
Croatia while the Serbian government promoted the Serb
movement in Bosnia-Herzegovina.

The Austro-Hungarian authorities pursued a definite
anti-Serbian policy, as evidenced by the trial in Zagreb
directed against 53 Serbs, and by the so-called Friedjung
Trial in Vienna, in which were involved the members of the
Croat-Serbian coalition accused of subversive activities on
behalf of Serbia. There can be no doubt that the Serbian national policy, when taken in conjunction with the general
evolution of the Southern Slav movement, menaced the integrity of the Habsburg Monarchy. However, Serbian actions
were not the only component of the anti-Habsburg activities
of Southern Slavs within the Empire. Nevertheless, they provided revolutionary-oriented Southern Slavs with ammuni-

tion for the attainment of their goals as well as those of the champions of a Greater Serbia.[32]

Revolutionary and subversive activities and propaganda were not confined to Macedonia and Southern Slavs in the first decade of the twentieth century. They were even manifest among the previously generally apolitical Albanians, whose traditional unrest assumed revolutionary characteristics as the turmoil in the Balkans was coming to a boil on the eve of the Balkan wars.

Albanian Insurrections and the Creation of Albania

At the beginning of the twentieth century, Albania was in a state of endemic anarchy. Jacqueries occurred in Kosovo and in the Sanjak, in which Montenegrins, Serbs, Greeks as well as consular agents from Austria-Hungary and Russia also participated. In 1900, the Albanians of Peć revolted; the discovery of a cache of arms among the Serbian population around Stari Kolašin (the so-called Kolaš Affair) in 1901 resulted in an Ottoman-Albanian raid directed against the Serbs; the Albanians of Kroya and Argirocastro rebelled in 1905; other insurrections broke out in 1906 and 1907 in southern Albania, in the region of Elbasan.

The activities of Albanian émigrées became more intense in those years as a result of their split into a radical and a reformist wing. A meeting of representatives of foreign Albanian societies took place in Bucharest in 1904. In that very year, three societies joined to form an organization known as *Bachkimi* (Union). The Albanian colony in the United States proclaimed in 1908, in Boston, the separation of the Albanian

199

Church from the Greek Church. Members of the Albanian national movement were in contact with the Young Turks and participated in the Young Turk Congress in Paris. Collaboration also occurred among committees in Albania proper—the committee of Debar joined the Young Turk committee and, in 1905, a committee was set up at Monastir modelled on the Young Turks. Čete organized by this committee began to operate in southern Albania in 1906, and one company was even organized in Bulgaria.

The Young Turk revolution was initially approved of by the Albanians. Autonomy was discussed at meetings held in Albanian towns. Clubs were created at Janina, Scutari, Elbasan, and other localities, whose programs were based on the principle of nationality and equal language rights. Of these clubs, three were most active, those of Monastir, Salonika, and Constantinople. The *Bachkimi* at Monastir was opposed to the reformists at Salonika and Constantinople and worked for the national emancipation of southern and central Albania. To this end, it organized a congress in November 1908, which was attended by representatives of Albanian clubs and foreign societies. The Albanian movement for autonomy and national emancipation ran into conflict with the Young Turk regime as the latter initiated its policies of Ottomanization and Islamization. At the time of the attempted counterrevolution in Constantinople, in April 1909, conservative north Albanians supported the Sultan, while the Albanian clubs of the south offered their support to the Young Turks. However, new laws on universal military service, on political societies, on the interdiction of the formation of armed companies—all adopted in 1909—undermined Albanian support for the new Turkish regime. A rebellion took place in Kosovo during the summer of 1909, which was quelled by Ottoman military intervention. Several thousand Albanians assembled at the end of August at Ferisović to protest onerous fiscal measures; they too were chased away by Turkish artillery fire.

The ensuing Turkish attempts to appease the Albanians were generally unsuccessful, as demands for Albanian autonomy were reechoed first at the Albanian Congress of Debar and, later, by the congress of representatives of southern and central Albania, held at Elbasan in September 1909. In fact, the Albanian resistance movement gained momentum with the establishment of committees such as "Liberty and Death" in Constantinople and secret clubs at Berat, Elbasan, and other places. By the spring of 1910, the movement against the Young Turk regime assumed the character of a vast armed uprising in northern Albania and at Kosovo, which forced Constantinople to use regular troops against the insurgents.[33]

The activities of the Albanian committees abroad were considerably influenced by the policies of the countries in which they were formed. The committee in Rome was connected with the Italian organization, the Albanian Council; the committee in Sofia collaborated with Bulgarian clubs in Macedonia; the Serbian government had contacts with certain Albanian chiefs; the Albanian movement in Vienna was financed and supported by the Austro-Hungarian diplomatic service. This is why, parallel to its activities related to national emancipation, the Albanian movement became an instrument in the struggle of the Powers, and of Balkan states, for acquisition of Albanian territory and access to the Adriatic. The Albanian movement served Austria-Hungary in its drive toward Salonika, and in its political moves directed against Serbia and Montenegro. Italy used it to secure its position in southern Albania and to restrain Austria-Hungary. Serbia's goal was to undermine Ottoman power in Kosovo and to arrange for its union with Serbia. Several plans were devised in Cetinje to promote the union of Albania into Montenegro. The Albanian committee at Podgorica, formed by émigrés from the uprisings of 1909–10, edited, however, the "Red Book," in which the fundamental requirements of Albanian autonomy were stated: equality of national rights in the Ottoman Empire and national, political, cultural, and religious liberty for the Albanians.

In the fall of 1910, the Albanian committees undertook the necessary preparations for a general insurrection in Albania.[34] This action was led by the committee of Ismail Kemal Bey at Bari, in collaboration with his supporters on Corfu; by the committees of Sofia and Cetinje; and by those created in Albanian proper at Kortcha, Valona, Skadar, and Kosovo. The Italo-Albanian Dr. Terrenc Tocci promoted, with Italian assistance, the goal of a free and independent Albania among the Mirdite. To counteract these provocations, the Porte granted amnesty to all insurgents, in July 1911, as Sultan Mehmed V paid a solemn visit to Kosovo. However, the Italo-Ottoman war of the fall of 1911 affected the Albanian revolutionary movement in a manner detrimental to the interests of Constantinople.

Preparations for a general insurrection in Albania were carried out during the winter of 1911–12. Disturbances occurred first in May 1912 among the Mirdite and then spread to the east, into the western part of the vilayet of Kosovo, and toward the south, to Kortcha, Debar, and Elbasan. The in-

REVOLUTIONS AND WARS, 1878-1914

surgents were assisted by Turkish officers in the Monastir region, who had organized the subversive The Savior of the Fatherland. The rebels assembled their forces in the region of Djakovica and entered into negotiations with Constantinople. The autonomist contingent of the movement demanded, in a memorandum addressed to the Sultan on July 29, the recognition of administrative and cultural autonomy for Albania within the framework of the Ottoman Empire. A similar request was sent from Valona. As the Porte failed to respond, the Albanian masses joined the uprising, which moved rapidly toward Skopje—which fell on August 12—and threatened to reach Salonika. Thereupon the Porte accepted the demands of the insurgents. Hostilities were, however, resumed in the fall of 1912 as the First Balkan War broke out. It was during this conflict that Ismail Kemal Bey, the leader of the Albanian autonomist movement, engineered the creation of independent Albania with Vienna's assistance. The proclamation of Albania's independence at Valona in November 1912 thus represented the fruition of the efforts of Albanian revolutionary leaders, even though that achievement did little to calm the explosive situations prevailing in the Balkan Peninsula at the end of 1912.[35] For, in fact, the military successes scored by the Balkan allies against the Porte ended the historic rationale for national revolution within the Ottoman Empire and, at least in the case of Serbia, it shifted its focus more and more in the direction of the "liberation" of the Southern Slavs of the Habsburg Monarchy.

It seems essential, at this stage of analysis of the Balkan revolutionary tradition, on the eve of the ultimate effort which was to lead to World War I, to try to assess the nature

203

and significance of the socialist movement in the Balkans in the protracted struggle for liberation, which occurred in the Peninsula before the mutation of the conflict outside of the former confines of the Ottoman Empire.[36]

The Socialist Movement and the Liberation Struggle in the Balkans

The development of a capitalist economy in the Balkans, its inclusion in the European economy, the beginning of industrialization, the crisis in artisan and, especially, rural agricultural production: all conditioned the formation of Balkan societies. By the end of the nineteenth century, organized workers' movements contributed new ideas for the development of the political and social life of the Balkans.

The first workers' political organization appeared in Bulgaria during the 1880s. By 1894, the Bulgarian socialist movement crystalized in the Bulgarian Social Democratic Party, which was largely the creature of Blagoev's efforts. In Serbia, following the death of Svetozar Marković in 1875, a split occurred among his followers, which delayed the formation of a workers' party until the beginning of the twentieth century. The Serbian Social Democratic Party was established in July 1903. Several organized social democratic parties were established also in Southern Slav regions—in Croatia in 1894, in Slovenia in 1896, in Dalmatia in 1902, and in Bosnia-Herzegovina in 1909. The social democratic movement also developed in Macedonia, in the Voivodina, in Montenegro, in Albania, as well as in Romania and Greece.

The socialist movement, however, was affected by internecine crises, which were most clearly evident in Bulgaria, where the revolutionary Marxists (The Narrows) and the "opportunists" (The Broads) split into separate factions in 1903. The aspirations of the workers' movement were closely related to the national liberation movements in the Balkans, as the socialists advocated self-determination and sought to connect social revolution with national emancipation [37] The international socialist movement endorsed, toward the end of the nineteenth century, the peoples' rights to self-determination, and related proletarian interests to the achievement of national goals. By the beginning of the twentieth century, however, certain current appeared in the international workers' movement which either limited or opposed the validity of that position.

Divergence within the international socialist movement were evident in the conflicting positions adopted by Austro-Hungarian and by Balkan social democrats on matters affecting the Balkan Peninsula. Thus Austrian socialists such as O. Bauer, K. Renner, and V. Adler favored cultural and national autonomy within the framework of the multinational state, which amounted to the acceptance of a federative Austria. This Austro-Marxism exerted a powerful influence on the Southern Slav Social Democratic parties in the Dual Monarchy at the time of the annexation of Bosnia, and in the ensuing years, in that it envisaged solutions to the Southern Slav question within the framework of the Monarchy. Similar points of view on cultural autonomy were discussed at the conference of Southern Slav socialists, in Ljubljana in November 1909, to the detriment of the interests of the revolutionary elements of the Southern Slav movement.[38] By contrast, the views of the Balkan social democrats were influenced by nationalism and by the Balkan revolutionary

205

tradition. They were expounded at the First Balkan Social Democratic Conference, which took place in Belgrade in January 1910, with the participation of representatives from Serbia, Bulgaria, Macedonia, Montenegro, Croatia, Bosnia-Herzegovina, Slovenia, and the Voivodina. The key speakers, the Serbian D. Tucović and the Bulgarian D. Blagoev, condemned the militaristic and nationalistic policies of the Balkan bourgeoisie which, in their view, hindered the unification of the Balkan peoples. They also condemned interference by the European Powers in Balkan affairs as detrimental to the development of the peoples of the Peninsula. To them, the Southern Slav Question, and the Balkan Question in general, were part of a unique national liberation and anticolonial movement founded on the principle of national self-determination. The Balkan social democrats, however, were not immune to nationalism. Thus, Tucović condemned the annexation of Bosnia at the Second Congress of the International in Copenhagen, while the Bulgarian "Broads" were de facto supportive of Bulgarian activities in Macedonia, and Bulgarian and Greek socialists advocated opposing nationalist positions on the Macedonian Question.

Despite the general ineffectualness of the socialists, the workers' movement did seek political rights through demonstrations and organized strikes. Both strikes and demonstrations reflected and contributed to social instability, especially in times of military conflict, population movements, and economic crises. The utilization of strikes as a means of expression of the socialists' "revolutionary struggle" in the Balkans may be historically divided into three major chronological periods: an initial stage, from the beginning of the century to World War I, corresponding to the early phases of industrial development in the Peninsula; a second stage, immediately following World War I, reflective of the antagonisms, sufferings, and devastations caused by the war; and a third stage during the Greek Depression of the 1930s.

In the initial stage, strikes and demonstrations were often organized by socialists, with the support and collaboration of the political parties of the middle class. On occasion, such demonstrations and strikes paved the way for military coups. In Serbia, for instance, massive street demonstrations by socialists, craftsmen, and students, held in March 1903, encouraged the army officers to proceed with their planned assassination of Alexander Obrenović. The same kind of demonstrations in Greece, in December 1908 and March 1909, paved the way for the military coup of August 1909.[39] Much later, in 1936, strikes and the resulting fear of communism facilitated the establishment of General Metaxas's dictatorship.[40] Several of the strikes which occurred at the beginning of the twentieth century, such as that of the tobacco workers in Bosnia in 1906; of the railwaymen in Bulgaria during the same year; of the workers at Čukarica, in the suburbs of Belgrade, in 1907; of the workers in the harbor of Salonika in 1909; or that of the workers in Brăila in 1910, had all of the characteristics of modern strikes even though they were generally easily repressed.[41]

However, the main protests and strikes in the Balkans occurred only after World War I. The most radical and militant manifestations involved railway, mining, tobacco, and textile workers. Thus, the railwaymen in Bulgaria staged two major strikes, in 1919 and 1920, which facilitated the assumption of power by Stamboliski. In 1920 also, some 30,000 Yugoslav miners and railwaymen clashed with police and military forces in Slovenia, Croatia, and Bosnia, and such disorders continued in Yugoslavia throughout that year.[42] In Romania, a general strike of railway workers and miners in the Jiu Valley, which started in 1919, soon engulfed the oil workers of the Prahova Valley, and by 1920 almost 400,000 workers were participating in mass demonstrations.[43] After a lull of nearly a decade, ascribable to economic stabilization resulting from agrarian reform and general postwar economic reconstruction, strikes reoccurred during the depression years of the early thirties. The most notable manifestations were recorded in the relatively more industrialized Romania among miners, oil workers, and railway workers, culminating in the so-called Grivița uprising of 1933.[44]

Nevertheless, these manifestations of labor unrest, reflective primarily of the workers' dissatisfaction with onerous economic conditions and living standards, were of peripheral significance in the history of Balkan revolutions. The best explanation for this lies in the industrial undervelopment of the Peninsula, and in the general lack of appeal of social revolutionary, or even mere socialist, doctrines for the largely illiterate industrial working class. To the industrial proletariat, solutions to the socioeconomic—and as such to political—issues were to be found, as a rule, within the framework of traditionally paternalistic or nationalistic forms and manifestations.

It is also noteworthy that with rare exceptions, social revolutionary actions such as demonstrations, strikes, and formation of political organizations with radical tendencies did not entail significant participation by Jewish intellectuals, labor organizers, or activists. In fact, in the Balkan Peninsula, the Jews never held a role comparable to that of their confreres in Russia or even in the Habsburg Empire.

208

The special position which the Jewish communities enjoyed within the Ottoman millet system is largely responsible for the political quiescence of the Jewish population in the core provinces of the Ottoman Empire before the late nineteenth century. The lack of political rights accounted for similar developments in the Romanian provinces. The number of Jewish activists who posed a threat to the political stability of the Ottoman Empire was historically very small indeed. The actions of the legendary Sabbatai Zevi, whose messianism and millennialism in the seventeenth century have been regarded by a few historians as a revolutionary manifestation, may have been disruptive within the Jewish millet but were rightly regarded by the Porte as the actions of a religious fanatic rather than those of a revolutionary.[45] And his repentance in the face of execution for heresy also raises doubts as to the depths of his radicalism. Among the few Jewish political activists and social reformers and revolutionaries of later years, perhaps the most important, prior to World War I, were the organizers and leaders of the so-called Workers' Socialist Federation of Salonika, which was established by a group of militant Sephardic Jews, in association with militant Bulgarian radicals, in 1909.[46] Yet, despite the organizing of a series of strikes which started in 1909, their commitment to revolutionary action was tempered by Ottoman and Greek reaction; as well as by lack of encouragement and support from the Socialist International, which frowned on any form of radicalism that could entail reprisals and liquidation of socialist organizations in the Ottoman Empire.

And what was true of Jewish socialists in Macedonia was also true of Jewish socialists in Romania, where Constantin Dobrogeanu-Gherea, the main ideologist in the Old Kingdom, kept a low profile for fear of jeopardizing the fragile social-democratic movement, in the face of threats to its very existence from conservative forces in that traditionally anti-Semitic and paternalistic society. The weakness of the socialists in Romania was particularly evident during the so-called Great Peasant Revolt of 1907, when the spontaneous outbreak of peasant violence directed against Jewish entrepreneurs and absentee landlords in Moldavia and Wallachia failed to secure the endorsement of Dobrogeanu-Gherea and his associates.[47] It is doubtful that the failure of the socialists to assume a leading role in the uprising was due primarily to ideological considerations; rather, that failure should be ascribed to the assumption by rival Christian agrarian populists of the role of ideological and spiritual leaders of a revolutionary manifestation, depicted by them as one by Christian masses oppressed by Jews and other elements alien to the Romanian peasants' rights and aspirations.

All in all then, the historic impact of the socialists on the course of political and revolutionary events in the Balkans was rather insignificant—at least in the years antedating World War I. The role of the nationalists was far more decisive as evidenced, inter alia, by the activities of the revolutionary contingent of the Southern Slav movement and of their external supporters, which precipitated the outbreak of the First World War.

The Young Southern Slav Revolutionaries and the Sarajevo Assassination

At the beginning of the second decade of the twentieth century, the Southern Slav movement entered a revolutionary phase, provoked by the accentuation of the internal national and social crisis of the Habsburg Monarchy, and by the changes which occurred in the Balkans on the eve, during, after the Balkan wars.[48]

The internal economic, political, and national crisis of the Monarchy was caused in part by its inability to compete with industrialized Western Europe—and tho corollary gradual loss of Balkan markets, and, with them, of its leverage in Balkan affairs. The Balkan wars dealt a further blow to the Austro-Hungarian economy as the result of the territorial aggrandizement of Serbia, the virtual collapse of the Ottoman economy, and the related threat to Austrian capital investments in Eastern railroads. These economic setbacks were accompanied by internal political crises. The successes recorded by the social democrats in the elections of 1911, the increased militancy of the Hungarians seeking independence, Italian irredentism, the aggressive pursuit of Romanian national aspirations in Transylvania, and the exacerbation of the Southern Slav question, all bode ill for the Monarchy's future.

The impact of the Serbian victories of 1912 and 1913 on the Southern Slavs caused alarm to Vienna. Volunteers from Bosnia-Herzegovina had joined the Serbian army in 1912. The Serbian opposition in the Bosnian Assembly condemned Austrian policies toward Serbia as pro-Southern Slav, and anti-Austrian demonstrations were taking place in Dalmatia and in Dubrovnik. The Southern Slav youth cheered the Balkan allies in Zagreb as Montenegro sought close ties with Serbia.

The internal situation of the Habsburg Monarchy and corollary developments in the Balkans clearly affected the Southern Slav movement itself, most notably in the shifting

211

from political to revolutionary action advocated by new generations of Southern Slav youths.[49] Earlier generations sought to secure religious and cultural autonomy in Bosnia-Herzegovina, and to gain political and social rights by political means within the framework of the Monarchy. Young Southern Slavs had been traditionally opposed to compromises, favoring drastic solutions to outstanding problems. This opposition, however, became militant to the extent of creating public and secret companies of students only by 1905, when the secret society *Sloboda* (Liberty) was set up in Mostar. In 1912 National Union clubs were created by students in Sarajevo, Mostar, Tuzla, Banja Luka, Trebinje, and in other localities. Austro-Hungarian authorities discovered before and after the assassination of Sarajevo a series of secret student organizations even in locations outside the territorial confines of Bosnia-Herzegovina, in Split, Nov Sad, Zagreb; as well as at the universities of Prague, Graz, and Vienna. These youths expressed their inflamatory views in publications such as the *Young Serb*, the *New Serb*, the *Whirlwind, National Union*, the *Rebirth, Liberty*, the *Progressive*, and others, published in such various places as Sarajevo, Sombor, Ljubljana, Zagreb, Split, or Sibenik. In 1913 it was decided to combat Austro-Hungarian policies through overt revolutionary propaganda among the people of Bosnia-Herzegovina. However, as they were unable to accept the premises of Austro-Marxism on national and cultural autonomy, as they lacked confidence in the revolutionary zeal of the peasantry and mistrusted the old political leaders, the revolutionary-oriented youth chose the path of individual terrorism. In June 1910 Bogdan Žerajić tried to kill the governor of Bosnia, General Varešanin, as a sign of protest against the Habsburg administration. He committed suicide but his friends vowed to continue his work. In June 1912, Luka Jukić attempted to assassinate Ban Cuvay in Croatia. During the same year, Ivan Planinšćak repeated the attempt on Cuvay. Nine months later, in July 1913, Stjepan Dojčić attempted to kill the new Croatian ban, Baron Skerlecz. Another attempt was made on Skerlecz in May 1914 by Jakov Šeter and Rudolf Hercigonja, Veljko Čubrilović, M. Mehmedbašić, and G. Princip, participants in the subsequent assassination of Franz Ferdinand, plotted the assassination of Generals Potiorek and Varešanin in 1913.[50]

The young Southern Slav revolutionaries, especially those in Bosnia, sought Serbian support for their activities. They therefore made contact, in Belgrade, with the organization Union or Death. This organization was created in 1911 by a group of army officers, former conspirators in the successful coup of 1903, who regarded the internal and foreign policies of the Serbian government as too timid, indecisive, and prone to internal divisiveness. The views of the Union, expressed in their publication *Piedmont,* which was first published in the fall of 1911, gradually gained adherents; and because of the considerable influence which the Union enjoyed in the army, its leaders, such as Colonel Dragutin Dimitrijević-Apis of the General Staff, began to play a major role in the political life of Serbia. Following a period of collaboration with the government at the time of the conclusion of the Balkan alliance in 1912, the Union pursued independent policies as of 1913 because of its opposition to governmental actions in Macedonia. On matters related to the Southern Slavs, the Union preached and encouraged national revolution for the attainment of the goal of unification of all Serbs.[51]

The visit of Crown Prince Franz Ferdinand to Sarajevo,

planned for June 28 (*Vidov-dan*), the date of the destruction of the medieval Serbian state at the battle of Kosovo, was considered as an afront to Serbia by revolutionary circles. The Bosnian revolutionaries decided to react by assassinating the Archduke. The trio of Princip, Grabež, and Čabrinović was in Serbia and, with the approval and support of the Union, entered Bosnia secretly toward the end of May. The goals of the revolutionaries and of their supporters were accomplished on June 28, when Franz Ferdinand was killed by Princip.[52]

In the accusations which preceded the declaration of war, and which were repeated later during the bitter discussions over the responsibility for the First World War, Austria-Hungary sought to connect the Serbian ruling circles to the crime. These accusations were unfounded as such, as the Serbian government had no relations with the young revolutionaries of Bosnia. Nor was Union or Death the initiator of the action of Sarajevo, although it did serve as an instrument for the execution of the plans of the revolutionaries. The relation of Serbia to the crime of Sarajevo was ultimately rooted in Serbia's commitment to the attainment of the national goals of the Southern Slavs.

The crime of Sarajevo was, in a sense, just another expression of the tumultuous history of the Balkans. Its significance was ultimately related to a stage in the development of the Southern Slav movement and the prevailing international conditions in 1914. In a sense, too, it was the ultimate expression of the goals of the national revolutionary movements of the Balkan peoples of the nineteenth and twentieth centuries.

EPILOGUE: THE BOLSHEVIK
REVOLUTION AND BALKAN
REVOLUTIONS

If we were to believe contemporary interpretations of the role played by the Bolshevik Revolution first in influencing, and then in shaping, the course of Balkan revolutionary activities since World War I we would have to conclude that the triumph of communism in the Balkans in our times was entirely a function of the fulfillment of the revolutionary aspirations of the peoples of the Balkans, under the guidance and inspiration provided by the Russian prototype. Such a contention is essentially baseless. Nevertheless, given the outcome of the Balkan peoples' "struggle for independence," the relationship between the Soviet Union and the Balkan countries assumes paramount importance in any assessment of the relationship between the Bolshevik Revolution and Balkan revolutions.

Until 1917 Balkan revolutionary activities could be characterized primarily as movements designed to secure, first, national independence and, second, the loosely defined historic goals of the Balkan nations. Most of these goals were defined by the leadership as realization of the historic aspirations of the Balkan peoples, focusing on the peoples' right to enjoy once more the benefits of independence and well-being which their historic ancestors had enjoyed in preconquest times. The connotations were essentially nationalist, generally ignoring the social and economic desiderata of the masses. The subordination of the attainment of socioeconomic goals to the realization of national independence was willy-nilly tolerated by the Balkan peoples and, in such cases where the interests of the masses differed from those of the leadership, the leadership was either able to suppress the aspirations of the masses or the masses failed to lend full support to the revolutionary movements, with resultant failure of the leaders' goals. There were very few social revolutionary actions, at odds with the liberation struggles proclaimed by the leadership, recorded in the nineteenth and early twentieth centuries. In fact, probably the only such manifestation which attained more than ordinary status in the record of Balkan revolutionary activity, was the Great Peasant Revolt of 1907 in the Romanian Kingdom.[1]

To qualify the Revolt of 1907 as a social revolution is probably in error, in that it was a spontaneous jacquerie, albeit of major proportions. It was the ultimate expression of frustration by the Romanian peasantry, which of all peasantries in the Balkans received least satisfaction from the ruling class, despite formal emancipation in 1864 and massive peasant participation in the Romanian War of Independence in 1877–78. The suppression of the uprising by the Romanian army was more important than the vague promises of reform and eventual fulfilment of the basic demands of the rebels upon attainment of the ultimate national goal—the establishment of Greater Romania. This brief discourse on the Revolt of 1907 is essential in any attempt to link social revolutionary manifestations in the Balkans with the Bolshevik Revolution of 1917, since there was indeed an intimate relationship between the Bolshevik Revolution as manifested in Bessarabia in 1917 and the de facto revolution which occurred among the Romanian peasantry, drafted into the Romanian army, shortly after the outbreak of the October Revolution in Russia. The Bessarabian example served to provoke demands for genuine emancipation and distribution of Romanian land to the peasantry, voiced by the rank and file of the Romanian peasant army, and, in turn, led to acceptance of these demands by King Ferdinand and the ensuing social transformation of Romania at the end of World War I. But did this sequence of actions and events indeed represent a meaningful link between the Bolshevik Revolution and the Balkan revolutionary tradition? Our answer would have to be negative on at least two counts. The Romanian peasants had no perception of the character of the Bolshevik Revolution or of its aims. They responded in the same manner as the Russian peasants did when promised land and peace by the cynical leaders of the Bolshevik Revolution. Moreover, the Romanian peasantry had no love for left-wing political movements, since, despite the perception of the significance of the Revolt of 1907 by the leading Romanian socialist of the time, Constantin Dobrogeanu-Gherea, the socialists had no commitment to peasant uprisings or, for that matter, to satisfying the "petit-bourgeois" desires of the Romanian peasantry.[2]

The same question could also be asked with respect to the similar revolutionary manifestations which occurred in

Bulgaria in 1918, again allegedly under the impact of the October Revolution. It is true that the Bulgarian actions were far more political than the Romanian in that the Left-Wing Socialists and the Agrarians, who were behind the revolutionary movement, had greater political experience than the Social Democrats of Romania. It is noteworthy, however, that the Bulgarian peasant units in the army were far more responsive to the entreaties of the Agrarian Union than to those of the Left-Wing Socialists, and that ultimately the temporarily successful uprising of September 1918, headed by Raiko Dascalov, resulted in the assumption of power, again albeit temporarily, by the head of the Agrarian Union Aleksandr Stamboliski.[3] It is also noteworthy that after the defeat of the revolutionaries by the loyal army, supported by German forces, in October, it was the Agrarians, and not the Left-Wing Socialists (who had formed the Bulgarian Communist Party in 1919), who secured the support of the peasantry for the peaceful political revolution which brought Stamboliski to power as head of a legally elected government in October 1919. By that time, the Communists were suspect and uncooperative and the Bulgarian masses sought solutions to political and economic problems totally opposed to those advocated by the Bulgarian Communists and practiced by Moscow.

In fact, Stamboliski's governance was characterized by peasant rule for the peasantry in a manner radically opposed to the political aims of both the right and the left. Peasant democracy was intolerable to the Bulgarian Communist Party and to its mentors in the Kremlin, as it negated the assumptions and corollary policies adopted in the Soviet Union in a manner so detrimental to the aspirations of the peasant masses. Thus, when the Bulgarian right staged the coup of June 9, 1923, which overthrew the Agrarian government, put down ruthlessly the pro-Stamboliski peasant uprisings in various parts of Bulgaria, and in the process murdered Stamboliski himself, the Bulgarian Communist Party remained neutral. The neutrality was an expression of the antipeasant policies of the Communists as much as of the Party's realization that the peasants had no interest in a Communist solution to their problems. The belated attempt to refuel the revolutionary spirit of the pro-Stamboliski masses in September 1923 through the staging of a Communist, worker-led, revolution of the restless peasantry failed miserably. The defeat of the September Uprising by the military forces of the Tsankov government was indeed facilitated by the peasant support for the Communist-directed revolution as well as by greater identification of the peasants' interests with the "reactionary" Tsankov regime than with the "revolutionary" Bulgarian Communist leadership.

The only strata of Bulgarian, and for that matter also of Romanian, society which were in any way responsive to the ideology and practices of the Bolshevik Revolution were small segments of the industrial proletariat and of the intellectuals but, by and large, even within these groups there were defections to the right, or even outright identification with the radical revolutionary right, which strongly overshadowed a class commitment to left-wing revolutionary plans or programs. And there were good reasons for this.

The original illusions entertained by ignorant and restless peasants and "democratically" oriented intellectuals regarding the goals expounded by the Bolsheviks in Russia, and by President Woodrow Wilson in his master plan for the pacification of the world, were shattered by the realities of the Bolshevik order in Russia, and of the rejection of Wilsonianism by political leaders in the United States and Western Europe. As the forces of nationalism reemerged—with corresponding revival of territorial revisionism and small power imperialism—justification for rejection of democratic reforms with corresponding alterations in the socioeconomic structures of the Balkan countries was provided by revisionism and counter-revisionism, as well as by the threat of communism; the defense and propagation of national interests threatened by Russian communism and traditional foreign enemies became the raison d'être of the rulers of the Balkans. The overthrow of Stamboliski's regime was the watershed in Bulgaria and, for that matter, it was symbolic of Balkan developments in general. Tsankov's regime, supported by and supportive of the IMRO, provided the rationale for the pursuit of "revolutionary activities" by that revolutionary organization committed to the "liberation" of Macedonia and other disputed Bulgarian territories from "national enemies." And indeed, most of the conservative classes in Bulgaria, while not entirely supportive of IMRO extremism, did endorse the goal of defending and furthering Bulgarian national interests as most suitable to the attainment of their own social, economic, and political interests.[4] And this was also true in Romania, where the emancipation of the peasantry, the granting of political rights to Jews, and the threat of Soviet, Hungarian, and Bulgarian revisionisms were parlayed into political actions and organizations designed to maintain the interests of the conservative forces to the detriment of the peasants, Jews, and national minorities. In Romania, however, the left was weak and vulnerable on account of the heavily Jewish preponderance in the Communist and Social Democratic parties. The cause of the peasant, theoretically expounded by the various peasant parties, was advanced very precariously because of the intrinsic opposition to peasant interests by the conservative ruling groups. Therefore, a populist, revolutionary right emerged slowly in the early twenties as the forerunner of the radical revolutionary populist movement later identified with the Iron Guard. The forerunners of the Iron Guard, headed by the same Corneliu Zelea Codreanu and his young associates, advocated a radical anti-Semitic, anti-Communist program, ostensibly favoring the improvement of the economic and social conditions of the peasantry and the rallying of the masses for a national Christian crusade for the preservation of the integrity of Greater Romania threatened by a Judeo-Communist conspiracy, by pro-Jewish political leaders, and by foreign revisionists. And this extreme right-wing populist movement enjoyed, from its very inception in the twenties, a significant amount of support from disgruntled intellectuals, students, bureaucrats, and even the younger members of the peasantry. Thus, the IMRO and the Legion of Archangel Michael were, in their own ways, revolutionary organizations with a certain *prise* in their respective countries. And their bases of support were stronger than those of the revolutionary left.[5]

Rightist revolutionary actions and programs were not unique to Bulgaria and Romania. They were evident in Greece, when, at the height of the frustration over the defeat suffered at the hands of the Turks, the Revolutionary Committee headed by Colonel Nicholas Plastiras seized power late in 1922 ostensibly to defend the national interests and ambitions of the Greeks.[6] And again in 1926 and 1935, military revolts directed against democratic constitutionalism, and communism, and revisionism were recorded. It is true that the military movements were not necessarily representative of the interests of the majority of the Greek population, but they were not repudiated by that population either, as they were carried out in the name of supporting and reinforcing the ever-present Greek nationalism and its revendications.

Albania, too, was not free of nationalist-determined revolutionary activities after World War I.[7] The revolt organized by the Committee of National Defense in the district of Vlora in 1920 against Italian occupiers of several Albanian districts may not have been either rightist or leftist, considering the low level of political consciousness of the Albanians. But it was clearly an expression of Albanian nationalism. And even the far more political revolution of June 1924, directed against Ahmet Zog and his ruling "Zogist clique" by a motley coalition headed by Fan Noli, with the cooperation of regional military commanders and with the support of illiterate Albanian masses, was not devoid of nationalist overtones. Zog was indeed characterized by Fan Noli and his left-wing supporters as an oppressor of the rights and liberties of the Albanian people, and, in truth, Noli looked upon the uprising as a social revolution against rule by a dominant clique of landlords and conservative military forces. The other participants, however, were persuaded to join the movement on the basis of Zog's being a traitor to the interests of the Albanian people because of his ties with Yugoslavia, Greece, and Italy—all mortal foreign enemies of Albania. The actual defeat of the revolution by forces loyal to Zog was facilitated by the strains and stresses within the revolutionary camp when Noli's leftist tendencies clashed with the simpler social and economic demands of the peasantry and the distinctly anti-Soviet positions adopted by the conservative allies in the revolutionary coalition. In a sense, then, Noli's revolutionary program, moderate though it may have been, was as unacceptable to the majority of his followers as was his gradual abandonment of nationalist positions in favor of a distinctly pro-Soviet orientation.

It would be fallacious to argue that social unrest was not prevalent among various social groups, of which some favored communist-style solutions. There were strikes and other violent manifestations by workers, most notably in Romania. The so-called Grivița Uprising by Romania's railway workers in 1933 was indicative of the social and economic crisis of the working class, but it did not per se represent unequivocal acceptance of Soviet solutions. Rather, in Romania and, for that matter, also in Yugoslavia in the thirties, resolution of social and political conflicts were more readily sought within the framework of right-wing formulas. The Romanian Iron Guard flourished in the thirties and enjoyed much support from the working class and working peasantry. Similarly, Croat separatists enjoyed wide support from the population of Croatia in their attempts to assert the values of Croatian nationalism and to protect the interests of the Croatian population in the face of Serbian domination. And even in Greece, where the Communist Party had significant following among many an intellectual and the disgruntled proletariat, and in Bulgaria, where Dimitrov's heroics and adverse economic conditions evoked favorable responses from certain segments of the working class, Communist solutions—even when couched in nationalist formulas—were rejected by the overwhelming majority of the population. The

223

changing tactics of the left-wing revolutionaries in favor of united fronts and democratic action programs in defense of the national interests of the peoples of the Balkans were ineffectual until, indeed, the territorial integrity and national interests of the majority of the Balkan nations were placed in mortal jeopardy by the actions of the Axis powers. And those actions ultimately accounted for the success of revolutionary movements led by Communists in Greece, Albania, and Yugoslavia, and for the imposing of Communist revolutionary solutions to the problems of Romania and Bulgaria during World War II.

The crux of the matter in appraising the ties between Communist revolution and the Balkan revolutionary tradition lies in the appraisal of the nature of the anti-Fascist "wars of liberation" which occurred during the Second World War, and which paved the way to the establishment of Communist regimes in all of the Balkan countries except Greece. The claims and counter-claims are well-known but are worth summarizing. Official doctrine, as expounded by Balkan historians today, is simply that the armed opposition movements to German, Italian, and native "fascist" forces were in fact spontaneous social-revolutionary manifestations, triggered off by dissatisfied masses and by Communists, the latter as rightful representatives of the masses' interests. The wars of liberation were also national movements, reflecting the peoples' determination to rid their countries of fascist oppressors and their desire to assure the territorial integrity and national independence of sought-after Communist national states.

These claims are specious, as there is no evidence to substantiate the validity of the ultimate equation of national independence and Communist rule. It is true, at least in the case of Yugoslavia and Greece, and to a lesser extent also Albania, that the resistance movements to German and/or Italian occupation were spontaneous mass movements by patriotic and abused peasants, workers, intellectuals, and other social groups.[8] It is also true that the Communists soon assumed a primary role in the leading of the resistance movements and were successful in that role to the extent to which they expounded programs and goals originally compatible with the interests of the masses. The accent, in the decisive phases of the wars of liberation, was indeed on patriotic motivation and on eventual social reform rather than on Communist revolution. Only as leaders of patriotic movements could the Communist leaders of Tito's partisans, or of ELAS in Greece, hope to retain the support of their non-Communist followers. In fact, however, the essential goal of the Communists, from as soon as the defeat of the Axis could be anticipated, was to destroy all political forces which could oppose the transformation of the war of liberation into a war for the establishment of Communist rule in Yugoslavia, Greece, and Albania. Thus, the primary targets of the Communist leaders became the Četniks in Yugoslavia, EDDES and EKKA in Greece, and all potential internal opponents of the Balli Kombëtar in Albania—all grouped together with other "domestic reactionaries," such as the Ustasha, traditional political parties, or other ostensible supporters of the Italian or German forces still active in the Peninsula. And not far behind in the list of priorities was the consolidation of the bases of future political power of Communist leaders at the expense of the majority of their followers, whose postwar aspirations were, for the Communists, incompatible with their own. It mattered little whether in this process Soviet tutelage and advice

225

was to be sought, accepted, or received; what did matter was that the pattern of the wars of liberation in Yugoslavia, Albania, and Greece was tactically identical with that devised and used by the Bolsheviks first in 1917 and as needed thereafter.

The ultimate resolution of these overt and covert movements and conflicts was made not by the revolutionaries but by the allies themselves. In Greece, where the Kremlin was unable to press its advantage in the face of British and American opposition, the communists were unable to "liberate" the country in the manner which they had contemplated. In Yugoslavia the withdrawal of support from Mihailović's Četniks by the British and Americans paved the way for Tito's ultimate success. And as Albania, Romania, and Bulgaria were considered by the Western allies to be outside the sphere of their interests, these countries were "liberated" in a Communist manner. Liberation came to Albania mostly because of Yugoslav and Russian support of the "liberation" movement; and to Romania and Bulgaria, where resistance and "liberation" movements were indeed of minimal importance, by direct action by Stalin's armies and political representatives.[9] By 1945, imposed Communist revolutions became irreversible in the Balkans outside of Greece and, in theory, the bases for the ultimate achievement of the alleged eternal revolutionary goal of the peoples of the Balkans—national independence in a Communist state—had been laid in granite. And consolidation has continued ever since.

CONCLUSION

The Balkan revolutionary tradition in modern times was stamped by two factors: one external, the other domestic. Throughout history the Balkans played the role of a transit area exposed to confrontations between world empires and their civilizations, between domestic medieval states—and, in modern times, between European powers. The national renaissance of Balkan peoples, begun in the eighteenth century, was stamped by historical memories and the patriarchal structure of the Balkan peasant society. The modernization process in the Balkans implied both a confrontation and a symbiosis between European modernism and Balkan traditionalism. It was marked by the idea not to reform but to destroy the old. Thus it had to be abrupt and revolutionary.

Two aspects dominated the Balkan revolutionary tradition: the agrarian and the national. The agrarian resulted through the struggle of the peasantry to gain ownership of the land and to force agrarian reform. The national aspect required a more developed society and was imported from Europe, from the Balkan diaspora along the Danube, in the

227

Mediterranean and Black Sea areas. Nationalism represented the creed of the newly born middle class, the urban population and the intelligentsia. Both the agrarian and the national factors reflected the level of Balkan social development. With local specifics, they corresponded to similar trends of societies at the same level of development elsewhere in the world, in past and present times. All these movements directed against the existing social and political order are essentially revolutionary. They are revolutionary also because they have to reflect opposing trends in the modernization process, similar to the struggle of the human body in accepting a transplanted organ.

Patterns of development of the Balkan revolutionary tradition are rather easy to establish. The tradition originated in the confrontation between the Moslem and Ottoman landlord and the Christian peasant-serf. After an initial period of *Pax Ottomanica,* which succeeded the domestic feudal anarchy of the fourteenth century, the Ottoman Empire, starting in the late sixteenth century, entered a period of crisis which corroded its entire economic and political system. Lost wars, famines, and epidemics could but contribute to the desperation of the population. Opposed to this, contact and traffic with the rest of the world, periods of peace during which local prosperity boomed periodically, led to the formation of domestic national leadership and whetted the appetite of those desirous of improving the status quo. The volcaniclike revolutionary outbursts of the seventeenth and eighteenth centuries reflected the initial dynamism of young national societies in the process of formation. And the outbursts of the eighteenth century flooded the Balkans in the nineteenth century.

CONCLUSION

The national factor in the Balkan revolutionary tradition, which was to dominate and overwhelm the agrarian, was a product of social and political developments. Nationalism in the Balkans, as well as in the rest of Europe, was a product of the middle class, of the city, and of the new intelligentsia. It reflected varying trends within the evolving Balkan national society. First, it flowed from the periphery to the center of the Peninsula, from parts exposed to foreign influences to the ones hidden in the depths of the Ottoman Empire. Second, the emancipation process was applied gradually, step by step, radiating from the national center toward the national periphery. Such gradual application could but stimulate the nationalist appetite of young Balkan societies, turning it into a kind of *sui generis* Balkan imperialism during the second half of the nineteenth century. Again we can discover in this process similarities with the modern world of today in Southeast Asia and in Africa.

The Balkan revolutionary tradition evolved through three great periods in Balkan history: Ottoman rule, formation of Balkan national states, and inclusion of the Balkans into modern Europe. During the first period, which lasted until the beginning of the nineteenth century, the Balkan revolutionary tradition expressed peasant-agrarian trends, stimulated by European intervention and wars against the Ottomans. The violent reprisals which usually followed the wars augmented peasant desperation and resulted in explosions against local and/or state authorities. In this period the national leadership consisted of outlaws, of the Orthodox priesthood, and of Balkan merchants whose vision transcended that of the Balkan village.

The second period, which began in the nineteenth cen-

229

tury, was more complex. The Balkan movements expressed agrarian as well as clearly defined national trends. In due course, the latter gradually supplanted the former and dominated the political scene. Still, the agrarian factor was constantly present in revolutionary upheavals in the Balkans if for no other reason than that the peasantry comprised the overwhelming majority of the population of the Peninsula. It is thus difficult to separate peasant-agrarian from national goals in any meaningful characterization of Balkan revolutionary movements. The leadership of these movements originated outside the village and was recruited from among outlaws, such as *hajduks* and klephts, or from the ranks of urban dwellers, or from those of the intelligentsia, chiefly teachers and priests. The leaders reacted differently in specific situations: in some, they espoused the demands of the peasantry; while in others, they went beyond the aims of the peasants in stressing national rather than agrarian goals. The differentiating factors between national and agrarian components of Balkan revolutions were related to the scope and organization of the movements. When parochial, ill-coordinated, and directed against local authorities, they stayed within an agrarian framework. When they confronted state authorities and stressed ideas of a political nature, tending toward the establishment of a national state, the movements became national. They reflected nationalism, which required the existence of a more sophisticated society able to introduce and apply European patterns. Nationalism had to overcome peasant isolationism and particularism. It required an understanding of the historic legacy, of the linguistic and ethnic community, and, last but not least, a knowledge of geography. Conditioned by the village and the confrontation be-

230

tween the Moslem landlord and the Balkan peasant, early Balkan nationalism focused on the Holy War against the Infidel. This idea was present in European wars against the Ottomans, as well as throughout the Balkan national revolutions in the nineteenth century, up to the Balkan War of 1912. In its initial stage, this religious nationalism, combined with a common peasant interest in land ownership, offered a broader basis for collaboration among Balkan revolutionary movements of the first half of the nineteenth century. Nationalism based on the struggle between the Cross and the Crescent was, however, gradually superseded by historical nationalism, based on, and nourished by, historical memories and experiences. Historicism was to encourage, to stimulate, to offer perspectives. It had to justify and legalize Balkan peasant revolutions to the Europe of Metternich and of the Holy Alliance. It had to introduce the Balkan shepherd to the European aristocratic historic nations. The appearance of the Balkan state and its establishment introduced a new factor in Balkan nationalism: the state itself. It was represented through the interests of dynasties, bureaucracies, armies. It had to distinguish between the European and the Balkan balance of power and adopt the art of modern diplomacy. In ambiguous situations of ethnically mixed areas and ill-defined frontiers, the interest of the state had to replace the principle of ethnicity in establishing "strategic boundaries." This resulted in a specific kind of Balkan imperialism, a mimicry of its European counterpart.

In fighting for national emancipation, various tactics were applied. The initial religious war had to be replaced by the total, national war. The peasant revolution was not sufficient; it had to be seconded by the intervention of a regular

231

army. In other words, the peasant revolution had to be supplemented by a classical war. This tactic was applied as early as 1814 in the formulation of the plans of the Greek Society of Friends and culminated in the period of the First Balkan Alliance in the later 1860s. When attempts to organize a general Balkan peasant uprising failed, and when Italy and Germany set the example of national unification through war, the idea of a Balkan revolution was forgotten and replaced by that of action by a regular army, trained in barracks and equipped with modern weapons. The Balkan revolutionary tradition thus became only a tool, a legitimizing instrument for armed intervention and modern war. In 1912, the Balkan allies did not expect an uprising in the central Balkans, behind the Ottoman lines. A return to the strategy of revolution appeared only in the resistance movements of the Second World War, after the total collapse of national armies made other forms of action well-nigh impossible.

The Balkan revolutionary tradition was utilized as a legitimizing force not only for the attainment of national emancipation and of foreign policy goals, but also for the pursuit of domestic policies. The national factor was so strong that it dominated Balkan politics in the past and continues to do so in the present. The right, the center, and the left all exploited nationalism and fostered national issues. They differed in methods as well as in substance but, basically, followed the same national endeavors. Conservatives preached the establishment of a strong state as a prerequisite for a successful foreign policy: domestic unity for the sake of national unification. The liberals related freedom at home to freedom abroad. Socialists preached the fusion of both revolutions, the national and the social, into one. The social democrats were not

CONCLUSION

imune to nationalistic influences; in fact, Balkan social democracy, based on the revolutionary tradition, never understood nor had sympathy for Austro-Marxist theories of cultural and individual national autonomy.

Throughout the nineteenth century, chiefly because of domestic weaknesses, the Balkan revolutionary tradition was torn between the use of radical methods and political compromise. The primary trend was to exploit European rivalries in the Balkans, and to play upon the prestige and the sensitivity of individual European powers. The Greeks went so far as to have three political parties named for individual European powers. Compromise with the Ottoman Empire for the partial fulfilment of national programs was another formula which proved attractive to Balkan leaders. Finally, a third formula for success advocated the *fara da se* struggle, based on domestic forces or on common action with other peoples of the Peninsula. All these tactics were forged in the Balkan revolutionary tradition and survived until nowadays.

All Balkan revolutionary organizations of the nineteenth century which promoted the struggle for national emancipation were essentially nationalistic and thus limited in scope and program. Their leadership was recruited from the middle class and the intelligentsia. Calls to action were generally issued by individual "apostles"; they usually sought a general Balkan uprising which, in fact, never occurred. One shortcoming was the lack of any socioeconomic program which would attract the peasant. Moreover, the leaders also mistrusted the fighting ability of the masses. Nineteenth century Balkan organizations existed more on paper, and in the schemes elaborated by their promoters, than in reality. The Social Democrats and the Communists of later years were

233

the first to understand the revolutionary potential of the landless peasantry. In the absence of a developed proletariat of the Marxist type, they turned toward the poor and landless peasant in an attempt to transform the Balkan national revolutionary tradition into a social revolutionary one through exploitation of the peasantry's dissatisfaction with the existing order.

World War I opened a new chapter in the history of the Balkans. Balkan armies participated in war for more than ten years, from the Balkan campaign of 1912 until the end of the Greek-Turkish confrontation in Asia Minor in 1923. As the result of the establishment of new national frontiers, some 2,000,000 people were moved from their homes and resettled during that decade with resultant social dislocation and conflict and economic instability. Minorities incorporated within the newly established national frontiers by the victors introduced problems inherited from the defunct Ottoman and Habsburg empires into the new bodies politic. In addition, a clash of civilizations resulted from the joining of the Habsburg Yugoslavs with those from Serbia and Montenegro. And this was true also in the case of Romanians from Transylvania, the Bukovina, Bessarabia, and the Dobrudja, not to mention the Hungarians and other minorities incorporated into the Greater Romanian state. Similarly, the Greeks moved from Asia Minor to the Greek mainland had a difficult time in making the necessary socioeconomic adjustments in their new surroundings. The nationalistic idea, which equated number and space with strength and might, proved to be erroneous and corroded from the very beginning the cohesiveness of the new successor states in the Balkans. The war left a tragic heritage, particularly among the peasant masses

234

of the vanquished, who had sacrificed their lives for defeat and humiliation. Their dissatisfaction, as well as that of their leaders, contributed to the growing social and national discontent which became so manifest in the years following World War I The Béla Kun affair in Hungary, the activities of the Internal Macedonian Revolutionary Organization in Bulgaria, and the acceptance by certain groups in Yugoslavia of the propaganda line emanating from the Moscow Comintern all reflected the instability and the potentially explosive atmosphere prevalent in the postwar Balkans.

Agrarian reforms, carried out in all Balkan countries after the war, eased the tensions. Despite imperfections, the reforms were welcomed at least in Bulgaria, Romania, and Yugoslavia, and thus facilitated the restoration of political and socioeconomic stability under the leadership of moderate peasant parties. But the peasant parties failed to play a decisive role in Balkan politics in spite of the numerical preponderance of the Balkan peasantry. Their failure should be ascribed in part to problems related to the subordination of the village to the city and social stratification within the village itself, but also to the continuing domination of the political scene by forces committed to nationalism. And the problems of the Balkans were exacerbated by the economic depression of the 1930s.

The depression delivered a severe blow to the developing agricultural countries and aggravated their social problems. Without having time to catch their breath, the Balkan countries witnessed the polarization caused by the growth of Nazi Germany. Rightist Balkan governments favored, on the eve of World War II, a return to paternalistic monarchic dictatorships characteristic of the nineteenth century. The royal dictatorships of the thirties also reflected the reality of the Nazi economic imperialism in Southeast Europe, fear of communism, and the failure of the Western democracies to offer meaningful alternatives. Yet, despite the seriousness of the prevailing political and social problems, the Balkan Communist parties were unable to make headway in a political order characterized by nationalism and factionalism among "bourgeois" political organizations. The Balkan revolutionary tradition made its reappearance only as war, invasion, and destruction of the state establishments in Yugoslavia, Greece, and Albania rendered other forms of resistance impossible. It should be noted, however, that in Romania and Bulgaria, where the armies were in control, and where nationalist aspirations were satisfied, revolutionary manifestations were all but absent. In the other three Balkan countries, revolutionary actions still reflected political and social polarizations of prewar and wartime years, exacerbated, however, by the cruelty displayed by foreign forces of occupation and/or by Communist propaganda and indoctrination. Nevertheless, the revolutionary manifestations represented the first chapter of the Cold War which followed the victory of the anti-Fascist coalition. The civil war in the Balkans, which took place under foreign occupation, did not alter Balkan revolutionary traditions to any significant extent. The politically naïve peasantry supplied the manpower and "national liberation" was cynically used for pseudo-nationalistic goals and as an instrument for social revolution.

NOTES

1. PAX OTTOMANICA AND HOLY WAR: THE REVOLT OF MICHAEL THE BRAVE

1. A brief exposition of the problem, with ample bibliographical references, will be found in Dimitrije Djordjević, *Révolutions nationales des peuples balkaniques, 1804–1914* (Belgrade: 1965), pp. 11–16.

2. *Ibid.* See also L. S. Stavrianos, "Antecedents to the Balkan Revolutions of the Nineteenth Century," *Journal of Modern History* (1957), 29:335–48; and Stephen Fischer-Galati, "Revolutionary Activity in the Balkans from Lepanto to Kuchuk Kainardji," *Südost Forschungen* (1963), 21:194–213.

3. See in particular Ezel Kural Shaw, "The Ottoman Aspects of *Pax Ottomanica:* The Political, Practical and Psychological Aspects of *Pax Ottomanica*," in Béla K. Király, ed., *Tolerance and Movements of Religious Dissent in Eastern Europe* (Boulder, Colo., and New York: Columbia University Press, 1975), pp. 165–82; and Stephen Fischer-Galati, "Judeo-Christian Aspects of *Pax Ottomanica*," *ibid*, pp. 185–97.

4. The basic and essential documents for the study of Michael the Brave and his activities are contained in the massive Hurmuzaki Collection and specifically in Eudoxiu de Hurmuzaki, *Documente privitore la Istoria Românilor,* (Bucharest: 1880), 3(1); (Bucharest: 1888), 3(2); (Bucharest: 1892), 4(1); (Bucharest: 1900), vol. 11;

I. PAX OTTOMANICA AND HOLY WAR

(Bucharest: 1903), vol. 12. Supplementary documentary sources may be found in Andrei Veress, *Documente privitoare la Istoria Ardealului, Moldovei şi Ţării Româneşti,* (Bucharest: 1931–34), vols. 3–7; and P. P. Panaitescu, *Documente privitoare la Istoria lui Mihai Viteazul* (Bucharest: 1936).

5. Austrian policy is best explained by Alfons Huber, *Geschichte Österreichs* (Gotha: 1892), vol. 4. See also the major study by Bistra Cvetkova, *Pametna bitka na narodite* (Varna: 1969) and the important work by Alexander Randa, *Pro republica christiana. Die Wallachei im "langen" Türkenkrieg der katolischen Universalmächte (1593–1606)* (Munich: 1964).

6. The basic studies on the antecedents to and of the war itself are, in addition to Randa, *Pro republica christiana,* P. P. Panaitescu, *Mihai Viteazul,* and the lengthy article, endowed with a splendid list of references to primary and secondary sources, by Ion Ionaşcu, "Mihai Viteazul şi unitatea politică a Tărilor Române," in D. Berciu, ed., *Unitate şi continuitate in istoria poporului român* (Bucharest: 1968), pp. 143–85.

7. In addition to references given above consult also I. Corfus, *Mihai Viteazul şi polonii* (Bucharest: 1937) and Manfred Stoy, "Die Bedeutung der Moldau und Wallachei in den österreichischen Türkenkriegen des 16. und beginnenden 17. Jahrhunderts," *Bericht über den zehnten österreichischen Historikertag in Graz* (Vienna: 1970), pp. 209–19.

8. See in particular Ion Ionaşcu, "Mihai Viteazul şi autorii tratatului de la Alba Iulia (1595)," *Analele Institutului de Istorie Cluj* (1962), 5:120–24.

9. An excellent statement will be found in Panaitescu, *Mihai Viteazul,* pp. 43ff.

10. Hurmuzaki, *Documente privitoare,* passim, and Panaitescu, *Mihai Viteazul.*

11. A comprehensive study of these questions is contained in N. Iorga, "Sfătuitorul bizantin al lui Mihai Viteazul: Mitropolitul Dionisie Rali Paleologue," *Revista Istorică,* (1919), 5:26–35. See also Alois Hajek, *Bulgarien unter der Türkenherrschaft* (Berlin: 1928), pp. 28ff. and Mercia MacDermott, *A History of Bulgaria, 1393–1885* (New York: Praeger, 1962), pp. 40–41.

238

12. In addition to references under note 11 above, consult Bistra Cvetkova, "Haydutstvoto v balgarskite zemi prez XV–XVIII v.," *Istoricheski Pregled* (1968), 4:40ff. and Al. Ciorănescu, *Documente privitoare la istoria românilor culese din arhivele din Simancas* (Bucharest: 1940), pp. 110–11.

13. Panaitescu, *Mihai Viteazul*, pp. 44ff. contains valuable data on these and other schemes.

14. Best discussion in Panaitescu, *Mihai Viteazul*, pp. 219ff.

15. In addition to pertinent references given above consult also the important study by N. Iorga, "Moldavie et Pologne au commencement du XVII⁰ siècle," *Revue Historique du Sud-Est Européen* (1930), 7:139–49.

2. REVOLUTIONARY MOVEMENTS IN THE SEVENTEENTH CENTURY: NATIVE ROOTS AND FOREIGN INCITEMENT

1. A comprehensive discussion of the problems of the Ottoman Empire in the seventeenth century will be found in Peter F. Sugar, *Southeastern Europe under Ottoman Rule, 1354–1804* (Seattle: University of Washington Press, 1977), pp. 209ff., with ample bibliographical references. See also Traian Stoianovich, "Land Tenure and Related Sectors of the Balkan Economy 1600–1800," *Journal of Economic History* (1953), 13:398–411. On Romanian conditions see, in general, A. Oțetea et al., eds., *Istoria Rominiei* (Bucharest: 1964), 3:13ff.

2. For a comprehensive overview, consult V. Motogna, "Epoca lui Matei Basarab și Vasile Lupu," *Cercetări Istorice, Iași* (1940), 13–16:453–544.

3. Ion Sârbu, *Matei vodă Basarabas auswärtige Beziehungen 1632–1654* (Leipzig: 1899) remains the best work on the subject.

4. See especially Lidia Demeny-Maskova, "Despre participarea românilor în oastea căzăceasca a lui Bogdan Hmelnițki," *Studii* (1963), 16:1381–95.

5. The basic work on the revolt is Lidia A. Demeny, L. Demeny, and L. Stoicescu, *Răscoala șeimenilor sau răscoală populară? 1655* (Bucharest: 1968). See also N. Iorga, "Răscoala Șeimenilor în

239

potriva lui Mateiu Basarab," *Analele Academiei Române: Memoriile Şectiunii Istorice*, Series 2 (1910–11), 33:129–46.

6. N. C. Băjenaru, "Domnia lui Constantin vodă Şerban de la stabilirea supremaţiei lui Rakoczy asupra Ţării Românesti pînă la mazilirea lui," *Arhiva, Iaşi* (1925), 32: 196–221; Al. Ciorănescu, *Domnia lui Mihnea III (Mihnea Radu, 1658–1659)* (Bucharest: 1936).

7. P. P. Panaitescu, "Pribegia lui Constantin Şerban Basarab şi a lui Stefan Petriceicu şi testamentele lor," *Memoriile Secţiunii Istorice. Analele Academiei Române*, Series 3 (1939), 21:373–432; Andrei Veress, Pribegia lui Gligoraşcu vodă prin Ungaria şi aiurea (1664–1672)," *Memoriile Secţiunii Istorice. Analele Academiei Române*, Series 3 (1924), 2:269–336; Eugen Pavlescu, *George II Rakoczy Principe de Transilvania (1648–1660)* (Iaşi: 1924).

8. See notes 6 and 7 above with special reference to Pavlescu, *George II*.

9. William Miller, "Greece under the Turks, 1571–1684," *English Historical Review* (1904, 19:646–68; Bistra A. Cvetkova, "La situation internationale et le peuple bulgare à la fin du XVIe et le début du XVIIe siècle," *East European Quarterly* (1972), 6:321–36; N. Iorga, "La France dans le Sud-Est de l'Europe. III. La croisade à la fin du XVIe siécle. Voyageurs, mercenaires et aventuriers au commencement du XVIIe siècle," *Revue historique du Sud-Est européen* (1936), 13:105–46.

10. Miller, "Greece under the Turks"; G. F. Herzberg, *Geschichte Griechenlands* (Gotha: 1876–79), 3:42ff.

11. Cvetkova, *La situation internationale*, pp. 321–36; M. P. Ionov, "Po v'prosa za politikata na Austriia k'm Turciia i polĭticheskite dvizeniia v B'gariia na XVI do nachaloto na XVIII v," *Istoricheski Pregled* (1956), 12:34ff., F. Mareš, "Aufstandsversuche der christlichen Völker in der Türkei in den Jahren 1625–1646," *Mitteilungen des Instituts für österreichische Geschichtsforschung* (1882), 3:249ff., B. Rupčić, *Enstehung der Franziskanerpfarreien in Bosnien und der Herzegowina und ihre Entwicklung bis zum Jahre 1878* (Breslau: 1937), pp. 91ff.

12. In addition to references given in note 11, above see also J.

2. THE SEVENTEENTH CENTURY

Pejacsevich, "Peter Freiherr von Parchevich, Erzbischof von Martianopel," *Archiv für österreichische Geschichte* (1880), 59:343ff.

13. See especially Mareš, *Aufstandversuche*, pp. 248–52.

14. G. Stanojević, "Odnosi Venecije za Hercegovačkim, Brdskim i Crnogorskim plemenima od opsade Kotora 1657 do početka Morejskoga rata," *Istoriski Časopis* (1959), 9:205ff.; G. Stanojević, "Crna Gora u doba Kandiskog rata (1645–1669)," *Istoriski Glasnik* (1953), pp. 25–28; F. Tajani, *Le Istoria Albanesi* (Salerno, 1886), pp. 18ff.; Miller, "Greece under the Turks," pp. 652ff.; Herzberg, *Geschichte*, 3:58ff.

15. See note 3, above and Pejacsevich, *Peter Freiherr von Parchevich*, 342ff.

16. See note 1 above, and also, Stephen Fischer-Galati, "The Peasantry as a Revolutionary Force in the Balkans," *Journal of Central European Affairs* (1963), 23:12ff.

17. G. Rosen, *Die Balkan Haiduken* (Leipzig: 1878); D. J. Popović, *O Hajducima* (Belgrade: 1930–31), 1:105ff.; J. W. Baggally, *The Klephtic Ballads in Relation to Greek History 1715–1821* (Oxford: Oxford University Press, 1937), pp. 2ff.

18. Otto Brunner, "Oesterreich und die Walachei während des Türkenkrieges von 1683–1699," *Mitteilungen des österreichisches Institut für Geschichtsforschung* (1930), 44:265–323; I. Radonic, "Situaţiunea internationalǎ a Principatului Ţǎrii Româneşti în vremea lui Ştefan Cantacuzino (1678–1688)," *Analele Academiei Române. Memoriile Secţiunii Istorice*, Series 2 (1913–14), 36:949–971; Virgil Zaborovschi, *Politica externǎ ale celor trei Principate, Ţara Româneascǎ, Transilvania şi Moldova de la asediul Vienei (1683) pînǎ la moartea lui Şerban Cantacuzino şi suirea pe tron a lui Constantin Brâncoveanu (1688)* (Bucharest: 1925); N. Iorga, *Viaţa şi domnia lui Constantin Vodǎ Brâncoveanu* (Bucharest: 1913); Ştefan Ionescu and Panait I. Panait, *Constantin vodǎ Brîncoveanu. Viaţa. Domnia. Epoca* (Bucharest: 1969); C. Şerban, *Constantin Brâncoveanu* (Bucharest: 1969); I. Mihnea, *Despre Dimitrie Cantemir. Omul—Scriitorul—Domnitorul.* (Iaşi: 1926); P. P. Panaitescu, *Dimitrie Cantemir. Viaţa şi opera.* (Bucharest: 1958).

241

2. THE SEVENTEENTH CENTURY

19. See note 18, above and Oțetea et al., *Istoria Rominiei*, 3:128ff.

20. G. D. Ionescu, "Tratatul încheiat de Gheorghe Ștefan cu Rușii în 1656," *Revista Istorică Română* (1933), 3:235ff.; P. Constantinescu-Iași, *Relațiile culturale romîno-ruse din trecut* (Bucharest: 1954), pp. 124ff.

21. I. C. Dostian, *Borba serbskovo naroda protiv turetskovo iga* (Moscow: 1958), pp. 79ff.; L. Hadrovics, *Le peuple serbe et son eglise sous la domination turque* (Paris: 1947), pp. 136ff.; J. N. Tomić, "Patrijarh Arsenje III Crnojević prema mlečicima i cesaru 1685–1695," *Glas Srpske Kraljevske Akademije* (1906), 70:119ff.; V. Klaic, *Geschichte Bosniens* (Leipzig: 1885), pp. 445ff.; H. Gerba, "Die Kaiserlichen in Albanien 1689," *Mitteilungen des K.K. Kriegsarchivs*, Neue Folge (1888), 2:117ff.

22. Gerba, *Die Kaiserlichen*, pp. 119ff.; I. Tomitch, *Les Albanais en Vieille-Serbie et dans le Sandjak de Novi-Bazar* (Paris: 1913), pp. 9ff.

23. See note 21, above and also C. Gianelli, "Lettere del Patriarca di Pec Arsenio III e del Vescovo Savatije all'Arcivescovo di Antivari Andrea Zmajevic," *Orientalia Christiana Periodica* (1955), 21:68ff.; R. M. Grujić, "Tri pisma cesara Leopolda I carigradskim patrijarsima," *Srpska Kraljevska Akademia. Spomenik*, series 2 (1913), 43:13ff.

24. Hadrovics, *Le peuple serbe*, pp. 136ff.; Tomic, *Patrijarah Arsenije III*, pp. 65ff.

25. J. Radonić, *Grof Djordje Branković* (Belgrade: 1911), pp. 5ff.; A. Ivic, "Aussiedlungen der Bulgaren in Ungarn," *Archiv für slawische Philologie* (1910), 31:414ff.; Ionov, *Po v'prosa*, pp. 45ff.; N. I. Milev, *Katolichkata Propaganda v Bulgaria prez XVII vek* (Sofia: 1914), pp. 18ff.; E. Fermendzin, ed., *Acta Bulgariae Ecclesiastica ab A. 1565 usque A. 1799* (Zagreb: 1887), pp. 304ff.

26. See note 25, above and Pejacsevich, *Peter Freiherr von Parchevich*, pp. 343ff.

27. W. Miller, "The Venetian Revival in Greece, 1864–1718," *English Historical Review* (1920), 35:343ff; A. A. Bernardy, *Venezia e il Turco* (Firenze: 1902), pp. 84ff.

3. REVOLUTIONARY MOVEMENTS IN THE EIGHTEENTH CENTURY

1. Interesting new data on these points is contained in Bulgarska Akademia na Naukite, *Istoriia na Bulgaria* (Sofia: 1954), 1:269ff.; I. C. Dostian, *Borba serbskovo naroda protiv turetskovo iga* (Moscow: 1958), pp. 89ff.; P. P. Panaitescu, *Dimitrie Cantemir* (Bucharest: 1958), particularly pp. 259–265; B. H. Sumner, *Peter the Great and the Ottoman Empire* (Oxford: Oxford University Press, 1949), pp. 5ff.

2. Consult in particular Sumner, *Peter the Great*.

3. In addition to Panaitescu's careful review of Russo-Romanian relations in this period contained in *Dimitrie Cantemir*, pp. 8ff. consult also L. E. Semeonova, "Din istoria relaţiilor romîno-ruse de la sfîrşitul secolului XVII-începutul secolului XVIII," *Analele Romîno-Sovietice: Seria Istorie* (1959), 2:109 33.

4. The most detailed account of these events will be found in Spiridon Gopcevic, *Geschichte von Montenegro und Albanien* (Gotha: 1914), pp. 170ff.

5. The problems of Romanian history in this period have been carefully reexamined in recent years. For a summary statement of the status and latest findings of Romanian historiography consult *Studii* (1962), 15(6); *Bibliografia Istorică a României* (Bucharest: 1970), 1:134–38; and the excellent notes contained in Şerban Papacostea, *Oltenia sub stăpînirea austriacă* (Bucharest: 1971), an essential monographic study.

6. D. P. Bogdan, "Legăturile serdarului Lupu Anastasă cu Ruşii (1721–1751)," Academia Republicii Populare Române. Institutul de Istorie. *Studii şi Materiale de Istorie Medie* (1957), 2:345–89.

7. Characteristic of the numerous studies on Romanian activities in this period are those by Bogdan, "Lupu Anastasă" and by C. Şerban, "Relaţiile politice romîno-ruse în timpul războiului ruso-turc din 1735–1739," *Analele Romîno-Sovietice: Seria Istorie* (1956), no. 4, pp. 113–33.

8. The classic statement on these problems is by J. Langer, "Nord-Albaniens und der Herzegowina unterwerfungs-Anerbiete an

3. THE EIGHTEENTH CENTURY

Oesterreich (1737–1739)," *Archiv fur österreichische Geschichte* (1881), 62:239–304. Little new information of a supplementary nature has been provided by Yugoslav historical literature, although corrigenda and addenda are recorded in historiographic surveys such as J. Tadić's valuable *Ten Years of Yugoslav Historiography, 1945–1955* (Belgrade: 1955).

9. The best account of Albanian developments is Gopcevic, *Geschichte*, pp. 216ff. and I. Tomitch, *Les Albanais de la Vieille-Serbie et dans le Sandjak de Novi-Bazar* (Paris: 1913), pp. 43ff. Little information is available on Greek developments in this period other than the convenient summary by William Miller, *The Turkish Restoration in Greece, 1718–1797* (London: Macmillan, 1921) and the introductory statement to J. W. Baggally, *The Klephtic Ballads in Relation to Greek History, 1715–1821* (Oxford: Oxford University Press, 1937).

10. Good summary statements are contained in Bulgarska Akademia, *Istoriia*, pp. 311ff.; Dostian, *Borba*, pp. 105ff.

11. See in particular M. Matei, "Lupta ţăranilor impotriva exploatării în timpul războaielor ruso-turce din a doua jumătate a secolului XVIII-lea," *Studii şi referate privind istoria Romîniei* (1954), 1:927–43.

12. On these points consult the excellent article by M. B. Petrovich, "Catherine II and a False Peter III in Montenegro," *American Slavic and East European Review* (1955), 14:169–94.

13. The most detailed account of Greek developments is contained in G. F. Hertzberg, *Geschichte Griechenlands* (Gotha: 1876–79), 3:22ff.

14. Interesting new information in M. D. Matei, "Despre poziţia claselor sociale din Moldova şi Tara Romînească faţa de războiul ruso-turc din 1768–1774," *Studii* (1953), 6(3):53–77, and A. Víanu, "Consideraţii asupra caracterului administraţiei ruse în tările romîne (1769–1774)," Academia Republicii Populare Romîne. Institutul de Istorie. *Studii şi materiale de istorie medie.* (1956), 1:233–44. See also Matei, *Lupta*, pp. 927ff.

15. General conclusions may be found in Stephen Fischer-Galati, "Revolutionary Activity in the Balkans from Lepanto to Kuchuk-Kainardji," *Südost-Forschungen* (1962), 21:194–213, and

4. THE EARLY NINETEENTH CENTURY

L. S. Stavrianos, "Antecedents to the Balkan Revolutions of the Nineteenth Century," *Journal of Modern History* (1957), 29:335–48.
16. On these problems, consult the excellent study by Stanford J. Shaw, *Between Old and New: The Ottoman Empire under Sultan Selim III, 1789–1807* (Cambridge, Mass.: Harvard University Press, 1971).
17. Consult the several articles on the Enlightenment in the Balkans contained in *East European Quarterly*, (1975), 9:386–507, and Vlad Georgescu, *Political Ideas and the Enlightenment in the Romanian Principalities 1750–1831* (Boulder, Colo., and New York: Columbia University Press, 1971), pp. 7ff.

4. THE REVOLUTIONS OF THE EARLY NINETEENTH CENTURY

1. On the Serbian revolution, see in particular A. Ivić, *Spisi bečkih arhiva o Prvom srpskom ustanku*, 10 vols. 1804–1812 (Subotica-Belgrade: 1935–39, 1973); Istorijski arhiv Beograd, *Gradja iz zemunskih arhiva za istoriju Prvog srpskog ustanka*, vol. 1, 1804–8; vol. 2, 1809 (Belgrade: 1961); M. Gavrilović, *Ispisi iz pariskih arhiva* (Belgrade: 1904); G. Jakšić and V. Vučković, *Francuski dokumenti o Prvom i Drugom ustanku (1804–1830)* (Belgrade: 1957); D. Janković, *Francuska štampa o Prvom srpskom ustanku* (Belgrade: 1959); H. Šabanović, *Turski izvori o srpskoj revoluciji*, vol. 1, 1789–1804 Sarajevo: 1956)—all containing important documentary sources. Among secondary sources consult Vuk Karadžić, *Prvi i drugi srpski ustanak* (Belgrade: 1947); M. Vukičević, *Karadjordje*, 2 vols. (Belgrade: 1907–12); Stojan Novaković, *Vaskrs države srpske; političko-istorijska studija o Prvom srpskom ustanku, 1804–1813* (Belgrade: 1904); L. Ranke, *Die serbische Revolution* (Hamburg: 1829); G. Yakchitch, *L'Europe et la resurrection de la Serbie (1804–1834)* (Paris: 1907); L. Arsenijević-Batalaka, *Istorija srpskog ustanka* (Belgrade: 1899). For other annotated bibliographic references consult Michael B. Petrovich, *Yugoslavia: A Bibliographic Guide* (Washington, D.C.: 1974), pp. 31–33.
2. See above and also Stojan Novaković, *Ustanak na dahije 1804* (Belgrade: 1904).

245

4. THE EARLY NINETEENTH CENTURY

3. See especially Traian Stoianovich, "Russian Domination in the Balkans," in Taras Hunczak, ed., *Russian Imperialism from Ivan the Great to the Revolution* (New Brunswick: Rutgers University Press, 1974), pp. 198–238.

4. For a more detailed account see Dimitrije Djordjević, *Révolutions nationales des peuples balkaniques 1804–1914* (Belgrade: 1965), pp. 26–28.

5. M. Gavrilović, *Miloš Obrenović*, 3 vols. (Belgrade: 1908–12); G. Jakšić, *Akermanska konvencija zaključena izmedu Rusije i Turske 25. septembra 1826* (Belgrade: 1911); B. Kunibert, *Sprski ustanak i prva vladavina Miloša Obrenovića 1804–1850* (Belgrade: 1901); V. Čubrilović, *Istorija političke misli u Srbiji XIX veka* (Belgrade: 1958); VI. Stojančević, *Miloš Obrenović i njegovo doba* (Belgrade: 1966); as well as references under note 1 above.

6. K. Petrović, "Jedna epizoda iz odnosa Karlovačkih gradjana prema prvom srpskom ustanku u Austriji," *Rad vojvodjanskih muzeja* (1961), 10:163–64; "Prvi srpski ustanak i Srem," *Zbornik Matice srpske* (1954), vol. 7; M. Ristić, "Stefan Živkovic-Nišlija, prvi vojni liferant i zajmodavac obnovljene Srbije Karadjordjevog doba," *Istorijski glasnik* (1953), 1–2:89–96.

7. S. Gavrilović, "Agrarni pokreti u Sremu, Slavoniji i Moslavini početkom XIX veka," *Historijski zbornik* (1957), 1–4, 71–82, and "Epilog seljačke bune u Sremu 1807," *Zadružni arhiv* (1955), 3:131–40; "Teodor Avramović-Tican," *Rad vojvodjanskih muzeja* (1954), 3:107–18.

8. S. Gavrilović, "Dokumenti Karlovačkog arhiva o Krušičkoj buni 1808, godine," *Zbornik Društvenih nauka Matice srpske* (1956), 12:76–86.

9. Gavrilović, *Agrarni pokreti*, pp. 71–82; F. Šišić, *Karadjordje. Život i delo. (Karadjordje, Južni Sloveni i Napoleonova Ilirija)* (Belgrade: 1956), pp. 55–56.

10. M. Djordjević, "Bosna i Hercegovina u strategijskim planovima srpskih ustanika," *Pregled* (1954), Sarajevo, 1:1–97.

11. V. Čubrilović, *Prvi srpski ustanak i bosanski Srbi* (Belgrade: 1939), pp. 115–30; J. Tošković, *Odnosi izmedu Bosne i Srbije 1805–1806 i boj na Mišaru* (Subotica: 1927).

12. P. Šobajić, "Udeo dinarskih plemena u Prvom srpskom us-

4. THE EARLY NINETEENTH CENTURY

tanku," *Glasnik Etnografskog instituta Srpske akademije nauka*
(1957), 2–3:81–96; V. Stojančević, "Stanovništvo Srbije za vreme
Prvog ustanka," *Istorijski glasnik* (1955), 3–4:41–58; J. Jovanović,
"Crnogorsko-srpski odnosi za vrijeme prvog srpskog ustanka," *Istorijski zapisi* (1953), 2:321–26; L. Arsenijević-Batalaka, *Istorija*,
2:560–61, 774–75.

13. B. Kallay, *Geschichte des serbischen Aufstandes*,
1807–1810 (Vienna: 1910), p. 132.

14. Djordjević, *Révolutions nationales*, pp. 32–33.

15. V. Stojančević, "Prvi srpski ustanak prema Bugarskoj i
Bugarima," *Istorijski glasnik* (1954), 1–2:121–45; V. Čubrilović, "U
čemu je suština i kakva je istorijska uloga Prvog srpskog ustanka
1804," *Jugoslovenski istorijski časopsis* (1963), p. 3.

16. G. P. Henderson, *The Revival of Greek Thought 1620–1830*
(Edinburgh and London: Edinburgh University Press, 1971); Stephen Chaconas, *Adamantios Korais: A Study in Greek Nationalism*
(New York: Columbia University Press, 1942); Richard Clogg, *The
Movement for Greek Independence 1770–1821: A Collection of Documents* (New York: Harper, 1976); N. Botzaris, *Visions balkaniques
dans la préparation de la révolution grecque (1789–1821)* (Paris:
1962).

17. M. Lascaris, "Le rôle des Grecs dans l'insurrection Serbe
sous Karageorges," *Les Balkans* (1933), passim.

18. *Ibid.*, pp. 12–21.

19. S. I. Gârleanu, *Haiducul Nicolae Grozea* (Bucharest:
1968); S. Iancovici, "Materiale privitoare la haiducia lui Tunsu şi
Grozea," *Studii şi materiale de istorie modernă* (1960), 2:105–54; I.
I. Neacşu, "Haiducia în Ţara Românească între anii 1822–1828,"
Studii şi articole de istorie (1968), 11:221–31.

20. On the revolt of Tudor Vladimirescu, see A. Oţetea, *Tudor
Vladimirescu şi mişcarea eteristă în Ţările Românesti* (Bucharest:
1945); Marcel Romanescu, "Contribuţii la cunoaşterea lui Tudor
Vladimirescu," *Balcania* (1947), 5(1):3–32; *Documente privind istoria României. Răscoala din 1821* (Bucharest: 1959–62), vols. 1–5;
Dan Berindei and Traian Mutaşcu, *Aspecte militare ale răscoalei
populare din 1821* (Bucharest: 1962).

21. Novaković, *Vasrks države srpske*, pp. 186–88; P. Popović,

Francusko-srpski odnosi za vreme Prvog srpskog ustanka (Belgrade: 1933), p. 36; E. Driault, *La Question d'Orient* (Paris: 1921), p. 98; F. Slipičević, "Prvi srpski ustanak kao sastavni deo Istočnog pitanja," *Istorijski pregled* (1954), 2:47–56.

22. On the Greek Revolution, see George Finlay, *History of Greece* (Oxford: 1877), vols. 5–7; C. M. Woodhouse, *The Greek War of Independence: Its Historical Setting* (London: Russell, 1952); Douglas Dakin, *The Greek Struggle for Independence 1821–1833* (Los Angeles and Berkeley: University of California Press, 1973); Richard Clogg, ed., *The Struggle for Greek Independence: Essays to Mark the 150th Anniversary of the Greek War of Independence* (London: Shoe String, 1973); Nikoforos P. Diamandouros et al., eds., *Hellenism and the First Greek War of Liberation (1821–1830): Continuity and Change* (Thessaloniki: 1976).

23. In addition to references given in note 22 above, see Botzaris, *Visions balkaniques*, pp. 294–343; Finlay, *History of Greece*, 6:98–134; A. Oțetea, "Les Grandes Puissances et le mouvement Hétairiste dans les Principautés Roumaines," *Balkan Studies* (1966), 7(2):379–94.

24. Botzaris, *Visions balkaniques*, pp. 102–9.

25. N. Todorov, "La participation des Bulgares à l'insurrection hétairiste dans les Principautes Danubiennes," *Etudes balkaniques* (1964), 1:90ff.

26. Grgur Jakšić, *Evropa i vaskrs Srbije, 1804–1834* (Belgrade: 1933), pp. 275–84.

27. Todorov, "La participation," p. 75; *Istoriia na Bulgariia* (Sofia: 1954), 1:328; *Istoriia Bolgarii* (Moscow: 1954), 1:245.

28. Djordjević, *Révolutions nationales*, p. 42.

29. See note 20 above, particularly Berindei and Mutașcu, *Aspecte militare*, passim.

30. Oțetea, "Les Grandes Puissances," pp. 384ff.; N. Camariano," Planurile revoluționare ale eteriștilor din București și colaborarea lor cu Tudor Vladimirescu," *Studii* (1967), 20:1163–75.

31. See note 22 above.

32. See particularly Karl Mendelssohn Bartholdy, *Geschichte Griechenlands von der Eroberung Konstantinopels durch die*

Türken im Jahre 1453 bis auf unsere Tage (Leipzig: 1870–74), 1:238ff.

33. An excellent discussion of these issues is contained in John Anthony Petropulos, *Politics and Statecraft in the Kingdom of Greece 1833–1843* (Princeton: Princeton University Press, 1968), pp. 19ff. with ample bibliographic references.

34. See in particular Edouard Driault and Michel Lhèritier, *Histoire diplomatique de la Grèce de 1821 à nos jours* (Paris: 1925–26), vol. 1, passim, and C. W. Crawley, *The Question of Greek Independence: A Study of British Policy in the Near East, 1821–1833* (Cambridge: Cambridge University Press, 1930).

35. In addition to references in notes 31–34 above, consult the important study by C. M. Woodhouse, *Capodistria: The Founder of Greek Independence* (London: Oxford University Press, 1973) and the detailed account contained in Driault and Lhèritier, *Histoire diplomatique*, 1:143ff.

36. D. Lainović and V. Protopsaltis, "Les rapports entre la Grèce et le Monténégro dans le passé," *L'Hellenisme contemporain*, 8:320.

37. Djordjević, *Révolutions nationales*, pp. 50–52.

38. Botzaris, *Visions balkaniques*, pp. 171–176.

39. See especially N. G. Popov, "Dokumenti za grchkoto vustanie ot 1821. godine i za učastieto na Bulgarite v nego," *Izvestija* (1957–58), pp. 346–56.

40. Botzaris, *Visions balkaniques*, pp. 171ff.

41. Petropulos, *Politics and Statecraft*, pp. 107ff.

42. A very incisive analysis of these issues is contained in Michael Boro Petrovich, *A History of Modern Serbia 1804–1918* (New York: Harcourt Brace Jovanovich, 1976), 1:129ff.

43. Nicholas Kaltchas, *Introduction to the Constitutional History of Modern Greece* (New York: Columbia University Press, 1940), passim, and Petropulos, *Politics and Statecraft*, pp. 48ff., are exceptionally valuable studies on these topics. See also G. Daskalakis, "Die Verfassungsentwicklung Griechenlands," *Jahrbuch des öffentlisches Rechts* (1937), vol. 24; A. Manesis, *Deux états nés en 1830* (Brussels: 1959); Demetrios A. Petrakakos, *Koinobouleutike Historia tes Hellados* (Athens: 1935–46).

249

5. REVOLUTIONARY MOVEMENTS AND THE FORMATION OF MODERN STATES, 1830-1878

1. D. Pavlović, *Pokret u Bosni i Albaniji protiv reforama Mahmuda II* (Belgrade: 1923); M. Gavrilović, *Miloš Obrenović* (Belgrade: 1912), 3:102ff; F. A. Miler, *Mustafa pasha Bairaktar* (Moscow-Leningrad: 1947); V. Stojančević, "Severna Albanija pod turskom vlašću 1830-tih godina," *Istorijski časopis* (1957), 7:123-141.

2. F. Slipičević, "Sukobi izmedu bosanskih feudalaca i Porte u prvoj polovini XIX veka," *Nastava istorije u srednjoj školi* (1951-52), p. 3.

3. A. Ivić, *Ustanak popa Jovice Ilića (1834), i bune leskovačkih i vranjanskih Srba (1842),* (Zagreb: 1919); V. Čubrilović, "Revolucionarni pokreti u Bosanskoj Krajini u XIX veku," *Glasnik Jugoslovenskog profesorskog društva* (Belgrade: 1934); D. Stranjaković, "Buna hrišćana u Bosni 1834," *Godiš. Nik. Čupića,* 40 (1931), 40:122-69.

4. P. Popović, *Crna Gora u doba Petra I i Petra II* (Belgrade: 1951); D. Vuksan, *Petar I Petrović Njegoš i njegovo doba* (Cetinje: 1951); H. Kapidžić, "Odnosi Ali paše Rizvanbegovića i vladike Petra II," *Istorijski zapisi* (1952), 5(8):69-99.

5. Mihailo Gavrilović, *Miloš Obrenović,* 3:420-34.

6. V. Stojančević, *Knez Miloš i Istočna Srbija* (Belgrade: 1957), pp. 27-52, and "Istočna Srbija u periodu turske okupacije 1813-1832. godine," *Istorijski časopis* (1956), 6:109-38.

7. Dimitrije Djordjević, *Révolutions nationales,* pp. 62ff.

8. V. Stojančević, "Narodnooslobodilački pokret u niškom kraju 1833 i 1834/5 godine," *Istorijski časopis* (1955), 5:427-35.

9. V. Stojančević, "Politički pogledi Miloša Obrenovića na pitanje oslobodenja balkanskih naroda," *Istorijski časopis* (1959), 9-10:357.

10. V. N. Zlatarski, "Bulgarski vustania i opiti za vustania do sredata na XIX vek," *Bulgariia 1000 godini, 927-1927* (Sofia:

1930), p. 731; Akademiia nauk SSSR, *Istoriia Bolgarii* (Moscow: 1954–55), 1:237.

11. V. J. Vučković, *Srpska kriza u Istočnom pitanju, 1842–1843* (Belgrade: 1957), pp. 22–25.

12. See, in particular, Cornelia Bodea, *Lupta românilor pentru unitatea națională, 1834–1849* (Bucharest: 1967) with ample bibliographical references.

13. G. Zane, *Le mouvement revolutionnaire de 1840, prélude de la révolution roumaine de 1848* (Bucharest: 1964); G. Platon, "Documente privind ecoul în Moldova al mișcărilor revoluționare de la Brăila din anii 1841–1843," *Romanoslavica* (1965), 11:311–22; C. N. Velichi, *Mișcările revoluționare de la Brăila din anii 1841–1843* (Bucharest: 1958).

14. See especially John Anthony Petropulos, *Politics and Statecraft in the Kingdom of Greece 1833–1843* (Princeton: Princeton University Press, 1968), pp. 153ff.

15. Edouard Driault and Michel Lhéritier, *Histoire diplomatique de la Grèce de 1821 à nos jours* (Paris: 1925), 2:179ff.; Petropulos, *Politics and Statecraft*, pp. 344ff.

16. Driault and Lhéritier, *Histoire diplomatique*, 2:195–96, 214; Petropulos, *Politics and Statecraft*, 329–43; N. Svoronos, *Histoire de la Grèce moderne* (Paris: 1953), pp. 49–57; George Finlay, *History of Greece* (Oxford: Oxford University Press, 1877), 7:107–83.

17. Petropulos, *Politics and Statecraft*, pp. 434ff.

18. M. Handelsman, *Czartoryski, Nicolas I et la Question du Proche Orient* (Paris: 1934) and "La question d'orient et la politique yougoslave du prince Czartoryski après 1840," *Séances et travaux de l'académie des sciences morales et politiques* (Paris: 1929).

19. V. J. Vučković, *Srpska kriza u Istočnom pitanju,* pp. 138–39.

20. D. Stranjaković, "Jugoslovenski nacionalni i državni program kneževine Srbije iz 1844," *Glasnik istorijskog društva* (Novi Sad 1931), 6:392–418 and "Kako je postalo Garašaninovo 'Načertanije'," *Spomenik S.K.A.* (1939), 91:63–113; Čubrilović, *Istorija, političke misli u Srbiji*, pp. 159–177; V. J. Vučković, "Prilog prouča-

vanju postanka 'Načertanija' (1844) i 'Osnovnih misli' (1847)," *Jugoslovenska revija za medunarodno pravo* (1961), 8(1):49-79; R. Perović, "Oko 'Načertanija' iz 1844 godine," *Istorijski glasnik* (1963), 1:71-94.

21. Ljubomir Durković-Jakšić, *Srbijansko-Crnogorska saradnja, 1830-1851* (Belgrade: 1957), p. 67.

22. Vucković, *Prilog*, p. 67.

23. Djordjevic, *Révolutions nationales*, p. 74.

24. Petropulos, *Politics and Statecraft*, pp. 455ff.

25. *Ibid.*

26. See Driault and Lhèritier, *Histoire diplomatique*, 2:252-53; Svoronos, *Histoire de la Grèce moderne*, pp. 53ff.; Finlay, *History of Greece*, 7:194-206.

27. Driault and Lhèritier, *Histoire diplomatique*, 2:253-95.

28. Djordjević, *Révolutions nationales*, pp. 77ff.

29. R. Perović, *Grada za istoriju srpskog pokreta u Vojvodini 1848-1849* (Belgrade: 1952), pp. XIX-LI; A. Lebl, *Revolucionarni pokret u Vojvodini 1848-1849 godine* (Novi Sad: 1960); D. Popović, "Vojvodjanski gradovi u buni—prilog istoriji Vojvodjanskih gradova—Novi Sad u 1848 i 1849 godini," *Zbornik Matice srpske* (1953), 5-46.

30. Čubrilović, *Istorija političke misli u Srbiji*, p. 204.

31. Djordjević, *Révolutions nationales*, p. 81.

32. V. Bogićević, "Početak ustanka Luke Vukalovića 1852-1853," *Godišnjak istorijskog društ a BiH* (1952), 4:205-23; V. Ćorović, *Luka Vukalović i Hercegovački ustanci od 1852-1862* (Belgrade: 1923).

33. D. Kosev, "Vustanieto na selianite v severozapadna Bolgariia i negovite prichini," *Istoricheski pregled* (1950) 6(4); Zlatarski, *Bolgarski vustania*, pp. 733-35; S. Dimitrov, "Serbiia i krestianskoe vustanie 1850 godine v Bolgarii," *Etudes balkaniques* (1964), 1:49-68.

34. William Miller, *The Ottoman Empire and Its Successors* (Cambridge: Cambridge University Press, 1936), pp. 183-90.

35. Driault and Lhèritier, *Histoire diplomatique*, 2:323ff.; Svoronos, *Histoire de la Grèce moderne*, pp. 58-59.

36. See note 12 above and N. Iorga, *Histoire des Roumains*

5. FORMATION OF MODERN STATES, 1830-78

(Bucharest: 1944), pp. 141–222, 223–236; John C. Campbell, "The Influence of Western Political Thought in the Rumanian Principalities," *Journal of Central European Affairs* (1944), 4:262–73; Dan Berindei, *Bălcescu* (Bucharest: 1969).

37. G. Bogdan-Duică, *Viaţa şi ideile lui Simion Bărnuţiu* (Bucharest: 1924) and *Eftimie Murgu* (Bucharest: 1937); S. Dragomir, *Avram Iancu* (Bucharest: 1965); V. Netea, *George Bariţiu: Viaţa şi activitatea sa.* (Bucharest: 1965); V. Cheresteşiu, *Adunarea de la Blaj* (Bucharest: 1966); and references under note 36 above.

38. G. Georgescu-Buzău, *Aspectul agrar al revoluţiei din 1848 în Muntenia* (Bucharest: 1848); D. Kosev, "Otrazhenieto na Krimskata voina (1853–1856) v Bulgariia," *Istoricheski pregled* (1946–47), 3:183–199.

39. Driault and Lhèritier, *Histoire diplomatique*, 2:381–402; Finlay, *History of Greece*, 7:219–28; Miller, *Ottoman Empire*, pp. 220–21.

40. Djordjević, *Révolutions nationales*, pp. 88–89.

41. Ćorović, *Luka Vukalović*, pp. 33ff.; Vojnoistorijski institut JNA, *Bune i ustanci u Bosni i Hercegovini u XIX veku* (Belgrade: 1962), pp. 50–55; V. Djordjević, *Crna Gora i Austrija od 1814–1894* Belgrade: 1924); S. Ljubibratić and T. Kruševac, "Prilozi za proučavanje hercegovačkih ustanaka 1857–1862," *Godišnjak istorijskog društva BiH* (1954), 6:167–91.

42. V. Skarić, "Iz prošlosti Bosne i Hercegovine XIX veka," *Godišnjak istorijskog društva BiH* (1949) vol. 1: 7–41; T. Kruševac, *Od narodnog ustanka do austrijske okupacije* (Sarajevo: 1948).

43. B. Pavičević, *Crna Gora u ratu 1862 god* (Belgrade: 1963).

44. F. Hauptmann, "General Rodić i političke austrijske vlade u Krivošijskom ustanku 1869–70 godine," *Godišnjak istorijskog društva BiH* (1962), 13:59–93.

45. G. Jakšić and V. J. Vučković, *Spoljna politika Srbije za vlade kneza Mihaila (Prvi balkanski savez)* (Belgrade: 1963), pp. 33–34, 54–55, 173–74, 193–94; A. Tamborra, "La politica serba del regno di Sardegna (1856–1861) su documenti inediti," *Rasegna storica del Risorgimento* (1951), vol. 38, and *Cavour e i Balcani* (Turin: 1958).

46. H. Wendel, *Bismark und Serbien im Jahre 1866* (Berlin:

1927); J. A. von Reiswitz, *Belgrad-Berlin, Berlin-Belgrad 1866-1871* (Munich: 1936); Jakšić and Vučković, *Spoljna politika,* pp. 257-67.

47. Michael B. Petrovich, *The Emergence of Russian Panslavism 1856-1870* (New York: Columbia University Press, 1956); Hans Kohn, *Pan Slavism: Its History and Ideology* (New York: McClelland, 1960).

48. Djordjević, *Révolutions nationales,* pp. 91ff.

49. M. Ekmečić, "Spoljni faktor u procesu sazrevanja balkanskih revolucija 1849-1878 godine," *Jugoslovenski istorijski časopis* (1964), 3:14.

50. *Arhiv na G. S. Rakovski* (Sofia: 1952); D. Ignjatović, "Rakovski v Belgrad 1860-1863," *Sbornik G. S. Rakovski* (1963), 1:383-432; Jakšić and Vučković, *Spoljna politika,* pp. 505-6; L. S. Stavrianos, *Balkan Federation: A History of the Movement Toward Balkan Unity in Modern Times* (Northampton, Mass.: Smith College, 1944), pp. 92-94, 273-274; M. Piroćanac, *Knez Mihailo i zajednička radnja balkanskih naroda* (Belgrade, 1895).

51. Jakšić and Vučković, *Spoljna politika,* pp. 137-138, 241-246, 280, 339, 413-416.

52. Djordjević, *Révolutions nationales,* pp. 99-100.

53. See in particular Ivan D. Shishmanov, *Ot Paisiia do Rakovski; stati po bulgarskoto vuzrazhdane* (Sofia: 1943); Mikhail Arnaudov, *Bulgarskoto vuzrazhdane* (Sofia: 1944); Zhak Natan, *Bulgarskoto vuzrazhdane* (Sofia: 1949); Georgi Konstantinov, *Revolutsionna romantika v bulgarskoto vuzrazhdane: G. S. Rakovski, Liuben Karavelov, Vasil Levski i Khristo Botev* (Sofia: 1944).

54. Richard von Mach, *The Bulgarian Exarchate: Its History and the Extent of Its Authority in Turkey* (London: 1907) and especially, B. H. Sumner, *Russia and the Balkans, 1870-1880* (Hamden, Conn.: Shoe String, 1962).

55. *Istoriia na Bulgariia* (Sofia: 1961), pp. 406-07.

56. V. Diculescu, "Rumänien und die Frage der bulgarischen Freischaren, 1866-1868," *Revue des Etudes Sud-Est Européennes* (1963),1(3-4):463-83; *Bulgariia; 1000 godini,* pp. 860-74.

57. Djordjević, *Révolutions nationales,* pp. 102-5; Mercia Macdermott, *A History of Bulgaria 1393-1885* (New York: Praeger 1962), pp. 236ff. See also references under notes 53 and 54 above.

58. D. Djordjević, "The Echo of the 1866 Cretan Uprising in Serbia," *Kretologikon Sinedrion* (Athens: 1975), 5:94–109, and Djordjević, *Révolutions nationales*, pp. 109–13. See also D. Dontas, *Greece and the Great Powers 1863–1875* (Thessaloniki: 1966) and Evangelos Kofos, *Greece and the Eastern Crisis 1875–1878* (Thessaloniki: 1975).

59. S. T. Lascaris, *Histoire diplomatique de la Grèce avant et après le Congres de Berlin 1875–1878* (Paris: 1924) as well as references under note 58 above.

60. T. W. Riker, *The Making of Roumania: A Study of an International Problem 1856–1866* (Oxford: Oxford University Press, 1931); W. G. East, *The Union of Moldavia and Wallachia 1859* (Cambridge: Cambridge University Press, 1929); *Studii Privind Unirea Principatelor* (Bucharest: 1960); Gerald J. Bobango, *The Emergence of the Romanian Nation State* (Boulder, Colo., and New York: Columbia University Press, 1979).

61. In addition to Jakšić and Vučković, *Spoljna politika;* Stavrianos, *Balkan Federation;* Driault and Lhèritier, *Histoire diplomatique*, 3:225ff.; see also S. Jovanović, *Druga vlada Miloša i Mihaila* (Belgrade: 1933), pp. 347–58; G. Jakšić, *Prvi grčko-srpski savez 1867–1868* (Belgrade: 1924); S. T. Lascaris, "La première alliance entre la Grèce et la Serbie," *Le Monde Slave* (1926), 9:1–50.

62. For the text of the treaty see Jakšić and Vučković, *Spoljna politika*, pp. 510–14; Stavrianos, *Balkan Federation*, pp. 277–81; Lascaris, *Première alliance*, pp. 428–37. The text of the military convention will be found in Jakšić and Vučković, *Spoljna politika*, pp. 515–19.

63. L. Aleksić, "O misiji Vuka Karadžića na Cetinju 1860–1861. godine," *Istorijski glasnik* (1958), 1–2:77–84; Pavičević, *Crna Gora*, pp. 84–89.

64. The text of the treaty will be found in Jakšić and Vučković, *Spoljna politika*, pp. 486–89.

65. Jakšić and Vučković, pp. 234–38, 408–13, 452–55.

66. J. Skerlić, *Omladina i njena književnost 1848–1871* (Belgrade: 1906) and *Istorija nove srpske kniževnosti* (Belgrade: 1953), pp. 211ff.; Čubrilović, *Istorija Političke misli u Srbiji*, pp. 240–45; Sl. Jovanović, *Druga vlada Miloša i Mihaila*, pp. 393–403; K. Milu-

tinović, "Crna Gora i Primorje u Omladinskom pokretu," *Istorijski zapisi* (1953), 9(1):1–46; Woodford D. McClellan, *Svetozar Marković and the Origins of Balkan Socialism* (Princeton, N.J.: Princeton University Press, 1964), pp. 51ff.

67. The statute is published in Milutinović, *Crna Gora*, pp. 32–34.

68. K. Milutinović, *Mihailo Polit Desančić kao istoričar* (Novi Sad: 1936); V. Popović, "Istočno pitanje u Politovoj političkoj ideologiji," *Letopis Matice Srpske* (1933), no. 337; K. Milutinović, *Politova interpretacija istočnog pitanja* (Belgrade: 1931); Čubrilović, *Istorijas Političke misli u srbiji*, pp. 257–64; D. Djordjević, "Projects for the Federation of South-East Europe in the 1860s and 1870s," *Balcanica* (1970), 1:119–49; N. Petrović, *Svetozar Miletić* (Belgrade: 1958), pp. 87–99, 182–85; Gale Stokes, *Legitimacy Through Liberalism: Vladimir Jovanović and the Transformation of Serbian Politics* (Seattle: University of Washington Press, 1975).

69. N. Kondarev, *Ideologiiata na Liuben Karavelov* (Sofia: 1957); H. Batowski, "Le mouvement panbalkanique et les différents aspects des relations interbalkaniques dans le passé," *Revue des études balkaniques*, 2(2):pp. 6, 233; K. Milutinović, "Tri projekta balkanske konfederacije," *Knjiga o Balkanu* (Beograd, 1937), 2:186–87.

70. Veselin Masleša, "Svetozar Marković," *Dela* (Sarajevo: 1956), vol. 3; Svetozar Marković, *Sabrani spisi* (Belgrade: 1960); J. Skerlić, *Svetozar Marković: Njegov život, rad i ideje* (Belgrade: 1922); McClellan, *Svetozar Marković*; D. Prodanović, *Shvatanje Svetozara Markovića o državi* (Belgrade: 1961).

71. Konstantinov, *Revolutsionna romantika*; K. N. Derzhavin, *Khristo Botev* (Moscow: 1962); Ivan N. Undzhiev, *Vasil Levski* (Sofia: 1945); A. Stekol'nikov, *Vasil Levskii* (Moscow: 1955).

72. V. Čubrilovič, *Bosanski ustanak 1875–1878* (Belgrade: 1930); M. Ekmečić, *Ustanak u Bosni 1875–1878* (Sarajevo: 1960).

73. On the preparations for the uprising and on Serbian propaganda in Bosnia, see Ekmečić, *Ustanak*, pp. 36–52; Čubrilović, *Bosanski ustanak*, pp. 14–22; M. Vukčević, *Crna Gora i Hercegovina uoči rata 1874–1876* (Cetinje: 1950).

74. Ekmečić, *Ustanak*, pp. 63–64; K. Milutinović, "Novi Sad

kao žarište socijalističkog pokreta 1872. godine," *Rad vojvodjanskih muzeja* (1952), 1:69-78.

75. R. Proroković, *Nevesinjska buna 1874 i početak ustanka u Hercegovini 1875* (Belgrade: 1905).

76. See notes 72-75 above and also consult M. Radoičić, *Hercegovina i Crna Gora 1875-1878* (Nevesinje: 1961).

77. In addition to references given in notes 72 and 73 above, see Vasa Pelagić, *Istorija bosansko-hercegovačke bune 1875-1878* (Sarajevo: 1953).

78. Note 77 above and Djordjević, *Révolutions nationales*, pp. 131-32.

79. The most detailed account of the Bulgarian uprising is contained in Dimitur T. Strashimirov, *Istoriia na Aprilskoto vuzstanie* (Plovdiv: 1907-9) in three volumes. See also Aleksandur Burmov, ed., *Aprilsko vustanie 1876: Sbornik ot dokumenti* (Sofia: 1954-56) also in three volumes. For the most recent interpretation of related events, consult Nikolai Todorov, "The Russo-Turkish War of 1877-1878 and the Liberation of Bulgaria: An Interpretive Essay," *East European Quarterly* (1980), 14(1):9-21.

80. See note 79 above and Djordjević, *Révolutions nationales*, pp. 132-35.

81. V. Djordjević, *Srpsko-turski rat* (Belgrade: 1907), vols. 1 and 2; J. Ristić, *Diplomatska istorija Srbije za vreme srpskih ratova za oslobodenje i nezavisnost 1875-1878* (Belgrade: 1896).

82. Čubrilović, *Bosanski ustanak*, pp. 270-77; Ekmečić, *Ustanak*, pp. 303-17. See also *Balcanica*, Belgrade: 1978, the entire volume dealing with the Eastern Crisis.

83. B. H. Sumner, *Russia and the Balkans 1870-1880* (Oxford: Oxford University Press, 1937), P. K. Fortunatov, *Voina 1877-1878 gg. i osvobozhdenie Bolgarii* (Moscow: 1950); Todorov, *Russo-Turkish War*, pp. 9ff.; George Georgiev and V. Topalov, *Kratka istoriia na osvoboditelnata voina, 1877-1878* (Sofia: 1958).

84. See especially Evangelos Kofos, *Greece and the Eastern Crisis 1875-8*, (Thessaloniki, Institute for Balkan Studies, 1975), pp. 111ff.

85. Driault and Lhèritier, *Histoire diplomatique*, 3:448-49; S. Th. Lascaris, *La Politique exterieure de la Grèce avant et après le*

5. FORMATION OF MODERN STATES, 1830–78

congrès de Berlin 1875–8, Paris 1924, pp. 119–20; Kofos, *Greece*, pp. 178ff.

86. Lascaris, *Politique exterieure*, pp. 118–19; Miller, *Ottoman Empire*, p. 381; Kofos, *Greece and the Eastern Crisis*, 174–77.

87. M. Iorga, *Războiul pentru independenţa României* (Bucharest: 1927); N. Adăniloaie, *Cucerirea independenţei de stat a României 1877–1878* (Bucharest: 1973); L. Login and C. Ucrain, *Plevna, 1877* (Bucharest: 1967); R. V. Burks, "Roumania and the Balkan Crisis of 1875–78," *Journal of Central European Affairs* (1942), 2:119–34, 310–20.

6. REVOLUTIONS AND WARS, 1878–1914

1. Joseph Swire, *Bulgarian Conspiracy* (London: Ryerson Press, 1939); Slavko Dimevski, *Makedonskoto nacionalno osloboditelno dviženie i Egzarhijata, 1893–1912* (Skopje: 1963); K. Silianov, *Osvoboditelnite borbi na Makedoniia*, 2 vols. (Sofia: 1933–43).

2. L. Lape, "Razlovečkoto vostanie vo 1876 godina," *Godišen zbornik na Fil. fak* (Skopje, 1950), 3(4):3–28; I. Katardžiev, *Serskata oblast 1780–1879* (Skopje: 1961), pp. 192–95.

3. J. Hadži-Vasiljević, *Ustanak Srba u Kumanovkoj i Palanačkoj Kazi u 1878. godini* (Belgrade: 1906) and *Pokret Srba i Bugara u Turskoj posle srpsko-turskih ratova 1876 i 1877–8 godine i njegove posledice, 1878–1882* (Belgrade: 1908); K. Džambazovski, "Za nekoi nacionalni makedonistički tendencii na makedonska emigracija vo Srbija kon krajot na XIX vek," *Glasnik na Inst. za. nac. istorija* (Skopje, 1961), 5(2):165–77.

4. Katardžiev, *Serskata oblast*, pp. 198–255; Kiril, Patriiarch bulgarski, *Suprotivata sreshu Berlinskiia dogovor. Kresneskoto vuzstanie* (Sofia: 1955); N. G. Levintov, "Kresnenskoe vosstanie," *Voprosy istorii*, (1951), 4:74–86.

5. Jovan M. Jovanović, *Južna Srbija od kraja XVIII veka do oslobodenja* (Belgrade: 1939), p. 142; I. Katardžiev, "Ustanci makedonskih seljaka u drugoj polovini XIX veka," *Nastava historije u srednjoj školi* (Zagreb, 1951), 1(3):198.

6. The best study on Albanian problems is Stavro Skendi, *The Albanian National Awakening 1878–1912* (Princeton: Princeton

6. REVOLUTIONS AND WARS, 1878–1914

University Press, 1967) with ample bibliographical references. See also Kristo Frasheri, *The History of Albania* (Tirana: 1964) and Basil Kondis, *Greece and Albania 1908–1914* Thessaloniki: 1976).

7. Skendi, *Albanian National Awakening*, pp. 31ff.

8. V. Stojančević, "Prilike u zapadnoj polovini Kosovskog vilajeta prema izveštajima austro-ugarskog konsula u Skoplju 1900 i 1901. godine," *Istorijski časopis* (1961–62), 12–13:287–316: V. Ćorović, *Diplomatska prepiska kraljevine Srbije* (Belgrade: 1933), vol. 1 (1902–3).

9. H. Kapidžić, *Herecegovački ustanak 1882* (Sarajevo: 1958), pp. 11–15; V. Čubrilović, *Bosanski ustanak 1875–1878* (Belgrade: 1930), pp. 329–78; M. Ekmečić, *Ustanak u Bosni 1875–1878* (Sarajevo: 1960), pp. 348–61; R. Jeremić, "Oružani otpor protiv Austro-Ugarske 1878–1882," *Napor Bosne i Hercegovine za oslobodenje i ujedinjenje* (Sarajevo: 1929), pp. 66–70.

10. Kapidžić, *Hercegovački ustanak*, pp. 85ff.; N. Vojinović, "Otpor vojnom zakonu Poborima i Boki Kotorskoj 1882. godine," *Godisnjak istorijskog društva BiH* (1960), 11:289–96; I. Zloković, "Iz drugog Krivošijskog ustanka," *Istoriski zapisi* (1957), 1–2:315–20; Jeremić, *Oruzani otpor protiv*, pp. 71–78; D. Tunguz-Perović, *Ustanak hercegovačko-bokeljski 1882* (Sarajevo: 1924).

11. See note 10 above and Dimitrije Djordjević, *Révolutions nationales des peuples balkaniques 1804–1914* (Belgrade: 1965), pp. 157–62.

12. See especially C. E. Black, *The Establishment of Constitutional Government in Bulgaria* (Princeton: Princeton University Press, 1943); Alois Hajek, *Bulgariens Befreiung und staatliche Entwiklung unter seinem ersten Fürsten* (Munich: 1939); Charles Jelavich, *Tsarist Russia and Balkan Nationalism: Russian Influence in the Internal Affairs of Bulgaria and Serbia, 1879–1886* (Berkeley: University of California Press, 1958).

13. See above note 12 and Bulgarska akademiia na naukite, *Istoriia na Bulgaria* (Sofia: 1962), 2:57–80; Akademiia nauk SSSR, *Istoriia Bolgarii* (Moscow: 1954), 1:262–377.

14. V. Vučković, *Diplomatska istorija srpsko-bugarskog rata* (Belgrade: 1958); V. Djordjević, *Istorija srpsko-bugarski rata, 1885* (Belgrade: 1908) in two volumes; Sl. Jovanović, *Srpsko-bugarski rat,*

(Beograd, 1933); M. I. Madzharov, *Istoriia na Srubsko-bulgarskata voina 1885 god* (Sofia: 1925).

15. See note 1 above as well as important bibliographic references in Michael B. Petrovich, *Yugoslavia: A Bibliographic Guide* (Washington, D.C.: 1974), pp. 49ff., and Marin V. Pundeff, *Bulgaria: A Bibliographic Guide* (Washington, D.C.: 1965), pp. 25ff.

16. Katardžiev, *Serskata oblast*, pp. 171ff.; S. Dimevski, *Prosvetnata politika na Egzarhijata* (Skopje: 1960); S. Papadopoulos, "Ecoles et associations grecques dans la Macedoine du nord durant le dernier siècle de le domination turque," *Balkan Studies* (1962), 3:397–442; Douglas Dakin, *The Greek Struggle in Macedonia* (Thessaloniki: 1966).

17. K. Džambazovski, *Kulturno-obštestvenite vrski na Makedoncite so Srbija kon tekot na XIX vek* (Skopje: 1960), pp. 172–73.

18. H. Andonovski-Poljanski, "Nekoi prašanja od voenata organizacija na makedonskoto nacionalno-revolucionarno dviženje vo predilindenskiot period," *Glasnik na Inst. za nac. istoriju* (Skopje, 1960), 4:1–2; *Istoria na makedonskiot narod* (Skopje: 1969), 2:157–70; D. Zografski et al., eds., *Egejska Makedonija vo našata istorija* (Skopje: 1951); Stephen Fischer-Galati, "The Internal Macedonian Revolutionary Organization: Its Significance in 'Wars of National Liberation'," *East European Quarterly* (1973), 6(4): 459–72.

19. William Miller, *The Ottoman Empire and Its Successors 1801–1921* (Cambridge: Cambridge University Press, 1927), pp. 432ff.; E. Driault and M. Lhèritier, *Histoire diplomatique de la Grèce de 1821 à nos jours* (Paris: 1926–30), 4:301ff.; G. Papadopoulos, *England and the Near East, 1896–1898* (Thessaloniki: 1969).

20. See note 19 above and J. S. Dutkovski, *L'occupation de la Crète 1897–1909* (Paris: 1953).

21. Djordjević, *Révolutions nationales*, pp. 180–86.

22. On the Hungarian crisis and its ramifications, see especially Vladimir Ćorović, *Odnosi izmedu Srbije i Austro-Ugarske u XX veku* (Belgrade: 1936).

23. M. Gross, *Vladavina hrvatsko-srpske koalicije 1906–1907* (Belgrade: 1960) provides much information on these problems.

24. Djordjević, *Révolutions Nationales*, pp. 190ff., with particular reference to archival sources contained in notes 23ff.

25. *Ibid.*, pp. 190–191 and notes 28ff.

26. *Ibid.*, p. 192.

27. Ljuben Lape et al., eds., *Ilindenski zbornik, 1903–1953* (Skopje: 1953); Ljuben Lape, *Izveštai od 1903 godina na srpskite konsuli, mitropoliti i učilišni inspektori vo Makedonija* (Skopje: 1954); Dančo Zografski, ed., *Izveštai od 1903–1904 godina na avstriskite prestavnici vo Makedonija* (Skopje, 1955). See also Wayne S. Vucinich, *Serbia between East and West: The Events of 1903–1908* (Stanford, Calif.: Stanford University Press, 1954).

28. Djordjević, *Révolutions nationales*, pp. 198–202; Jerry Augustinos, "The Dynamics of Modern Greek Nationalism: The 'Great Idea' and the Macedonian Problem," *East European Quarterly* (1973), 6(4):444–53; Leonard Bushkoff, "Marxism, Communism and the Revolutionary Tradition in the Balkans," *East European Quarterly* (1968), 1(4):371–400.

29. S. Story, ed., *The Memoirs of Ismail Kemal Bey* (New York: 1920); E. E. Ramsaur, Jr., *The Young Turks: Prelude to the Revolution of 1908* (Princeton: Princeton University Press, 1957); B. Lewis, *The Emergence of Modern Turkey* (New York: Oxford University Press, 1961), pp. 193ff.

30. D. Vlahov, "Makedonija i Mladoturska," *Istorijski glasnik* (1949), 3:34ff.; Papadopoulos, *Ecoles, pp.* 403ff.; D. Xanalatos, "The Greeks and the Turks on the Eve of the Balkan Wars," *Balkan Studies* (1962), 3:277–96.

31. Č. Popović, "Organizacija 'Ujedinjenje ili smrt'–Uzroci i način postanka," *Nova Evropa* (1927), 15:12, and "Rad Organizacije 'Uledinjenje ili smrt'—Granični oficiri," *Nova Evropa* (1927), 16:5. See also the excellent account of the history of this period contained in Michael Boro Petrovich, *A History of Modern Serbia* (New York: Harcourt Brace Jovanovich, 1976), 2:534–611.

32. Djordjević, *Révolutions nationales*, pp. 214–17.

33. Skendi, *Albanian National Awakening*, pp. 405ff.; Kondis, *Greece and Albania*, pp. 63ff.; Frasheri, *History of Albania*, pp. 163ff.

34. See note 33 above, especially Frasheri, pp. 163–170.

35. Skendi, *Albanian National Awakening*, pp. 438ff.

36. Djordjević, *Révolutions nationales*, pp. 222ff.

37. *Ibid.*, pp. 223–26; Woodford D. McClellan, *Svetozar Marko-*

vić and the Origins of Balkan Socialism (Princeton: Princeton University Press, 1964), passim and especially pp. 275–96.

38. Vlado Strugar, Socijalna demokratija o nacionalnom pitanju jugoslavenskih naroda (Belgrade: 1956), pp. 13–81; Z. Priklmajer-Tomanović, "Srpska socijalna demokratija i nacionalno pitanje," Istorijski glasnik (1956), 3–4:77–83 and Srpska socijalna demokratija u aneksionoj krizi 1908 (Belgrade: 1953); K. Milutinović, "Anekcija Bosne i Hercegovine i socijalna demokratija," Pregled (1964), 2:213–37.

39. Dragiša Vasić, Devetstotreća (Belgrade: 1925); Victor Papacosma, The Military in Greek Politics: The 1909 Coup d'Etat (Kent, Ohio: Kent State University Press, 1977).

40. See especially Richard Clogg, A Short History of Modern Greece (Cambridge: Cambridge University Press, 1979), pp. 133ff., with ample bibliographical references.

41. D. Kosev, H. Hristov, D. Angelov, Kratka istoria na Bulgaria (Sofia: 1969), pp. 242–48 and 252–58; Dragiša Lapčević, Istorija socijalizma u Srbiji (Belgrade: 1922), N. G. Munteanu and G. Breaz-Tudoran, "Luptele muncitorilor din portul Brăila în anul 1910." Analele Institutului de Istorie P.M.R., 1 (1955), 1:63–81.

42. V. Dedijer, I. Božić, S. Ćirković, M. Ekmečić, History of Yugoslavia (New York: McGraw-Hill, 1974), p. 522.

43. Ioachim Crăciun et al., Bibliografia istorică a României, 1944–1969 (Bucharest: 1970), 1:212ff. provides exhaustive references.

44. Ibid., pp. 222–28.

45. See Ezel Kural Shaw, "The Political, Practical and Psychological Aspects of Pax Ottomanica," in Bela K. Kiraly, ed., Tolerance and Movements of Religious Dissent in Eastern Europe (Boulder, Colo., and New York: Columbia University Press, 1975), pp. 165–82; Stanford J. Shaw, "The Ottoman Millet System: An Evaluation," in Kiraly, pp. 183–84; Stephen Fischer-Galati, "Judeo-Christian Aspects of Pax Ottomanica," in Kiraly, pp. 185–97.

46. P. Dumond, "Une organisation socialiste ottomane: le fédération ouvrière de Salonique (1908–1912)," Etudes Balkaniques (1964), 1:76–88; Georges Hapupt, "Introduzione alla storia della Federazione Operaia Socialista di Salonicco," Movimento Operaio e Socialista, (1972), 13(1):99–112; Joshua Staar, "The Socialist Fed-

eration of Saloniki," *Jewish Social Studies* (1945), 7(4):323–36. See also George B. Leon, *The Greek Socialist Movement and the First World War: The Road to Unity* (Boulder, Colo., and New York: Columbia University Press, 1976).

47. Crăciun et al., *Bibliografia*, 1:193–95; Institutul de studii istorice și social-politice de pe lîngă C.C. al P.C.R., *Documente din istoria mişcării muncitoreşti din România 1900–1909* (Bucharest: 1975).

48. On the relevant problems of the Austro-Hungarian Monarchy, see "Joseph Redlichs das politische Tagebuch," *Schicksaljahre Österreichs 1908–1919*, vols. 2 and 3 (1953–1954); M. J. Baernreither, *Fragmente eines politischen Tagebuches* (Berlin: 1928).

49. V. Masleša, *Mlada Bosna* (Belgrade: 1945); V. Zaninović, "Mlada Hrvatska uoči I svetskog rata," *Historijski zbornik*, (1960), 11–12:65–104; B. Jevtić, *Sarajevski atentat* (Sarajevo: 1924); V. Dedijer, *Sarajevo 1914* (Belgrade: 1966); Joachim Remak, *Sarajevo* (New York: Phillips, 1959).

50. See above note 40 and V. Bogićević, "Atentat Bogdana Žerajića 1910 godine," *Godišnjak istorijskog društva Bosne i Hercegovine*, (1954), vol. 4. D. Ljubibratić, *Gavrilo Princip* (Belgrade: 1959) and *Vladimir Gaćinović* (Belgrade: 1961); D. Jevdjević, *Sarajevski atentatori* (Zagreb: 1934).

51. See above notes 31, 40, and 41, as well as Č. Popović, "Sarajevski atentat i organizacija 'Ujedinjenje ili smrt'," *Nova Evropa* (1932), 25:8.

52. Djordjević, *Révolutions nationales*, pp. 238–40.

EPILOGUE: THE BOLSHEVIK REVOLUTION AND BALKAN REVOLUTIONS

1. *Marea răscoală a ţăranilor din 1907* (Bucharest: 1967); Philip G. Eidelberg, *The Great Rumanian Peasant Revolt of 1907* (Leiden: Brill, 1974).

2. V. Liveanu et al., *Relaţii agrare şi miscări ţărăneşti în România 1908–1921* (Bucharest: 1967).

3. Joseph Rothschild, *The Communist Party of Bulgaria: Ori-*

263

THE BOLSHEVIK AND BALKAN REVOLUTIONS

gins and Development, 1883–1936 (New York: Columbia University Press, 1959); Nissan Oren, *Bulgarian Communism: The Road to Power, 1934–1944* (New York: Columbia University Press, 1971); John D. Bell, *Peasants in Power: Alexander Stamboliski and the Bulgarian Agrarian Union, 1899–1923* (Princeton: Princeton University Press, 1977).

4. See especially Joseph Swire, *Bulgarian Conspiracy* (London: Ryerson, 1939).

5. Note 4 above and Henry L. Roberts, *Rumania: Political Problems of a Agrarian State* (New Haven: Yale University Press, 1951) and Eugen Weber, "Romania," in Hans Rogger and Eugen Weber, eds., *The European Right: A Historical Profile* (Berkeley: University of California Press, 1965), pp. 501–74.

6. Michael Llwellyn Smith, *Ionian Vision: Greece in Asia Minor 1919–1922* (London: St. Martin's Press, 1973); D. George Kousoulas, *Revolution and Defeat: The Story of the Greek Communist Party* (London: Oxford University Press, 1965).

7. Kristo Frasheri, *The History of Albania* (Tirana: 1964), pp. 213ff.

8. John Hondros, *Occupation and Resistance: The Greek Agony, 1941–1944* (New York: 1979); Dominique Eudes, *The Kapetanios: Partisans and Civil War in Greece, 1943–1949* (London: Monthly Review, 1972); Peter R. Prifti, "The Labor Party of Albania," in Stephen Fischer-Galati, ed., *The Communist Parties of Eastern Europe* (New York: Columbia University Press, 1979), pp. 5ff.; Frasheri, *History of Albania*, pp. 267ff.; Jozo Tomasevich, *The Chetniks: War and Revolution in Yugoslavia, 1941–1945* (Stanford, Calif.: Stanford University Press, 1975).

9. Thomas T. Hammond, ed., *The Anatomy of Communist Takeovers* (New Haven: Yale University Press, 1975), pp. 244–338.

264

INDEX

INDEX

Branković, George, 39-40
Brsjačka Buna, 166
Brvenicsky, Stephan, 53
Bulgaria: revolutionary activities in, 94-95, 105, 109-10, 114, 127-32, 174-76, 218-20; revolutionary plans, 122, 125-26; uprising of *1876,* 141, 152-55; and revolutionary activities in Macedonia, 165, 179-80, 190, 192-93, 195
Bulgarian Communist Party, as revolutionary force, 218-19, 223
Bulgaris, Leonidas, 134, 157-58
Bushatlya, Mehmet Pasha, 54-55

Callimachi, Grigore, 60-61
Cantacuzenos, Andronicos, 7
Cantacuzino, Şerban, 33-34
Cantemir, Antioh, 34
Cantemir, Constantin, 33, 36
Cantemir, Dimitrie, 33, 46-48
Capo d'Istria, John, 75, 79
Carol of Hohenzollern, King of Romania, 140
Catherine the Great, Tsarina, 60
Cavour, Camillo di, 120
Charles II of Gonzaga, Duke of Nevers, 24-25
Čiprovec, uprising of, 40
Clement VIII, Pope, 27
Codreanu, Corneliu Zelea, 221
Communism, and revolutionary activities in the Balkans, 215-26, 233-35
Crete: revolt of *1866,* 133-34; revolutionary activities in, 140-41; revolt of *1876,* 158; revolt of *1896,* 180-81
Crimean War, 91, 116, 127, 136
Csáky, Grof Ladislas, 34

Čubrilović, Veljko, 213
Cuza, Alexandru Ioan, 130, 136, 140
Czartoryski, Adam, 100-1

Dabija, Eustaţiu, 24
Daskalov, Raiko, 218
Delčev, Goce, 190
Desančić, Mihailo Polit, 143, 148
Dimitrijević-Apis, Dragutin, 213
Dimitrov, Giorgi, 223
Dimitur, Hadji, 131
Djak, rebellion of, 72
Djerov, Spiro, 134
Djordjić, Pavel, 12, 14
Dobrogeanu-Gherea, Constantin, 209-10, 217
Dojčić, Stjepan, 213
Dragoumis, Ion, 180, 192, 196
Duca, Constantin, 34
Duca, Gheorghe, 33
Dučić, Nićifor, 146
Dyonisios of Trikala, 24

England, and revolutionary activities in Greece, 115-16
Epirus, revolutionary activities in, 115, 134, 157-58

Ferdinand I, Holy Roman Emperor, 6
Ferdinand II, Holy Roman Emperor, 20
Ferdinand of Coburg, King of Bulgaria, 189, 192
Ferdinand of Hohenzollern, King of Romania, 217
Filipov, Nikola, 114
Filiti, Dositei, 75
Forta, Salko, 173
France, and revolutionary activities in the Balkans, 66-68

INDEX

Franz Ferdinand, 213-14
Frasheri, Abdul, 168

Gaj, Ljudevit, 102
Garašanin, Ilija, 101-2, 107-8, 122, 124-25, 146
Garibaldi, Giuseppe, 120, 132-33
Garibaldi, Ricciotti, 134
George I, King of Greece, 133-34
Georgijević-Berovski, Pop Dimitrije, 163
Ghica, Grigore, 22-23, 52, 60-61
Giorgio, Paolo, 10
Glavaš, Stanoje, 72
Gligorijević, Hadji Prodan, 70, 79, 81
Gradaščević, Hussein, 92
Grdan, Voevod of Nikšić, 15
Greece: revolutionary activities in, 58-60, 77-89, 97-98, 102-5, 132-35, 157-58, 221-22; and revolutionary activities in the Balkans, 78-82, 86-89; and revolutionary activities in the Diaspora, 110-11, 114-16, 134, 140-41, 157-58, 180-81; and revolutionary activities in Macedonia, 180; war with Turkey of 1897, 180-81
Grivas, Bua, 5
Grivița, uprising of, 208, 223

Habsburg Monarchy, and revolutionary activities in the Balkans, 1-17, 33-35
Hadjivelkov, Vasil, 97
Hajduks, 10, 12, 14-15, 17, 31-32, 42, 69-71, 74-76, 114, 118, 121, 146, 164-65, 230
Hellenism, as a revolutionary idea, 103-4
Hercigonja, Rudolph, 213

Herzegovina: revolutionary activities in, 109, 116-19; insurrection of 1875, 141-43, 146-52, 154-56; insurrection of 1882, 171-74
Hitov, Panajot, 148
Holy League, 6-8, 13-15, 17; war of 1683-1699, 26, 30, 36, 41
Hristo, Hadji of Koprivišta, 87, 105

Ibrahim, Beyoli of Busciati, 5, 13
Ibrahim Pasha, 84-85
Ilinden, uprising of 1903, 190-91
Internal Macedonian Revolutionary Organization (IMRO), 178-80, 190, 192, 195, 220-21, 235
Ioan Vodă, cel Cumplit, 6-7
Ionian Islands, revolutionary activities in, 133-35
Iron Guard, as revolutionary force, 221-23
Ismail, Kemal Bey, 202-3

Jacchia, Sultan, 28
Jacqueries, 9, 21, 61, 199
Jančić, rebellion of, 73
Jews, participation in Balkan revolutionary activities, 209-10, 220-21
Joseph II, Holy Roman Emperor, 65
Jovanović, Vladimir, 143-44
Jukić, Luka, 213

Karadja, Stefan, 131
Karadjić, Vuk, 139
Karadjordje, Petrović, 69-70, 72-74, 78
Karadjordjević, Peter, 188
Karageorge, see Karadjordje, Petrović
Karano-Tvrtković, Pavle, 92

267

INDEX

Karavelov, Liuben, 2, 130-31, 144, 175
Karev, Nikola, 190
Karlowitz, Treaty of, 34, 36, 41, 43-45
Khmelnitsky, Bogdan, 20, 35
Klephts, 32, 41-42, 54, 59, 66, 75, 78, 230
Knićanin, Stevan, 107
Kolokotrones, Theodore, 84, 98
Kolonikos, Patriarch of Peć, 46
Koraes, Adamantios, 67
Kormanos, Ostoja, 150
Kossuth, Louis, 106, 119-20
Kovačević, Stojan, 173
Kresna, insurrection of, 163-65
Kuchuk Kainardji, Treaty of, 61-63, 66
Kumanduros, Alexander, 138-39
Kumanovo, insurrection of, 163-64
Kun, Béla, 235
Kutalija, Bey Ibrahim Čengić, 173

Latas, Omer Pasha, 109, 119, 134-35
Lazarević, Luka, 72
Leon, Radu, 22
Leopold I, Holy Roman Emperor, 34, 37-40, 46
Leopold II, Holy Roman Emperor, 2
Lepanto, battle of *1571*, 5-6
Levski, Vasil, 130-32, 145, 175
Ljubibratić, Mića, 146
Lupu, Anastasă, 50-51
Lupu, Vasile, 20, 35
Lusk, Treaty of, 47-48

Macedonia, revolutionary activities in, 134, 157-58, 161-66, 176-80, 190-96, 199
Mahmoud II, Sultan, 91
Makariopolski, Ilarion, 128-29

Mali, Stephen, 58
Mamarčev, Georgi, 95
Marinović, Jovan, 108
Marko, Deli, 14
Marković, Svetozar, 143-47, 151, 204
Mavrocordat, Nicolae, 49, 52
Mavrocordatos, Alexander, 84
Maximilian II, Holy Roman Emperor, 6
Mazzini, Giuseppe, 110
Megali Idea, 103-4, 115, 132, 137
Mehmed V, Sultan, 202
Mehmedbašić, Muhamed, 213
Michael, Prince of Serbia, *see* Obrenović, Michael
Michael the Brave, 5, 7-16
Mihali, Hadji, 80-81
Mihnea III, 22
Milan, King of Serbia, *see* Obrenović, Milan
Milanović, Mladen, 72
Miletić, Svetozar, 143, 148
Mohammed Ali, 95, 97
Montenegro: revolutionary activities in, 47, 57-58, 93, 149; and revolutionary activities in the Balkans, 109, 117-19, 148-59; war with Turkey of *1876*, 141, 150, 152, 154-55
Moralijata, Petar, 87
Morea, revolutionary activities in, 58-60
Movilă, Aron, 8
Movilă, Moldavian dynasty, 7, 16
Mustafa, Pasha of Scutari, 91-93

Nationalism, as factor in Balkan revolutions, 99-102, 216, 221-22, 227-36
Navarino, battle of *1827*, 85

268

INDEX